Spontaneity and Planning in Social Development

Spontaneity and Planning in Social Development

Edited by Ulf Himmelstrand

SAGE Studies in International Sociology 24
sponsored by the International Sociological Association/ISA

For information address

SAGE Publications Inc, 275 South Beverly Drive,
Beverly Hills, California 90212
SAGE Publications Ltd, 28 Banner Street, London EC1Y 8QE

British Library Cataloguing in Publication Data
Spontaneity and planning in social development.
   (Sage studies in international sociology; 24)
   1. Social change
   2. Economic development
   I. Himmelstrand, Ulf
   361.6   HM101   80-41957

ISBN 0-8039-9804-X

First Printing

CONTENTS

INTRODUCTION

Ulf Himmelstrand
University of Uppsala, Sweden

The **terms spontaneity and planning** would seem to have a variety of meanings in the debate about social development. Planning is usually supposed to be the opposite of spontaneity; yet spontaneity is also considered important for development, together with planning. Thus, the mixtures and combinations of spontaneity and planning are of crucial significance not only in sociological theories of development but also in the formulation of a variety of ideologies of development.

In ideologies words such as spontaneity and planning are imbued with affective power, and not only or predominantly with a descriptive or theoretical meaning. Such words become tools to be used in attack,

Author's note: This Introduction is a revised and considerably expanded version of an agenda-setting paper sent by me to the prospective contributors to the Plenary Session III held at the Ninth World Congress of Sociology in Uppsala, August 1978. The contributors to that plenary were E. O. Akeredolu-Ale, Nigeria; Albert Cherns, England; Bogdan Denitch, USA; Elizabeth Jelin, Argentina; K. S. Jomo, Malaysia; and Piotr Sztompka, Poland. Tatiana Zaslavskaya (USSR) served as *rapporteur* and discussant. For this volume I asked her to supplement her comments with some reflections on planning and spontaneity in the Soviet Union. The paper by Britta Jonsson, Sweden, was presented at another session of the World Congress of Sociology, but with her permission I have included it here. To attain a more complete coverage of themes belonging to the topic of this book, I have specially commissioned the contributions by Branko Horvat, Yugoslavia, and Lars Udéhn, Sweden. Furthermore, I have added a chapter of my own.

or in affirmation and defence. Since the word 'spontaneous' usually is considered as referring to something good, something to be affirmed, spontaneity cannot be attacked without re-baptizing it, for instance by calling it 'spontanistic'. For the term 'planning' there are similar verbal tricks which help to shift the emotive meaning of the term from positive to negative or vice versa. Often such words have acquired what Charles Stevenson (1944: 72) called an *independent emotive meaning*. Their references to real problems and events have become attenuated as a result of their use as symbols of affirmation or identity, or as weapons of attack and defamation. Whatever is the fact about a certain set of events matters little, if anything, if the corresponding symbols have an independent emotive meaning to their users or receivers.

But in some ideologies such symbolic terms may indeed relate to real problems, real events and real options, and may be used as tools of analysis rather than as weapons of attack, or symbols of affirmation or identity; they are then said to have a *dependent* emotive meaning. For instance, the leaders of a movement facing the necessity to co-ordinate the spontaneous forces which originated and sustain the movement, may decide that the co-ordination required to survive a difficult situation, or to push forward toward a decisive victory, re-quires unity and discipline. In such a context the term 'spontanistic' may be used to pin-point the problems and risks of a lack of co-ordination and unity, but without attempting to stigmatize and expel particular members of the movement.

In other situations characterized by an ossified and overdisciplined uniformity, we may find that the term 'planning' has acquired an independent emotive meaning of a laudatory type which makes it impossible to seriously criticize the very real dangers of bureaucratic ossification, and discuss different ways of combining planning and spontaneity.

When we look more closely at laudatory terms like planning and spontaneity, whether they are used instrumentally in persuasive com-munications of independent emotive meanings in order to hide real problems, or are perceived at the receiving end as encouraging or uplifting oratory, we often find that such independent emotive mean-ings fulfil the function of safe-guarding the hegemony of a certain social class. They do this by excluding real problems from the full view of classes suffering from such problems without understanding why.

On this point critical sociology has a role to play, and it would seem that this role can be most effectively fulfilled by combining critical sociology with a sociology of class. Who benefit and who suffer from a particular kind of ideological use of terms like spontaneity and planning, or of terms related to them? This question, in its turn, calls for further questions regarding patterns of social differentiation in the society within which we observe spontaneity and planning, and regarding the differential cultivation of independent emotive meanings of these terms. Several contributions to this book take this approach, most notably those written by K. S. Jomo, and by Elizabeth Jelin.

The contributors to the plenary session on Spontaneity and Planning in Social Development at the Ninth World Congress of Sociology had several things to accomplish. Some attention had to be given to definitions of spontaneity and planning, and to a scrutiny of how such terms have been used in the scientific debate. The contributions by Piotr Sztompka and Lars Udéhn address themselves to these problems of conceptual clarification and explication. But the topic of our plenary session also dealt with the *interplay* of spontaneity and planning in *social development.* Here various conceptions of social development, or social transformation are possible.

The difficulty of considering the meaning of spontaneity and planning separately from each other can be indicated by pointing out, for instance, that activities which appear as planned on the individual level, or on the micro level of firms or organizations, may appear as spontaneous when aggregated on the macro level, in the sense that they are unregulated by any overall plans. Business cycles, inflation and stagflation are not planned; they are spontaneous in this sense in spite of the fact that they add up a large number of activities which on the individual or micro level may have implied a considerable amount of planning. Similarly, but less easy to document in modern history, individual activities of a spontaneous nature may add up to *coincide* with an overall planning of social events.

But the fact that one and the same set of *activities* may seem spontaneous on the macro level while appearing as planned on the micro level, does not imply that the meaning of the concept spontaneity varies significantly between these levels. There must be a core meaning of this concept which applies at any level. Micro activities and macro events which are unregulated by any antecedent plans, or obviously contradict any such plans, are usually called spontaneous. Spontaneity, however, is not therefore unpremeditated. It springs from human predicaments and structural contradictions rather than from plans or normative regulation.

The term *planning* would seem to have much more variety of meaning than the term spontaneity. Of course it would be possible to restrict the use of this term to the construction of five-year plans and production targets within socialist societies. But this would leave unanalyzed the elements of planning both on the level of the state and enterprises which no doubt exists also in private capitalist societies. The planning system of big business in highly developed capitalist societies has been most convincingly depicted by John Kenneth Galbraith in his book *Economics and the Public Purpose* (1974, part three), and later by Alfred D. Chandler Jr. in *The Visible Hand* (1977). Since the present volume, unfortunately, does not contain any contribution on these capitalist planning systems, in their interaction with capitalist markets, we must refer interested readers to the two books just mentioned. Marginalist economists, due to their restricted and therefore somewhat unrealistic focus on spontaneous market mechanisms alone, have little or nothing to contribute on this point.

Given the variety of meanings of the term planning, I here venture two sociological generalizations:

(1) Planning can be based on two fundamentally different mechanisms which, however, can be combined: (a) achieving predictable and desirable results by CONSTRUCTING THE FUTURE; this can be achieved through centralized setting of *plan targets*, and by *legislating* or *organizing* the relevant sectors of economy or society to implement the plan through detailed co-ordinated *instruction* and *prescription*. (b) In the absence of such highly regulative means of 'constructing the future' through centralized planning, it is possible, at least to some extent, to introduce a certain element of planning by learning to CAUSALLY MANIPULATE AND PREDICT THE FUTURE, more precisely in information-gathering and processing which makes it possible to estimate and possibly to manipulate variables as well as parameters of socio-economic processes, for instance by changing interest rates and exchange rates, introducing tax-holidays, economic incentives, currency regulations etc. Spontaneity, in the sense of decentralized activity, can be allowed considerable degrees of freedom within such planning frameworks. Polish socialist economists such as Oscar Lange (1963) and Wlodzimierz Brus (1972) have described such combinations of centralized planning and decentralized spontaneity, and in the present volume Branko Horvat has dealt with the same problem, but from a somewhat different angle, namely that of workers self-management. My own contribution in the last chapter also touches on these problems.

(2) The predominant mode of production within a given society

determines the levels and types of planning possible in that society; more stringent centralized planning, obviously, is not possible within a capitalist mode of production, as Tatiana Zaslavskaya points out in her contribution to this volume.

The two types of planning indicated in the first generalization above are ideal types. In real societies we find various mixtures of patterns corresponding to these ideal types. Even in bourgeois capitalist societies we find elements of centralized regulation, for instance through legislation of rules for traffic, and through the bureaucratic rules that make the conduct of public administration predictable. And in socialist societies we may find that some activities make use of mechanism (b) — predicting and causally manipulating the future — rather than mechanism (a) — constructing the future — as specified above.

However, there are also other types of complications which must be added to our scheme. The distinction between spontaneity and planning does not exhaust the universe of action. There are activities such as habitual or compliant action which may be neither spontaneous nor planned from the micro perspective of the actor, but which fit beautifully into macro-planning schemes. Another complication deals with the relevance of the so-called *private sphere* in macro sociological analysis, and the *time element* in social development. It could be maintained that there is a completely private type of spontaneity which does not fit into any macro processes, nor relies to any considerable extent on macro conditions. Such privatized spontaneity may seem completely irrelevant to our topic of spontaneity and planning, and could thus be disregarded here. I do not take this view. When the time element is considered even the most private may become publicly significant.

Not only is the element of time involved in the transition from one predominant ideal-typical situation to another, with all the various aspects and combinations of incremental versus dialectical change which may operate over time. What may at one time seem as a highly private type of spontaneity, following its own internal rhythm determined by psychological rather than sociological laws, may at a later time become a social not to say societal issue. Such a private process is the *quest for personal identity among individuals or groups.* Sometimes such a quest for identity may seem unrelated to broader social issues, but if shared by sufficiently many people, it inevitably feeds its tributaries into the mainstream of social history. For instance, the private quest for personal identity may be transformed into so-called counter-culture, and such deviations may in their turn become politicized or commercialized; the private has thus become public; spontaneity has become an issue which could be considered by planners.

The social prompting and the societal effects of more-or-less-widespread private spontaneity could thus be explored in the so-called counter-cultures which have emerged in some highly developed capitalist societies. Such counter-cultures may sometimes appear as a withdrawal to sanctuaries or 'cultural reservations' with their own alternative style of life largely unrelated to outside society and culture. The numerical size, insulation, visibility or outward activities of such counter-cultures (including the extent to which the paraphernalia of counter-culture turn out to be marketable on the commercialized arenas of youthful leisure-time activities) would seem to determine the effects of counter-culture on society at large. Planning issues which may arise at this point deal with questions like the following.

Is counter-culture functional to the pacification and diversion of youth, and thus desirable to planners worried by the activism of youthful 'trouble makers' who do not care to isolate themselves from society but wish to change it? Or is counter-culture a cradle of things to come at the crossroads of today? Do counter-cultures generate innovative impulses which spread in society at large thus confronting social planners with new issues that do not fit into old plans? The paper by Britta Jonsson, which was presented at another session of the Ninth World Congress of Sociology, touches on the sociological meanings of counter-culture. I have included it here in spite of the fact that it is not couched in terms of spontaneity and planning, to provide food for thought about the relationships between private and group spontaneity, and public issues and concerns.

It is obvious that many of the themes of spontaneity and planning indicated in this introduction come rather close to the themes of *decentralization* and *centralization* so often discussed by political sociologists, and sociologists of economic life. Just like spontaneity and planning, decentralization and centralization seem to represent opposite principles. Even though this is the case at the level of definitions, few sociologists today would consider these principles unreconcilable in society. Centralization may be necessary for effective co-ordination and equalization of social conditions. Decentralized spontaneity is needed for human fulfilment, creativity and self-realization, and for motivation and mobilization. Both are thus considered necessary in most modern societies. Furthermore, one set of principles advocating decentralization and spontaneity often introduces strains, negative externalities and inequality which call for centralized measures to check these effects, and centralized planning pursued in the extreme may close off the mainsprings of motivation and personal involvement, thus calling for more decentralization and spontaneity. Here the questions arise what modes of production, which social structures and what historical junctures in social development allow what combinations of spontaneity and planning, decentralization and centralization. None of the papers in this volume address and answer these questions conclusively, but these questions should still be raised. However, it seems appropriate on this point to state these questions in a somewhat more systematic manner. In the course of doing this, I will have an opportunity to place the various contributions to this book within a more systematic framework.

In the figure on page 8 I have indicated a number of possible combinations of centralistic planning (CP), and decentralistic spontaneity (DS) without in any way claiming to have exhausted the possibilities. Some of the types indicated can be specified in quite different ways, and thus will render several sub-types due to historical conditions not incorporated in the formulation of this typology. The sequence of types in the figure is not meant to be historical. However, in our comments we will mention a few cases of historical transitions from one type to another. The first types — (a) and (b) — contrast two rather different cases — participatory planning and the so-called command economy. The Yugoslav economy based on workers self-management seems to be working toward participatory planning, as indicated by Branko Horvat in his contribution. The Soviet system is usually conceived in the West as a command economy with a very limited range for spontaneity (as indicated by the brackets around DS); but Tatiana Zaslavskaya in her contribution claims that the Soviet system more recently has been introducing significant elements of participatory planning as well. Obviously no real case is a pure case, in terms of our ideal types; but even so great differences remain between Yugoslavia and the Soviet Union.

Type (c) refers to the kind of market socialism described, for instance, by W. Brus (1972). The socialist state does not in this case regulate the economy in detail, but only sets the most important parameters of decentralized spontaneous economic activities, for instance prices on factors of production, and some commodities, interest rates and the like. Some methods by which such a socialist planning can be carried out are discussed by Lars Udéhn in his paper, and Branko Horvat also deals with related problems. Such setting of parameters of decentralized economic activities is also rather common on a more limited scale in some non-socialist so-called mixed economies today.

FIGURE
Types of Relationships between Centralized Planning and Decentralized Spontaneity

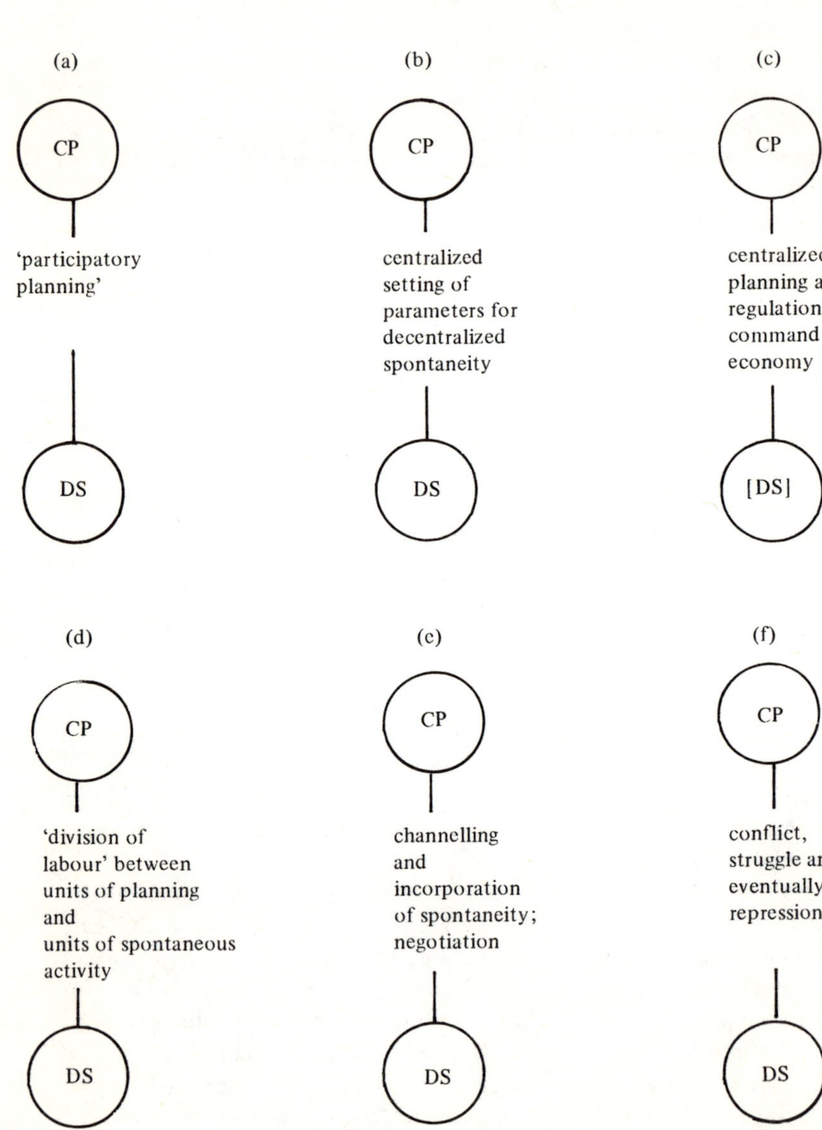

I will here skip type (d) for the time being since it can be better understood after introducing types (e) and (f). All of these three last-mentioned types relate mainly to capitalist economies even though, as we will show, type (e) can be illustrated also with the early stages of post-war Yugoslav developments.

Type (e) — a planned channelling and incorporation of spontaneous movements — fits rather well with Bogdan Denitch's description of the emergence of early post-war Yugoslavia. The spontaneous mobilization of popular forces in the guerilla warfare against the Nazi occupiers in World War II was the historical foundation of the new Yugoslav federation, and could be channelled and incorporated into a new system by the Yugoslav Communist party under Tito's leadership.

But also in Elizabeth Jelin's description of the case of Argentina in the first period of Peronism, we find this pattern of channelling of spontaneous movements, and their incorporation — more precisely of the trade union movement — and a subsequent pattern of state-union negotiations. Such patterns of negotiation can also be found in Yugoslavia in relationships between federal or regional agencies, and decentralized enterprises under the system of workers self-management. In capitalist Argentina, however, the system did not proceed toward a pattern of participatory planning as in socialist Yugoslavia, but toward increasing class conflicts and eventually repression of decentralized spontaneous movements — that is from type (e) to type (f). The broader contextual conditions for type (e) in Argentina — according to Elizabeth Jelin — was the existence of a political legitimacy assured by a bourgeois class hegemony. When this legitimacy and hegemony broke down as a result of the emerging contradictions of peripheral capitalism (another significant contextual condition) then a transition from (e) to (f) took place.

K. S. Jomo's and E. A. Akeredolu-Ale's papers on Malaysia and Nigeria respectively also deal with problems of state-planning and spontaneous developments in so-called peripheral capitalist economies. But due to the historical and local specificities of these two countries, the structural contradictions involved manifested themselves in ways which in some if not all aspects differ from the Latin American scene reviewed by Jelin. In Nigeria manifest class conflict is still less rampant than in Latin America, and Akeredolu-Ale therefore approaches the problems of planning within the framework of what he calls organizational theory. What he has in mind is a 'division of labour' between the management of public affairs, and the spontaneous dynamics of entre-preneurial activities, as indicated by type (d) in our figure. The role of the state is to take control over the residual tasks which the capitalist economy cannot resolve on its own. In Nigeria these tasks are not only the attainment of professed political goals such as self-reliance, egalitarianism, social justice, freedom and democracy, according to Akeredolu-Ale, but also the setting-up and management of enterprises for which the Nigerian capitalist economy turned out to have little capacity, or for which transnational corporations had little incentive in the Nigerian context. Akeredolu-Ale's paper emphasized firstly the structural necessities of state intervention in Nigerian industrialization, due to the weaknesses of indigenous spontaneous forces, or to the disincentives operating on them, and secondly the structural constraints which limit the effectiveness of state-interventions within peripheral capitalist economies like Nigeria.

Jomo describes a country — Malaysia — which seems somewhat more developed than Nigeria in terms of modern entrepreneurial activities, but he also emphasizes the role of state interventions. They can support and encourage selected elements in an otherwise capitalist economy. Being more developed along capitalist lines than Nigeria, Malaysia also exhibits more of manifest class conflict. A transition from type (d) under which we have subsumed both Nigeria and Malaysia to types (e) and (f) would seem likely in the case of Malaysia, and may already have started. However, there are a number of specific local conditions in Malaysia — not the least being its small size, and its neighbours, which could make such a transition take on characteristics rather different from those found in Latin America.

It may seem rather paradoxical that the division of labour between the state and decentralistic spontaneous forces which define type (d) can be illustrated not only by less developed countries like Nigeria and to some extent Malaysia, but also by highly developed European welfare states. Such a paradoxical coincidence is of course a result of our rather crude and ahistoric typology. In Europe, and particularly in Scandinavia, the strength of labour movements and their institutionalized incorporation in political and labour-market structures, has made class conflict, for instance in the form of strikes, less manifest (Korpi and Shalev, 1979), and made it possible for the state to concentrate on caring for the 'residual tasks' which the capitalist economy cannot resolve on its own, in the kind of 'division of labour' indicated by Akeredolu-Ale. What our typology does not take account of, then, is the fact that class conflict in the Nigerian case still is rather undeveloped and therefore not particularly intense, while historical processes in Scandinavia have allowed the strength of the working-class to express itself politically in such a manner as to reduce the intensity of certain forms of class struggle. This historical process could be seen as another sub-type of type (e), in addition to the sub-types illustrated by the cases of early, post-war Yugoslav developments, and the first period of Peronism in Argentina.

However, as I indicate in my own paper toward the end of this book, the contradictions of capitalism have not been resolved by a division of labour between state and economy within the framework of mature welfare capitalism, but are in fact now manifesting themselves with new force. In Sweden this has led the trade union movement and the Social Democratic Party to call for a system of 'wage-earners' funds offering more direct control to collective labour over the use of capital, not through a nationalization of enterprises by a labour government but in a more decentralized fashion. My paper will illuminate how this proposed solution may relate spontaneity and planning in social development in a manner which combines types (a) and (c).

As contextual conditions affecting the emergence and transition of different types of combinations of spontaneity and planning, I have mentioned more or less interrelated structural and historical conditions such as modes of production (socialist or capitalist), position in the world economy (central or peripheral), type of neighbouring countries, early or late periods of development, type of class hegemony, extent of political legitimacy, and extent of manifest class struggle. All of these are macro-conditions. One distinguished contribution to this book, however, treats micro-, or perhaps rather intermediate-level conditions, namely the paper on technological planning and spontaneity by Albert Cherns. It helps us to fill in a linkage between the macro-level conditions and the micro-processes of spontaneity.

But as Tatiana Zaslavskaya has emphasized in her comments, a technology is not chosen willy-nilly with reference to idealistic aims such as 'more room for spontaneity', but rather on the basis of the dominant mode of production. She would seem to imply that capitalism is less free to enter into technological planning *for* spontaneity than is socialism, due to the strictures of capital accumulation and the profit-making characteristic of the capitalist system. However, in actual fact the industrial technologies of socialist countries — even of Yugoslavia with its workers self-management — would seem to be very similar to those of capitalist countries, from the point of view indicated by Cherns. Perhaps level of industrial development is as crucial as mode of production on this point. Perhaps the technological change needed to give more room for spontaneity will come about only when a highly developed capitalist country goes socialist? As Karl Marx said: 'No social order ever disappears before all the productive forces for which there is room in it have been developed; and new higher relations of production never appear before the material conditions of their existence have matured in the womb of the old society.'

I would like to conclude my introduction on this hopeful note. Let me only add that the reader who believes that he knows what this book is all about after having read this introduction is mistaken. The introduction may have added structure to the book; but I have not provided texture. The wealth of information and insight contained in the following chapters now waits for the reader's attention.

REFERENCES

BRUS, W. (1972) *The Market in a Socialist Economy*. London: Routledge and Kegan Paul.

CHANDLER, A. D., Jr. (1977) *The Visible Hand*. Cambridge, Mass.: The Belknap Press of Harvard University Press.

GALBRAITH, J. K. (1973) *Economics and the Public Purpose*. London: André Deutsch.

KORPI, W. and SHALEV, M. (1979) 'Strikes, Power and Politics in the Western Nations, 1900-1976', *Political Power and Social Theory* 1: 299-332.

LANGE, O. (1963) *Political Economy. Vol. I: General Problems*. New York: Macmillan.

STEVENSON, C. L. (1944) *Ethics and Language*. New Haven: Yale University Press.

I
CONCEPTS AND PROCESSES

1

THE DIAECTICS OF SPONTANEITY AND PLANNING IN SOCIOLOGICAL THEORY

Piotr Sztompka
Jagiellonian University, Poland

> Most, if not all, revolutions have produced societies very different from those desired by the revolutionaries. Here is a problem, and it deserves thought from every serious critic of society.
>
> *Karl R. Popper*

1. INTRODUCTION

The focus of this paper is meta-theoretical. Taking it for granted that some phenomena, events and processes in social life are deliberately planned, and some others are spontaneous, I attempt to discuss the differential capability of several sociological theories to incorporate this crucial dichotomy in their respective conceptual frameworks.

The purpose of the paper is to show that:

(a) spontaneity and planning are two aspects of social reality which exist side by side in every and any transformation of the social system, for reasons not only factual (extrinsic), but also, and preeminently principal (intrinsic);

(b) various sociological theories (orientations, traditions, 'paradigms', 'schools' etc.) possess differential capability for meaningfully conceptualizing, and validly accounting for the spontaneous and planned aspects of social reality, and consequently they would have differential utility for explanatory, predictive and controlling purposes (for adequate social science and realistic social practice);

(c) dialectic sociology, approximated most closely by the Marxist theory of society, presents a unified image of spontaneity and planning at the three interlinked levels: the level of individual action (microsociological), the level of social structure, and the level of historical process (macrosociological) and therefore it provides the best theoretical foundation for effective social policy.

The course of the argument includes the following steps:

(a) at the beginning I attempt to introduce some initial definitions, clarifying the meanings in which the relevant terms, 'spontaneity' and 'planning', will be understood in further discussion. I also venture a tentative typology of factors responsible for the notorious co-presence of both spontaneity and planning in the majority of social phenomena and processes;

(b) as I believe that any concept or proposition of a sociological theory is meaningful only within the context of some more or less explicit assumptions (conceptual model), I attempt to reveal those assumptions which are relevant for the discussion of spontaneity and planning. Those assumptions are of the ontological sort (specifying the fundamental features of social reality: of man, society and history), and of the epistemological sort (specifying the fundamental properties of social cognition);

(c) then I attempt to show how the choice of particular assumptions prejudges the way in which the factors of spontaneity and planning are treated in a sociological theory. Three ideal-types of sociological theories are outlined: positivistic, subjectivistic and dialectical. The first is shown to over-emphasize the possibility of manipulation and planning, the second — to over-emphasize the factor of freedom and spontaneity. Only the third — the dialectic model — is capable of incorporating the interplay of spontaneity and planning, paying their due to both interlinked factors;

(d) finally, the dialectic solution to the riddle of spontaneity versus planning is shown to entail specific directives for the planning activity itself. Some hints for the dialectical approach to planning are suggested at the end of the paper.

2. CONCEPTUAL CLARIFICATIONS

Obviously, spontaneity and planning are mutually relative concepts; the meaning of one is the obverse of the meaning of the other. There are two strategies available for constructing the meaning of mutually relative concepts of this sort: one can either define 'spontaneity', and then construct 'planning' as a residual category within a certain class of events and processes, or one can define 'planning' and then construct 'spontaneity' as a residual category within that class of events and processes. I am choosing the second strategy, and therefore two steps must be taken: first — a class of 'planned' events and processes must be singled out within the universe of all possible events and processes, and second — a residual class of 'spontaneous' events and processes must be specified as covering the remaining part of the selected universe.

By the procedure of successive approximations one may narrow down the universe of events and processes, coming down to the class of 'planned' events and processes. The following steps may be mentioned:

(a) the widest class conceivable is the universe of all events and processes in the world;

(b) within that class the narrower one will be made of *humanly relevant* events and processes, i.e. those causally effective with respect to human beings and those with respect to which human beings are causally effective;

(c) the next, narrower class is made of events and processes *subjected to human impact*, i.e. created, shaped or modified either by human actions, or by the sheer presence of human beings;

(d) within that class, the narrower one will be made of events and processes subjected to conscious and purposeful *human intervention*. Of such events and processes it can meaningfully be said that they were 'intended' or 'expected' by somebody (an individual, some agency, a group of individuals etc.);

(e) but obviously human conscious and purposeful interventions in the course of events and processes may either be successful or may fail. This brings us to the narrowest class of those events and processes which are the result of a *successful human intervention*, i.e. have been created, shaped or modified by human beings exactly in line with their purposes, intentions or expectations. Such events and processes 'reproduce' in reality the plans conceived in advance by conscious and purposeful agents (in microscale — human individuals; in macroscale — planning agencies of all sorts), and thus may be referred to as 'planned'.

I propose to reserve the term 'planned' for this class of events and processes. To repeat — by PLANNED I mean those events and processes which have been created, shaped, or modified by a successful human intervention; or to put it otherwise — the results of successful planning.

Now, 'spontaneous' events and processes must be constructed as a residual category, by opposition to 'planned' events and processes. Thus, by SPONTANEOUS I mean those events and processes which have been created, shaped, modified or at least encountered in the course of human intervention, but have not been intended by the planning agents, or to put it otherwise — the results of unsuccessful planning. In this case the plans conceived by some conscious and purposeful agents or agencies are not reproduced in reality. The discrepancies may be of at least three types: first — something qualitatively different than planned may be obtained; second — something quantitatively more than planned may be obtained (note that this sort of spontaneity may sometimes be welcome, but by no means always; compare the surplus production of oil, with the unexpected rise of juvenile delinquency); or third — something less than planned may be obtained (again, most often this situation is negatively evaluated by a planner, but it is not always the case; consider the situation when expected and accepted side-effects failed to appear).

To sum up my terminological conventions: by PLANNING I mean any deliberate, conscious and purposeful intervention of human agents or agencies in the course of events and processes. The successful planning results in PLANNED events and processes. The unsuccessful (or not fully successful) planning produces unintended, unaccepted, unrecognized side-effects, or simply results different from or contrary to a plan, which shall be named SPONTANEOUS. According to such understanding of the relevant terms, one may speak of spontaneity only if there has been some effort at planning, and the effort failed. The problem of spontaneity appears as the problem of limitations to the human mastery over the world (and particularly the social world).

3. EXTRINSIC VS. INTRINSIC SPONTANEITY

Spontaneity understood in this way is certainly an ubiquitous factor of human experience. Human efforts at purposeful control notoriously fail. Now, why is it the case? There seem some analytically possible answers to this query. Two quite distinct sources of spontaneity may be mentioned, and consequently one may speak of two types of spontaneity: extrinsic and intrinsic.

In the case of *extrinsic* spontaneity something is wrong with the tools utilized by the planning agent (or agency). First, the agent may possess inadequate knowledge of the 'know-that' type, i.e. the theories or empirical data taken as the basis for planning may be wrong, or at least incomplete. Such an inadequate knowledge may refer either to the target system of planning (an object which is to be created, shaped or modified), or to the strategies of effective action (so called 'socio-technical', or 'engineering', or 'praxiological' knowledge). Second, the agent may possess inadequate knowledge of the 'know-how' type, i.e. the technological methods of implementation of the conceived plans may either be ineffective or unrealistic (not fit to the actual manipulative possibilities of the planner). Third, the planning process itself may be carried out in a sub-optimal way. After all, planning is a human activity, and planners are human, too. All the dilemmas of human action may be encountered in planning and lead to spontaneous effects (e.g. ambiguity of values taken as the guiding standards for planning, conflicts between tactical and strategic considerations, conflicts between long range and short range goals etc.).

In all cases discussed above the spontaneity is apparent rather than real; something which we do not understand or cannot manipulate appears as spontaneous. Spontaneity in this sense is the epiphenomenon of our ignorance or our impotence or both. Each can be overcome, at least in principle. Therefore extrinsic spontaneity must be conceived as factual only and not a basic limitation of planning efforts.

The situation becomes radically different in the case of intrinsic spontaneity. Here the problem is much more fundamental; some properties of the target system invalidate our planning efforts, making them ineffective, partly effective, or even counter-effective. This failure cannot be corrected, even potentially, because it is brought about by the inherent, ontological properties of reality. No improvements of our knowledge or planning techniques will do, the only solution is to adapt our planning techniques to those fundamental limitations, and to curb our expectations as to foolproof and totally effective planning.

Needless to say, the limitations of this sort become particularly pronounced when the society itself becomes the target-system of planning. In this case the following ontological factors may be tentatively suggested as responsible for intrinsic spontaneity:

(a) the reflexive character of social reality, i.e. the ability of human beings to react in some way to the plan itself, even before it is implemented in practice (e.g. self-fulfilling prophecies, suicidal predictions, boomerang effects etc.);

(b) the emergent character of some social phenomena, i.e. the inability to account for them beforehand, even on the basis of most adequate and complete knowledge of component (or lower-level) phenomena, and their regularities (e.g. interaction-effects, composition-effects, macro-scale effects of micro-scale activities, aggregate-effects etc.);

(c) the complexity of social reality, and particularly the multiplicity of planning agencies and planning efforts simultaneously operating (the attempts of one planner may invalidate the attempts of the other);

(d) the openness of the social system (environmental effects caused by other systems — ecological, geographical, natural, technological, personality etc.);

(e) the stochastic or probabilistic nature of intra-systemic links in a society;

(f) the internal contradictions, antinomies, conflicts between components or subsystems within society, and between the social system and other systems;

(g) the random, irregular, 'capricious' nature of human conduct (of some actors most of the time, and of all actors some of the time); it is suggested by such terms as 'free will', 'dynamic assessment', 'independent factor of choice', 'definition of a situation' etc.

So far I have given the basic definitions of 'spontaneity' and 'planning', and have substantiated the belief that both concepts are necessary for the adequate account of social reality. Now, the question is: which sociological theories are able to incorporate both concepts in their frames of reference. This obviously depends on the explicit content of those theories, as well as on the implicit philosophical assumptions they accept. Let us begin with the latter.

4. PHILOSOPHICAL DILEMMAS

The meaningful discussion of the issue of spontaneity and planning presupposes some standpoint on two philosophical questions: first — on the ontological question of the role of human action in the functioning of society and in the course of history (because social planning is after all, a form of action intended to influence society and history); and, second, on the epistemological question of the potentialities and limitations of social cognition (because social planning is a form of application of sociological knowledge). Those questions give birth to double philosophical dilemmas. I shall argue that traditional solutions to those dilemmas are inadequate, because they entail the one-sided emphasis either on the factor of planning or the factor of spontaneity. I shall introduce in each case, the alternative, dialectic solution, which shall be able to incorporate both factors simultaneously. Let me start with the ontological dilemma.

The question of the role of man in society and history is phrased as the dilemma of *freedom* vs. *necessity*. The standpoint emphasizing the factor of freedom may be called VOLUNTARISTIC, and the standpoint emphasizing the factor of necessity may be called FATALISTIC.

But there are two, rarely noticed, but definitely distinct meanings of VOLUNTARISM:

(a) $VOLUNTARISM_1$ = the belief in the causal effectiveness of human intervention, if the intervention is decided upon and executed. To put it otherwise — man is omnipotent, and by his action can influence all social phenomena and social processes ('Man can do everything'):

(b) $VOLUNTARISM_2$ = the belief in the irregularity and indeterminacy of social phenomena and processes. To put it otherwise — society is made of plural, random, irregular, indetermined events ('In society, everything is possible, everything can happen').

Similarly, there are two, rarely noticed, but definitely distinct meanings of FATALISM:

(a) $FATALISM_1$ = the belief in the absence of any causal effectiveness of human intervention, even if such an intervention is undertaken and attempted. Man is impotent with respect to the 'invisible hand' of Nature, History, Deity etc. which rules all social phenomena and processes ('One can do nothing about it');

(b) $FATALISM_2$ = the belief in the regular, deterministic character of social phenomena and processes. Society is made of orderly, regular, law-governed, causally-connected events. Only such things are possible in a society which do not contradict social laws ('There are things which cannot be done').

When those distinctions are taken into account, the contradiction of VOLUNTARISM and FATALISM appears as spurious. Some inter-combinations of both traditional standpoints are possible, as well as some more extreme formulations. And thus:

(a) $VOLUNTARISM_1$ + $VOLUNTARISM_2$ = EXTREME VOLUNTARISM entailing some form of 'chaotic activism', as the only possible social policy;

(b) FATALISM$_1$ + FATALISM$_2$ = EXTREME FATALISM entailing some form of enlightened resignation, as the only possible social policy;

(c) FATALISM$_1$ + VOLUNTARISM$_2$ = a standpoint which entails some form of ignorant, helpless passivism, as the only possible social policy;

(d) VOLUNTARISM$_1$ + FATALISM$_2$ = POSSIBILISM entailing some form of creative activism, as a prescribed social policy.

The assumption of possibilism with the attached directive of creative activism is a standpoint to be encountered within the dialectic model of society and social development, as formulated in the Marxist tradition. In Marxism, as interpreted in this paper, man is seen as the creative agent, the constructor of a society, and society — at the same time — as the producer of objective, structural constraints on human action. A certain range of possibilities for creative action is open for every individual. But his action can be effective only within the range of those possibilities if it is carried out in accord with social laws. A role of planning is therefore acknowledged, but so is the necessity of spontaneously-arising constraints.

Let me now move to a second, epistemological dimension. The problem of the nature of social knowledge is phrased as the dilemma of *theory* vs. *practice*. The standpoint emphasizing the theoretical aspects of knowledge may be called COGNITIVISTIC, and the standpoint emphasizing the practical aspects of knowledge may be called ACTIVISTIC.

But there are two, rarely noticed, but definitely distinct meanings of COGNITIVISM:

(a) COGNITIVISM$_1$ = the belief that social knowledge is (should be) abstract and general (nomological). It provides simplified and one-sided models of reality (theoretical idealizations);

(b) COGNITIVISM$_2$ = the belief that social knowledge is (should be) detached from valuations and practical applications. It provides simplified, objective, value-free descriptions and interpretations of basically intellectual relevance.

Similarly, there are two, rarely noticed but definitely distinct meanings of ACTIVISM:

(a) ACTIVISM$_1$ = the belief that social knowledge is (should be) concrete and particular (idiographic). It provides the full-fledged picture of 'living, real human beings' in their everyday activities, and in their real social environment. Social knowledge is meaningful and immediately relevant for human actors.

(b) ACTIVISM$_2$ = the belief that social knowledge is (should be) infused with valuations and oriented toward change. It implies normative prescriptions, proscriptions, suggestions, directives of immediate relevance for practical action.

When those distinctions are taken into account, the contradiction of COGNITIVISM and ACTIVISM appears as spurious. Some inter-combinations of both traditional standpoints are possible:

(a) $COGNITIVISM_1 + COGNITIVISM_2 = EXTREME COGNITIVISM$ entailing some 'ivory tower', or 'academic', or 'scholastic' image of social science;

(b) $ACTIVISM_1 + ACTIVISM_2 = EXTREME ACTIVISM$ entailing some 'down-to-earth' narrowly-practical orientation;

(c) $ACTIVISM_1 + COGNITIVISM_2 = FACT\text{-}ORIENTED OBJEC\text{-}TIVISM$, or 'statistician's sociology' entailing inductive, fact-gathering attitude;

(d) $COGNITIVISM_1 + ACTIVISM_2 = THEORETICAL AND COM\text{-}MITTED SOCIOLOGY$.

The image of theoretical and committed sociology is to be encountered within the dialectic conception of social knowledge as 'human praxis', typical for the Marxist orientation in social theory. Knowledge of society conceptualized in abstract and general terms is here conceived as directly functional for practical social changes, and conversely, the transformations of society are seen as directly reflected in the constantly growing and modified body of a theory. Theory appears as a tool for planning, and a reflection of spontaneity.

The dialectical assumptions of POSSIBILISM and COMMITMENT seem to provide the only proper philosophical framework for the meaningful consideration of spontaneity and planning in their close, dialectic interplay.

5. SOCIOLOGICAL THEORIES

Now, the substantive content of sociological theories must be examined from the same point of view: are they able or not to account for the factors of spontaneity and planning? For the purposes of the present discussion sociological theories may be considered as systematic attempts to solve three related questions: what is a man as a member of society, what is a society, what is history of a society. Taking into account the typical answers to those questions three distinct 'models of sociology' can be sketched: positivistic, subjectivistic and dialectical.

The *positivistic sociology* involves:

(a) the image of man as a passive, reactive creature; responding either to environmental stimuli or internal drives (illustrations: behavioristic theory, learning theory, instinct theory, psychoanalytic theory, the 'over-socialized conception of man' etc.);

(b) the image of society as a mechanical or organic system, functioning in an orderly fashion (illustration: structural functionalism);

(c) the image of history as a strictly determined, orderly sequence of events (illustration: evolutionary theory, also so-called 'orthodox' or 'vulgar' Marxism, as read — mistakenly — by some interpreters).

It can easily be seen that positivistic sociology places a one-sided emphasis on orderliness, determinacy, regularity, non-randomness of social phenomena. For this reason it is unable to incorporate spontaneity in its conceptual framework, except perhaps in the form of deviant behavior.

The *subjectivistic sociology* involves:

(a) the image of man as a freely-active, illogical, irrational, emotional, affective creature; interpreting and defining situations, negotiating decisions with himself, and executing actions in a constantly modified manner (illustrations: symbolic interactionism, 'ethogenetics' etc.);

(b) the image of society as a fluid, constantly changing network of multiple interactions (illustrations: ethnomethodology, dramaturgical theory);

(c) the image of history as a set of separate, individual events with no perceivable regularities, no causal interconnections, and no totality.

It can easily be seen that subjectivistic sociology places a one-sided emphasis on disorderliness, indeterminacy, irregularity, randomness of social phenomena. For this reason it is unable to incorporate planning in its conceptual framework.

The *dialectical sociology* involves:

(a) the image of man as freely-active but within the scope of structural constraints, creative but in the closed field of opportunities and limitations, partly determining and partly determined, subject and object simultaneously. I shall refer to such a standpoint by the name of CREATIVISM (illustrations: Marxian theory of human species nature, theory of alienation as the pathology of human nature etc.);

(b) the image of society as a morphogenetic, open system, generating a network of structural relationships within which the elements are implicated (illustrations: Marxian theory of socioeconomic formation, Marxian theory of classes etc.). I shall refer to such a standpoint by the name of STRUCTURALISM.

(c) the image of history as a regular, directive, endogenous development, moved by a human social praxis (illustrations: Marxian theory of class consciousness, theory of revolution, theory of the proletarian party). I shall refer to such a standpoint by the name of HISTORISM.

The dialectical assumptions of CREATIVISM, STRUCTURALISM and HISTORISM seem to provide the only proper sociological framework for the meaningful consideration of spontaneity and planning in their close, mutual interdependence.

6. SOME HINTS FOR DIALECTICAL PLANNING

Pervasive spontaneity is no reason for despair but should rather be conceived as the eternal challenge, stimulating human creative efforts. In order to face and exploit this opportunity, the planning activity itself must be properly structured. The dialectical philosophical assumptions, as well as the dialectical sociological orientation entail certain requirements that have to be met by planning activities.

First, planning should be STRUCTURAL rather than COERCIVE, i.e. it should create structural opportunities for the people to behave in certain ways, and prevent them from acting in different ways; it should channel their living space by means of economic structures, norms, rules, patterns of behavior, rather than compelling them to action by direct orders, enforcement, manipulation. Planners should rely on meta-power rather than naked power.

Second, planning should be FLEXIBLE rather than RIGID, i.e. it should allow for changing circumstances, for unexpected reactions to previous decisions, for long-range side-effects etc. It should include 'planning for spontaneity', i.e. come to terms with the unavoidable factor of spontaneity. It should be a dynamic adaptive process utilizing feedbacks of all sorts.

Third, planning should be CONCRETE rather than ABSTRACT, i.e. it should specify goals and means within the realistically available resources and opportunities, and not rest content with vague declarations and wishful thinking. It should be immediately translatable into specific, practical activities of specified agents (whether individuals or collectivities).

Fourth, planning should be SELECTIVE rather than TOTALISTIC, i.e. it should focus on the strategic societal variables (e.g. the economic sphere), and leave the secondary, less significant fields for the free play of spontaneous factors.

Planning of such a dialectic sort allows for the full implementation of human creative powers; transforming the course as well as the mechanisms of social development toward growing self-consciousness and self-direction, within the inescapable limitations of the human condition.

REFERENCES

AFANASYEV, V. G. (1968) *Scientific Management of a Society*. Moscow: International Publishers.

BAUMGARTNER, T. et al. (1975) 'A Systems Model of Conflict and Change in Planning Systems', *General Systems* 20: 167–183.

BENNIS, W. G. et al. (1969) *The Planning of Change*. New York: Holt.

BURNS, T. (1973) 'A Structural Theory of Social Exchange', *Acta Sociologica* 16: 188–208.

——, W. BUCKLEY (eds.) (1976) *Power and Control*. London: Sage.

BUCKLEY, W. (1967) *Sociology and Modern Systems Theory*. Englewood Cliffs, NJ: Prentice-Hall.

DAHRENDORF, R. (1968) 'Market and Plan', pp. 215–231 in *Essays in the Theory of Society*. Stanford: Stanford University Press.

DOBROWOLSKI, K. (1973) *Theory of Spontaneous Processes* (in Polish). Krakow: Ossolineum Publishers.

GIBSON, Q. (1960) *The Logic of Social Enquiry*. London: Routledge & Kegan Paul.

GOULDNER, A. (1957) 'Theoretical Requirements of the Applied Social Sciences', *ASR* 22(1): 92–102.

HARE, P., M. F. SECORD, (1972) *Explanation of Human Behavior*. Oxford: University Press.

MERTON, R. K. (1936) 'The Unanticipated Consequences of Purposive Social Action', *American Sociological Review* 1: 894–904.

——(1948) 'The Self-Fulfilling Prophecy', *Antioch Review*, Summer: 193–210.

——(1967) 'Manifest and Latent Functions', in *On Theoretical Sociology*. New York: Free Press.

OSSOWSKI, S. (1968) 'Social Consequences and Conditions of Social Planning' (in Polish), in *Collected Works of S. Ossowski*, vol. V. Warszawa: Polish Scientific Publishers.

POPPER, K. R. (1976) 'Reason or Revolution', pp. 288–300 in T. W. ADORNO (ed.), *The Positivist Dispute in German Sociology*. London: Heinemann.

SCHUTZ, A. (1970) 'Acting and Planning', pp. 125–145 in *On the Phenomenology and Social Relations*. Chicago: Chicago University Press.

——(1970) 'The Problem of Rationality in the Social World', in D. EMMET (ed.), *Sociological Theory and Philosophical Analysis.* New York: Macmillan.

SWINGLEWOOD, A. (1975) *Marx and Modern Social Theory.* London: Macmillan.

SZCZEPAŃSKI, J. (1974) 'Reflections on the Planning of Social Life' (in Polish), in *Przemiany czasu teraźneijszego.* Warszawa: KiW.

SZTOMPKA, P. (1971) 'Some Conditions of the Applicability of Sociological Knowledge', *The Polish Sociological Bulletin* 1: 5–16.

——(1973) 'On the Spurious Dilemma of Theory and Practice' (in Polish), in *Practical Applications of the Social Sciences.* Warszawa: Ossolineum Publishers.

——(1974) *System and Function: Toward a Theory of Society.* New York: Academic Press.

——(1979) *Dialectical Sociology: Overcoming Theoretical Dilemmas.* New York: Academic Press.

TOPOLSKI, J. (1978) *Rozumienie historii* (Understanding history). Warszawa: Polish Editorial Institute.

WIATR, J. (1973) *Marxist Theory of Social Development* (in Polish). Warszawa: Polish Scientific Publishers.

2

CENTRAL PLANNING: POSTSCRIPT TO A DEBATE

Lars Udéhn
University of Uppsala, Sweden

1. THE TREND TOWARDS CENTRAL PLANNING

One of the most conspicuous features of twentieth century development is the increasing role of the state in the management of society. Closely connected with this development is the increasing use of planning methods to move society in a desired direction, or, at least, to avoid some undesired consequences of its spontaneous development. The trend is not continuous, however, and there are great differences between countries. In the West, the discontinuous character of the trend is closely associated with the occurrence of crises in the economic and political systems. In times of depression and war, the state extends its control over the economy, but does not always give it up at the end of a crisis. There are also some differences between countries in the West. So, for instance, France and Sweden have gone further in their use of central planning than have USA, Great Britain, and West Germany. These minor differences are probably due to differences in ideology and tradition.

A big leap in the trend towards central planning was taken by the countries of Eastern Europe when they introduced large-scale central planning of the economy. In later years there have been some reforms in these countries pointing in the direction of a more decentralized economic system, making more use of the market mechanism and less use of central control. This change, which should not be overrated, has led to some speculation about a convergence of the economic systems in East and West (see, for instance, Linneman et al., 1967: 58, 120).

A precondition for efficient planning on the part of the state is a powerful state apparatus. In the capitalist countries of the West, the power of the state is still limited by the institution of private property, but is constantly increasing as a result of the extension of the public sector. The extension of the public sector means, first of all, that an increasing part of society comes under the direct control of the state, and secondly, that the state comes to control an increasing part of society's total resources, which it can use to influence the private sector indirectly. Planning in the West is, of course, very different from planning in the East. It is far less comprehensive and far less detailed. It is less centralized and less imperative. Planning in the West has for a long time been confined to physical planning of cities, but ventures successively into new fields, and, at the same time, becomes more and more institutionalized. The latest example is the introduction of long-range economic planning in several capitalist countries of Western Europe (Shonfield, 1965: 67).

The trend towards central planning in most capitalist countries is undeniable, and there is no disagreement over the fact that there is such a trend.[1] But if there is total agreement over the fact that central planning is increasing, there is an equally total disagreement about the desirability, and the causes and effects of this development. Since the beginning of the twentieth century there has raged an intense debate between liberals and socialists on these matters. This paper will deal with some aspects of this debate.

2. CENTRAL PLANNING AND ECONOMIC CALCULATION

The problem of economic calculation in a centrally planned economy is part of a wider problem which might be called 'the epistemological problem of central planning'. It is a problem that concerns the principal possibility of gaining the kind of knowledge necessary for central planning of society.[2] I will not deal with this general problem in this paper, but concentrate on the more narrow problem of economic calculation in a centrally planned economy.

The idea of central planning is usually associated with that of socialism. Indeed, 'socialism' is often taken to be synonymous with 'central planning'. Although it would be wrong to identify the two, and so reduce socialism to central planning, it is true that most socialists have advocated a centrally planned economy. In fact, one claim for the superiority of socialism over capitalism is based on a belief in the superiority of a centrally planned economy over a market economy. The idea that the socialist economy will have to be a centrally planned economy goes back to Marx and Engels. They did not develop this idea in any detail, however, but gave only a few hints as to the question of economic organization under socialism. The Polish economist Wlodzimierz Brus has gathered from the works of Marx and Engels some propositions about the socialist economy. According to him (1972: 18-19), it is characterized by:

1. direct, *ex ante*, regulation of the social distribution of labour;
2. direct determination of labour input coefficients, for both living and embodied labour...;
3. equilibrium of supply and demand in physical units;
4. the distribution of social product in accordance with the satisfaction of general needs, and, at the same time the allocation of the fund intended for individual consumption according to the amount of labour contributed;
5. centralization of the saving and investment decisions.

It is the third proposition, that equilibrium of supply and demand should be obtained in physical units only, that is the most controversial from the economist's point of view. It seems to exclude the possibility of economic, as distinguished from physical, calculation in the socialist economy.

There is a tendency among early socialist writers to take lightly the problem of socialist economic organization. According to Engels (1878: 367), 'People will be able to manage everything very simply, without the intervention of much-vaunted "value".' The same attitude can be found in Lenin's writings before the revolution.

> The accounting and control necessary for this [the correct functioning of communist society] have been simplified by capitalism to the utmost and reduced to the extraordinarily simple operations — which any literate person can perform — of supervising and recording, knowledge of the four rules of arithmetic, and issuing appropriate receipts. (1918a: 361)

After the revolution there was a complete change in attitude. Lenin had to admit that the problems were enormous.

> The organization of accounting, the control of large enterprises, the transformation of the whole of the state economic mechanism into a single huge machine, into an economic organism that will work in such a way as to enable hundreds of millions of people to be guided by a single plan — such was the enormous organizational problem that rested on our shoulders. (1918b: 580)

The prospect of a communist society was more and more displaced into the distant future, while the transition period — the dictatorship of the proletariat — was placed in the foreground (Lenin, 1918c and 1918d).

Closely associated with the idea that calculation will be in physical terms only, is the idea that there will be no money under socialism. With the end of commodity production, exchange of products will come to an end, hence, no need for money. This was supposed to hold, at least, for the 'higher phase' of communist society, when consumption takes the form of free sharing. In the 'lower phase' of communist society, money, in the form of a certificate or voucher, would be used in the sphere of consumption (Marx, 1875: 15). This was for a long time the orthodox Marxist view (cf. Bucharin and Preobrazenski, 1919: 37). The idea of a future communist society without money, but with free sharing of the products of society, is based on the assumption that there is plenty of everything, so that there will be no problem of choice. It is easy to understand why this assumption should give rise to such a fierce attack from certain economists. The whole concept of 'economy', according to the dominant tradition, is based on the contrary assumption; that there is scarcity of resources. Economics is defined by Lionel Robbins (1932: 16) as 'the science which studies human behaviour as a relationship between ends and scarce means which have alternative uses'.

The debate about economic calculation under socialism started with Ludwig Mises' famous article 'Die Wirtschaftsrechnung in Sozialistischen Gemeinwesen' (1920, translated into English as 'Economic Calculation in the Socialist Commonwealth', 1935). In this article, Mises argues that economic calculation, and, therefore, rational production, is impossible under socialism. Since there is no exchange of capital goods, these goods will have no price, and without a price mechanism no rationality is possible in the economy.

> It is an illusion to imagine that in a socialist state calculation *in natura* can take the place of monetary calculation. Calculation *in natura*, in an economy without exchange, can embrace consumption-goods only; it completely fails when it comes to deal with goods of higher order. And as soon as one gives up the conception of a freely established monetary price for goods of a higher

> order, rational production becomes completely impossible. Every step that takes us away from private ownership of the means of production and from the use of money also takes us away from rational economics. (p. 104)

Mises also criticizes the Marxian idea to calculate value in terms of labour-time. It is supposed to be inadequate on two grounds: first, it leaves the employment of material factors of production out of account. Secondly, it ignores the different qualities of labour (p. 113). Another line of attack is that a socialist economy will lose the efficiency of the capitalist economy due to the lack of private initiative and individual responsibility (p. 114).

A treatment of the problems with a socialist economy, very similar to, but independent of, Mises' was made by Max Weber in his *Wirtschaft und Gesellschaft* (1922, the first part translated into English as *The Theory of Social and Economic Organization*, 1947). Like Mises, he argues that rational accounting is impossible without the market (pp. 194, and 204-205). But unlike Mises, Weber is careful to distinguish between *formal* rationality and *substantive* rationality. It is only formal rationality, the extent of quantitative calculation or accounting which is technically possible and which is actually applied (pp. 184-185), that is secured by the market and the use of money. Substantive rationality, 'the degree in which a given group of persons,...is or could be adequately provided with goods by means of an economically oriented course of social action' (p. 185), has nothing to do with formal rationality. 'This course of action will be interpreted in terms of a given set of ultimate values...' (p. 185). It is a fact, however, that a market economy, maximizing formal rationality, presupposes certain substantive conditions, that is, a certain type of society; a society not necessarily maximizing substantive rationality (p. 212). It is this substantive rationality which is later to become the subject matter of welfare economics.

After the attack from Mises, it was agreed by socialist and non-socialist economists alike, that a socialist economy would have to deal with the problem of economic calculation. But with this, the agreement came to an end. Some considered the difficulties insurmountable, while others considered them of minor importance, or no importance at all. Already in 1908 — in an article translated into English as 'The Ministry of Production in the Collectivist State' (1935) — the Italian follower of Pareto, Enrico Barone, had provided what might be called a 'theoretical solution' of the problem. This 'solution' consisted in showing that on certain assumptions, constituting a model of a socialist economy, it is possible to determine 'the equilibrium perfectly, with as many equations as unknowns' (p. 56). One of Barone's conclusions was that a socialist economy would have to run production in a way similar to that of the capitalist economy. 'If the Ministry of Production proposes to obtain the collective maximum — which it obviously must, whatever law of distribution may be adopted — all the economic categories of the old regime must reappear though maybe with other names: prices, salaries, interest, rent, profit, saving, etc.' (p. 73)

The next attack from a liberal economist on the centrally planned economy was something of a retreat from the position of Mises. Possibly under the influence of Barone, Hayek, in his 'The Present State of the Debate' (1935), can see no principal impossibility in the attempt to use economic calculation under socialism. The difficulties are rather of a practical nature. Hayek sees two fundamental difficulties with economic calculation in a centrally planned economy. The first difficulty concerns the information needed for economic calculation. The task of collecting all the information necessary for economic calculation at the central level is beyond human capacity. Secondly, even if this information were available, there remains the problem of solving 'hundreds of thousands' of differential equations, and this cannot be done in a life-time (p. 212).

The next move in the debate came from the socialist economist Oscar Lange. In his article 'On the Economic Theory of Socialism' (1935-37, reprinted in Lippincott, ed., *On the Economic Theory of Socialism*, 1938), he sets out to answer the critique of Mises and Hayek. His solution to the problem is a kind of 'market socialism', with decentralized decision-making about production. His answer to Mises, is that he fails to distinguish two different meanings of the term 'price'.

> Professor Mises seems to have confused prices in the narrower sense, i.e., the exchange ratios of commodities on a market, with prices in its wider sense of 'terms on which alternatives are offered'. As in consequence of public ownership of the means of production, there is in a socialist economy no market on which capital goods are actually exchanged, there are obviously no prices of capital goods in the sense of exchange ratios on a market. And, hence Professor Mises argues, there is no 'index of alternatives' available in the sphere of capital goods. But this conclusion is based on a confusion of 'price' in the narrower sense with 'price' in the wider sense of an index of alternatives. It is only in the latter sense that 'prices' are indispensable for the allocation of resources, and on the basis of the technical possibilities of transformation of one commodity into another they are also given in a socialist economy. (p. 61)

The essential element in Lange's model is that decisions about production are taken at the level of the enterprise, while the central planning board has the function of setting prices only. The central planning board, then, performs the function of the market (pp. 82-83). The managers of production are guided in their decisions by rules, whose function is to replace the profit-motive. These rules are: (a) to combine factors of production in such a way as to minimize average cost of production, and (b) to determine the scale of output so that marginal cost equals the price of the product (p. 76). Equilibrium of supply and demand is to be attained by the method of trial and error. At first, prices are fixed quite arbitrarily by the central planning board. If any error is made, this will show itself clearly in the form of either a surplus or a shortage. The central planning board then changes the price so as to correct the mistake, a procedure which goes on until equilibrium is obtained.

Lange also denies that the central planning board — as Hayek claimed — has to solve hundreds of thousands of equations. On the contrary, he claims superiority for the socialist economy regarding the ability to reach equilibrium.

> Indeed, it seems that this trial and error procedure would, or at least could, work much better in a socialist economy than it does in a competitive market. For the Central Planning Board has a much wider knowledge of what is going on in the whole economic system than any private entrepreneur can ever have, and, consequently, may be able to reach the right equilibrium prices by a much shorter series of successive trials than a competitive market actually does. (p. 89)

Here it must be pointed out, however, that Lange's model is built upon a system with decentralized decision-making, whereas Hayek's critique was directed at a system where decisions about production are taken by the central planning board, which is the traditional socialist model. The following remark by Hayek is, therefore, not wholly unjustified: 'It is merely a reminder of how much of the original claim for the superiority of planning over competition is abandoned if the planned society is now to rely for the direction of its industries to a large extent on competition. Until quite recently, at least, planning and competition used to be regarded as opposites...' (1940: 186)

A socialist blueprint, more in accord with traditional socialism, but otherwise rather similar to Lange's, was advanced by Joseph Schumpeter in his *Capitalism, Socialism and Democracy* (1943). In Schumpeter's model, the actual buying and selling of factors of production is handled by the central planning board, whereas in Lange's model this was done by the individual enterprises. Like Lange, Schumpeter believes that the task of management will be easier under socialism, since every price will be fixed and known in advance, so that there will be no uncertainty surrounding the decisions of management (p. 186). But in the opinion of Hayek, it is precisely this stability of prices, which is the main disadvantage of this kind of socialist economy (1940: 192-193).

I think that this disagreement between leading economists reflects, besides ideological differences, different approaches to economic problems and economics as a science. Hayek draws his conclusions from a *micro-analysis*. For him, the problem of rationality is tackled from the angle of the individual enterprise. Rationality, from this perspective, depends on the ability of the enterprises to adjust themselves 'to the daily changing conditions in different places and different industries' (1940: 188). Other economists are more *macro-oriented*. They attach little, or no, importance at all, to these small adjustments at the margin. Maurice Dobb (1969: 121), for instance, calls this preoccupation with marginal adjustments and optimality the 'perfectibility fallacy'. According to the more macro-oriented economists, economic efficiency depends more on technological revolutions, large-scale organization and the possibility to plan in advance with relatively stable prices. From this point of view, the constant fluctuations on the market are wholly irrational. According to Schumpeter, the superiority of socialism over capitalism, does not depend upon its greater rationality, but on the fact that its rationality concerns a higher level (1943: 196).

The controversy about the possibility of economic calculation under socialism has come to an end. Liberal economists have dropped their original argument against central planning, i.e., that it is wholly irrational, and turned to other arguments of an ethico-political nature. (c.f. Brus, 1972: 34) It is today more or less generally agreed that there are different levels of rationality; that the free market economy is not necessarily the most rational from the point of view of society as a whole and with regard to long-range economic development (c.f. Tinbergen, 1964: 43). A contributing factor behind this development is, of course, that central planning has been introduced also in the capitalist economies, so that there is need for a theory to guide economic policy also in the capitalist countries.

Another reason why central planning is no longer deemed impossible, or even irrational, is the development of new tools and techniques for central planning. The most important theoretical tools are input-output analysis and linear programming. A practical tool of great importance for the future is the computer. Oskar Lange (1967: 401-402) makes the following remarks when looking back at the debate in the thirties.

> Were I to rewrite my essay today my task would be much simpler. My answer to Hayek and Robbins would be: so what's the trouble? Let us put the simultaneous equations on an electronic computer and we shall obtain the solution in less than a second. The market process with its cumbersome *tatonnements* appears old-fashioned. Indeed, it may be considered as a computing device of the pre-electronic age.

This is undoubtedly an exaggeration and Lange adds:

> All this however, does not mean that the market does not have its relative merits. First of all, even the most powerful electronic computers have a limited capacity. There may be (and there are) economic processes so complex in terms of the number of commodities and the type of equations involved that no computer can tackle them. Or it may be too costly to construct computers of such large capacity. In such cases nothing remains but to use the old-fashioned market servo-mechanism which has a much broader working capacity.
>
> Managers of socialist economies today have two instruments of economic accounting. One is the electronic computer..., the other the market.

As a final comment on the problem of economic calculation and central planning, I would like to point out that no solution is absolute, i.e., independent of space and time. The best solution, which today seems to be some combination of plan and market, depends upon the level of the productive forces; the level of technology and organization (c.f. Bettelheim, 1968). I have already argued that central planning is made easier by the development of new tools and techniques of planning. It is also made easier by a 'higher' level of organization of the economic system; by larger units of production and more integration between units (ibid.: 21-31 and 74-78). This is so not only under socialism, but also under capitalism as J. K. Galbraith (1967: ch. 3) has pointed out. The reason why this is so, is that larger units and more integration between units reduces the number of market relations, that is, the number of links where actual exchange takes place, and, therefore, the number of equations that has to be solved at the centre.

3. CENTRAL PLANNING AND
ULTIMATE ENDS

Among the values dominating our political scene, security, equality, democracy, and freedom seem to be recognized by large groups of people as the most important ones. While it is generally agreed that security, equality, and freedom are ultimate or absolute values, there is some disagreement about the status of democracy. Some fail to see any intrinsic value in democracy. 'However strong the general case for democracy, it is not an ultimate or absolute value and must be judged by what it will achieve. It is probably the best method of achieving certain ends, but not an end in itself' (Hayek, 1960: 106). According to this view, democracy is valued positively only because it is a method for peaceful change, because it is a safeguard for individual liberty, and because of its educational effects upon the citizens (ibid.: 107-108). Since Tocqueville wrote his *Democracy in America*, it is generally believed among liberals that democracy, if extended too far, may become a threat to individual liberty. Democracy, therefore, must be limited. More specifically, democracy has to stop where private property begins. I do not share this view. I regard democracy as an end in itself, as an ultimate end.

For the laissez-faire liberals, freedom is the only end, or, at least, the supreme end. Central planning is attacked, above all, because it is a threat to individual freedom. The ends of security and equality are abandoned because they cannot be achieved without central planning, or, at least, a far-reaching interventionism. The free market economy is supposed to give us freedom, and for this, security and equality have to be sacrificed. The argument that central planning reduces individual freedom or autonomy cannot be dismissed easily. Central planning is a threat to individual freedom in at least two ways: first directly, because central planning presupposes that the planning agency has control over those subject to planning. To be controlled is always to lose some freedom. Secondly, central planning is an indirect threat to freedom, because it presupposes a large administrative apparatus with far-reaching authority, and such power-centres are always a latent threat to freedom in society. There is no absolute guarantee against the abuse of power, and planning presupposes power. But to admit this, is not to reject central planning. First of all, it can be denied that freedom is the only end. Secondly, there are many ways to check and reduce the power of the planning agency. Thirdly, it may be doubted that the alternative to central planning, i.e., the market, can secure freedom any better. In what follows, I will discuss briefly, the relation of security, equality, democracy, and freedom to central planning.

Security

Social security is a basic value for socialism and social liberalism alike, but rejected by laissez-faire liberals. They will accept nothing that cannot be achieved on the free market. Every man, therefore, must look after his own security by way of private insurances. Security is also regarded as an unworthy goal for human beings to strive for, since it is really an escape from freedom and responsibility.[3]

This criticism is not unjustified if directed at an all too paternalistic state. But when – as is actually the case – the criticism is directed at the purely economic security provided by social insurance against loss of income through unemployment, illness and old age, it must be regarded as downright cynical, or at best, due to lack of imagination as regards the situation of the poor. There are probably all too many people round the world who would readily give up their alleged freedom for just a little amount of security. In order to be fair, however, it must be pointed out that some laissez-faire liberals argue that the market would be able to solve the problem of economic insecurity much better than the state. According to these arguments, the state and the labour unions fail to achieve their ends with a remarkable regularity, and are really victims of an illusion in believing that the conditions of the poor could really be improved in any other way than by the free play of the market.[4]

I do not think that security should, or could, in any sense be sacrificed for freedom. I don't even think that freedom without security is worth having. On the contrary, I think that economic security is a precondition for true freedom.[5] That real freedom depends upon economic security is also admitted indirectly by the laissez-faire liberals when they stress the importance of 'the man of independent means' for freedom in society (see, for instance, Hayek, 1960: ch. 5). Otherwise they would deny this interdependency.

Equality

Equality, like security, is an important value for socialism, but rejected by the laissez-faire liberals, except in the form of equality before the law and equal political rights, i.e., democracy. Equality as understood by socialists has a more substantial character. It means, I believe, primarily, equal possibilities for everyone to satisfy his material needs. The ideal distribution under socialism is, according to Marx (1875: 17):

'From each according to his ability to each according to his needs'. Thus, socialist equality is not equal treatment – it is obvious that equal treatment of unequal individuals leads to inequality in material conditions, so that equality in material standard presupposes unequal treatment – but, above all, an equal material standard for all. But equality of material standard is not only an end in itself, it is supposed to give opportunities for all to realize their freedom. Socialist society, then, is 'an association, in which the free development of each is the condition for the free development of all' (Marx and Engels, 1848: 105).

The main reason for liberals to reject equality as a value, is its supposedly negative effects on freedom and individuality. The first theorist to see the dangers of equality and predict the coming of mass-society was Tocqueville. According to him, democracy and equality are roughly the same thing, or perhaps, one should say that democracy is the means by which the great masses want to reach equality. I will quote at length from his *Democracy in America* (1835-40, vol. 2: 380-81) a passage which is unsurpassed as a picture of the paternalistic state.

> I seek to trace the novel features under which despotism may appear in the world. The first thing that strikes the observation is an innumerable multitude of men all equal and alike, incessantly endeavouring to produce the petty and paltry pleasures with which they glut their lives....Above this race of men stands an immense and tutelary power, which takes upon itself alone to secure their gratifications, and to watch over their fate. That power is absolute, minute, regular, provident and mild. It would be like the authority of a parent, if like that authority, its object was to prepare men for manhood; but it seeks, on the contrary, to keep them in perpetual childhood: it is well content that the people should rejoice, provided they think of nothing but rejoicing. For their happiness such a government willingly labours, but it chooses to be the sole agent and the only arbiter of that happiness: it provides for their security, foresees and supplies their necessities, facilitates their pleasures, manages their principal concerns, directs their industry, regulates the descent of property, and subdivides their inheritances – what remains, but to spare them all the care of thinking and all the trouble of living?...After having thus successively taken each member of the community in its powerful grasp, and fashioned them at will, the supreme power then extends its arm over the whole community. It covers the surface of society with a network of small complicated rules, minute and uniform, through which the most original minds and the most energetic characters cannot penetrate, to rise above the crowd. The will of man is not shattered, but softened, bent and guided: men are seldom forced by it to act, but they are constantly restrained from acting: such a power does not destroy, but it prevents existence; it does not tyrannize, but it compresses, enervates, extinguishes, and stupefies a people, till each nation is reduced to nothing better than a flock of timid and industrious animals, of which the government is the shepherd.

This frightening picture has ever since been a nightmare to many defenders of individual freedom and the main theme of innumerable books, both novels and more scholarly works. This critique has been directed, with little discrimination, against egalitarianism, democracy, interventionism, and socialism. But is it justified? Must equality in material standard lead to this state of affairs? I don't think so. Only those, who believe that economic activity is the only activity where man can realize his freedom, have reason to be afraid of equality. It is easy, when witnessing the constant increase of state-interference in the private sphere, to get the impression that we are moving in the direction of a state of affairs which permits no freedom or individuality. But, it is equally easy to forget all the new possibilities that open up for an ever larger part of the population as a result of increased economic security and equality. Freedom and individuality are not part of zero-sum games. There is no finite amount of freedom and individuality in society. Freedom may increase if the state or some other public organ takes over some of 'the trouble of living'. This is not to deny, however, that Tocqueville's mass-society is a real threat to individuality. Nor can it be denied that some of its features are realized today. But as to the causes of this, there are different opinions. For my part I doubt that it has much to do with economic security and equality. Perhaps, it has something to do with the economic market, its commercialism and persuasive advertising, its mass-production and mass-consumption.[6]

There is another, and more radical, argument against equality as a form of distributive justice. According to this argument, the concept of 'distributive justice' is simply meaningless (Hayek, 1966; see also 1968).

> The essential points of this conception of justice are (a) that justice can be meaningfully attributed only to human action and not to any state of affairs as such without reference to the question whether it has been, or could have been, deliberately brought about by somebody;...(p. 166)

> There is only a justice of individual conduct but not a separate 'social justice'. (p. 175)

> ...it is meaningless to describe the manner in which the market distributed the good things of this world among particular people as just or unjust. This, however, is what the so-called 'social' or 'distributive' justice aims at in the name of which the liberal order of law is progressively destroyed. (p. 167)

> That the concept of justice is nevertheless so commonly and readily applied to the distribution of incomes is entirely the effect of an erroneous anthropomorphic interpretation of society as an organization rather than as a spontaneous order. (p. 171).

If I have rightly understood Hayek, his main point is that the concept of 'social' or 'distributive' justice presupposes that society exists as some sort of subject over and above the individuals, to whose actions the value of justice can legitimately be attributed. According to this view, the concept of 'distributive justice' is an instance of what Myrdal (1932: 54 and ch. 6; cf. also Albert, 1964: 399) has called the 'communistic fiction'. Hayek's conclusion is that, since the concept of 'distributive justice' is meaningless, every distribution imposed upon society from above must be arbitrary. It is tacitly assumed, of course, that the distribution of the market is natural in some sense, and, therefore, excepted from moral evaluation.

I will readily agree with Hayek that the concept of 'justice' is not meaningful, if applied to anything else than individual human beings and their relations. The concept of 'justice' derives all its meaning from its implications for individuals. If it is true, as Hayek asserts, that the term 'just' is only applicable to human action, a change of meaning would be involved in its application to distribution. But it is not true, as Hayek also wants us to believe, that the application of justice to distribution, presupposes any transcendental being over and above society. In a democracy, distributive justice is imposed by the majority, all of whom are concrete human beings, and it is imposed because of the effect on individual human beings and their relations. I fail to see anything mystical or metaphysical about it.

I suspect that what is involved in this argumentation is not so much a communist as an individualist fiction. A peculiar thing with many liberals is that they regard every act of the government, except the institution of the laws of property and contract, as arbitrary. They fail to see that property rights — which determine distribution on the market — are as arbitrary as anything else imposed on society by the state. Liberals tend to regard the institution of private property as the only natural order of things. The individual has a natural and sacred right to his property. Ownership is seen as a relationship between an individual and the things he owns. This is the individualist fiction; the failure to understand that ownership is a social relation between men. No-one has a natural right to the riches of the earth or the products of social labour.[7] It is one of Marx's greatest achievements to have unveiled this individualist fiction in his analysis of commodity fetishism (1967: 71-83).

Democracy

As I have said before, laissez-faire liberals attach no intrinsic value to democracy. One reason for this might be that democracy, if extended to economic matters, could mean the abolition of private property. Another reason is that democracy — as Tocqueville suggested — might lead to totalitarianism. Democracy and totalitarianism are not incompatible. It is perfectly possible to have a government that is elected in a truly democratic way, but whose power pervades every corner of society, so as to become totalitarian. It is quite another matter that in reality, democracy is the best safeguard for individual freedom. This is so, because people generally don't want to live under a totalitarian regime. According to Hayek (1960: 104), democracy may be extended in two ways: through extending the range of persons entitled to vote and the range of issues that are decided by democratic procedure. From this, it follows — I don't know whether Hayek would agree or not — that democracy is extended if 'society' takes over the means of production, thereby extending the range of issues under democratic control. This is, of course, the strongest argument in favour of socialism and central planning; that the economic sphere would be subjected to democratic control and not in the hands of private persons.

There are also those who deny that social control of the economic sphere means an extension of democracy, as compared to private property. Democracy, they say, is only a method, it is completely neutral as to content.[8] This view of democracy, however, leads to some absurd consequences. It would permit a country to call itself democratic even if the democratic method was applied only in a limited or very small range of issues — educational or religious matters, for instance — while leaving the rest to private initiative or an autonomous administrative apparatus. This will not do. It must be admitted that democracy is extended when the range of issues under democratic control is extended, and, consequently, that democracy is extended when it comes to include decisions in the economic sphere.

The most important argument against extending democracy to the economic sphere is the pluralistic argument. It is argued that the extension of democracy to the economic sphere is dangerous, since it leads to a monolithic state, the concentration of all power in one hand. With private property, on the other hand, power is diffused over many, separate hands, preventing its abuse. To illustrate the importance of this argument, Hayek (1960: 118ff.) takes the example of an employee coming into conflict with his employer. When there are many employers it is no problem. The employee can turn to another employer. When, on the other hand, there is only one employer, i.e., the state, the problem is acute for the individual if he comes into conflict with his superiors. He is wholly dependent upon the state and cannot take the risk of falling in disgrace. The dependency on a single employer will give rise to such unworthy phenomena as opportunism and bootlicking. This argument against central planning cannot be dismissed easily. I don't think, however, that the danger is overwhelming as long as democracy is strong. The dangers may also be reduced through the conscious creation of a pluralistic power-structure; a constitution with built-in checks and balances. First of all, it is possible to separate different powers at the central level, with the object to check each other. The classical division of the judicial, the legislative, and the executive powers may be retained and improved in various ways. Secondly, it is possible to have a highly decentralized system, with a high degree of self-management at the communal- and enterprise-levels.

Finally, there is the argument against central planning, that democracy is best achieved with the help of a free market. According to the doctrine of consumer sovereignty, the market is a kind of voting system, where consumers vote for certain products by way of demanding them. The market is supposed to have the advantage over central planning, of being much more sensitive to the diversity of individual tastes and values, and to the demand of minorities. Under central planning, on the contrary, a hierarchy of ends – imposed from above – determines what goods are to be produced. There will be no sensitivity to the diversity of tastes, and minorities will be neglected.[9]

Of some importance, in relation to this, is K. J. Arrow's demonstration that there is no way to move from individual orderings of ends to a collective hierarchy of ends, without paradoxical results. This fact has been known for a long time as the 'paradox of voting'. According to Arrow (1951: 18), the collective hierarchy of ends must be either 'imposed' or 'dictatorial'. Behind this seemingly dramatic conclusion lies the simple fact, that different people order 'social states' according to different preference-scales, and, unless you permit interpersonal comparisons, it is impossible to obtain one single preference-scale for the whole collectivity. Incidentally, however, Arrow's analysis gives a negative result also for the market, as a mechanism for 'rational social choice' (loc. cit.). This would perhaps disturb some defenders of the market, but not the extremely individualistic laissez-faire liberals. They flatly deny that there is such a thing as rational social choice. The idea of a rational social choice, like that of distributive justice and the whole discipline of welfare economics, is rejected as an expression of the 'communist fiction'.

Behind Arrow's conclusion, lies the assumption that individuals have both 'tastes', which they express on the market, and 'values', pertaining to social states and guiding their political voting (1951: 18). To most men, I believe, it is commonplace that there *are* values pertaining to social states, and that these values should determine the shape of society. But this is exactly what the laissez-faire liberals deny. They want to restrict the impact of moral values to the private sphere. If, for instance, an individual wants a more equal distribution of incomes, and is rich, then he should give some of his money to the poor. If, on the other hand, he is poor, and still wants a more equal distribution of incomes, this desire is deemed immoral, since it is based on envy. The laissez-faire liberals, as true individualists, prefer private charity before social insurances, because it involves free choice and individual responsibility. (cf. Friedman, 1962: 195, and Hayek, 1960: ch. 5). If, however, we recognize the existence and importance of values pertaining to social states, the market can be shown to have serious shortcomings as a democratic institution. It completely fails, for instance, to meet the 'demand' for social states. Another, and more obvious, shortcoming of the market as a democratic institution is that different persons have unequal possibilities to vote. A universal suffrage, favouring the wealthy, is no better than the pre-democratic system of privileges. Still another shortcoming of the market is the limitation of consumer sovereignty through the persuasive power of advertising. Some economists go so far as to regard 'consumer sovereignty' as nothing but a myth.[10] It may also be pointed out that consumer sovereignty is in no way incompatible with central planning. It may be that a central planning agency is less sensitive to the diversity of tastes than is the market — especially so, since diversity is to a large extent created by the market — but this is no serious deficiency considering the superficiality of this diversity.

Freedom

Individual freedom or liberty is the cardinal value of liberalism. Other values may be realized only if they are compatible with freedom. But freedom is the most important value for socialism too, and yet socialists advocate central planning. The difference between liberalism and socialism lies in the conception of freedom and in the understanding of the causes of restrictions on freedom in society.

The prevailing opinion among liberals is that their concept of 'freedom' is negative, while the socialist concept of 'freedom' is positive

(Berlin, 1958). The negative concept of 'freedom' means freedom *from* coercion or restraint. But only the restraint imposed upon us by other men, not the restraint imposed upon us by nature. (Hayek, 1960: 12, 16) The positive concept of 'freedom' means primarily self-mastery or self-determination (Berlin, 1958: 131ff.; Petrovic, 1967: 125).

> The 'positive' sense of the word 'liberty' derives from the wish on the part of the individual to be his own master. I wish my life and decisions to depend upon myself, not on external forces of whatever kind. I wish to be the instrument of my own, not of other men's, acts of will. I wish to be a subject not an object,...(Berlin, loc. cit.)

Freedom, in this sense, comes to be much the same as power, at least in the restricted sense of power over one's own fate. Most liberals deny that there is any affinity between freedom and power, but to me, it seems almost self-evidently true that there must be such an affinity. The freedom for me to do what I want in my interaction with other men is, of course, power. This interpretation of freedom is also implicit in the so-called 'paradox of freedom', which says that freedom destroys itself if unlimited, since 'Unlimited freedom means that a strong man is free to bully one who is weak and rob him of his freedom' (Popper, 1945, vol. 2: 124). Such liberals as Hayek and Berlin, however, lay much stress on the difference between the negative and positive concepts of freedom, trying to show that an identification of freedom with power leads to unreasonable consequences. They fail to see that the positive and negative concepts of 'freedom' are but two sides of the same coin, which is what the paradox of freedom tries to tell us.

Isaiah Berlin's argument is intended to make us believe that the positive concept of 'freedom' leads to an application on society as a whole, resulting in some sort of mystical, metaphysical holism. He mentions, in passing, that this might be done with the negative concept too,

> but the positive conception of freedom as self-mastery, with its suggestion of man divided against himself, has, in fact, and as a matter of the history of doctrines and of practice, lent itself more easily to this splitting of personality into two: the transcendent, dominant controller, and the empirical bundle of desires and passions to be disciplined and brought to heel. (1958: 134)

> Presently the two selves may be represented as divided by an even larger gap: the real self may be conceived as something wider than the individual (as the term is normally understood), as a social 'whole' of which the individual is an element or aspect: a tribe, a race, a church, a state, the great society of the

> living and dead and the yet unborn. This entity is then identified as being the
> 'true' self which, by imposing its collective, or 'organic', single will upon its
> recalcitrant 'members', achieves its own, and therefore their, 'higher' freedom.
> (132)

This is the argument of Isaiah Berlin. But exactly how self-mastery
suggests a man divided against himself, and why this should lead to a
projection of man's real self on society as a whole, we are not told.
The example of German romanticism is not enough to prove the point
that the positive concept of 'freedom' leads to dictatorship.

Hayek begins with rejecting the interpretation of freedom as the
' "ability to do what I want", the power to satisfy our wishes, or the
extent of choice of alternatives open to us' (1960: 16). His ground for
doing this, is that our ability to do what we want, is largely determined
by our physical environment, which is irrelevant for freedom.

> This kind of 'freedom' appears in the dreams of many people in the form of
> the illusion that they can fly, that they are released from gravity and can
> move 'free like a bird' to wherever they wish, or that they have the power to
> alter their environment to their liking. (loc. cit.)

Hayek is careful to point out that

> 'freedom' refers solely to a relation of men to other men, and the only infringe-
> ment on it is coercion by men. This means, in particular, that the range of
> physical possibilities from which a person can choose at a given moment has
> no direct relevance for freedom. (p. 12)

So far, I agree with Hayek. It is important to distinguish restraints
imposed by men from restraints imposed by nature. But then comes the
decisive and erroneous move in Hayek's argumentation. 'This confusion
of liberty as power with liberty in its original meaning inevitably leads
to the identification of liberty with wealth; and this makes it possible
to exploit all the appeal which the word "liberty" carries in support for
a demand for the redistribution of wealth' (p. 17). The error is obvious.
Hayek rejects the concept of 'freedom' as power on the ground that it
includes power over nature. But when this is done, he rejects the identification of liberty with wealth, because it follows from the erroneous
interpretation of liberty as power. Does Hayek really mean that wealth
is part of nature, like the law of gravity, to which he appealed when
rejecting the interpretation of freedom as power? If he does not, his
argument against the positive concept of 'freedom' is invalid.

To conclude, there is nothing wrong with the positive concept of 'freedom'. The liberals use it themselves in their highly, and rightly, praised 'Bill of Rights', which is nothing but a bundle of positively defined rights or freedoms. The positive concept of 'freedom' is inseparably linked to the negative concept of 'freedom'. They are correlative concepts. What is more, the socialist concept of 'freedom' may very well be defined negatively, as freedom from alienation. The difference between the liberal and socialist concepts of 'freedom' is not to be found in this distinction. The difference is that socialism has a much wider concept of 'freedom' than has liberalism. But being wider has nothing to do with being positive. According to the socialist concept of 'freedom', freedom has as many forms or dimensions as there are forms of alienation. This wide conception of freedom has the disadvantage of being less precise, but the advantage of making possible an analysis and critique of society on several levels. The liberals, with their restricted concept of 'freedom', are completely unable to produce a critique of culture or social structure. They can only provide a critique of state interference in the private spheres of individuals. And this, of course, is what their concept of 'freedom' is intended to achieve. Liberalism and socialism differ also in the view of the causes of unfreedom in society. Liberals, we have just seen, tend to see state activity as the only threat to freedom in society. The conflict is between civil society and the state. Socialists, on the other hand, see the all-important cause of unfreedom in the institution of private property. The most important conflict – that between classes – is within civil society, and the state is only a superstructure deriving its power from civil society.

There is no doubt that liberalism is right in seeing the state as a potential threat to individual freedom, but there is equally no doubt, that there is something superficial with this view. The most remarkable characteristic of the liberal ideology is its inability to see any cause of unfreedom in the institution of private property. Economic exchange on the market is supposed to take place under 'freedom of contract', entered into on equal terms. Hayek is quite clear about it; ownership of the means of production is no means to coerce other people, except under extreme cases of monopoly, such as ownership of a spring in an oasis (1960: 136). This is very far from the truth, of course. It need not be a matter of life or death for coercion to take place. The threat of unemployment and the power to influence wages and working conditions are very effective means of coercion. Jobs, and even less, good jobs, do not grow on trees, especially not in a free market economy.

There is a good deal of truth behind the Marxist distinction between 'formal' and 'real' freedom.

4. CENTRAL PLANNING AND SOCIALISM

I asserted at the beginning of this paper that there is a trend towards central planning in the capitalist countries of today. To Marxists, and some others, this is the expression of a more or less 'necessary' development; the result of tendencies inherent in the capitalist system itself.[11] If this is true, the case against central planning would be quite meaningless. Consequently, liberals deny that there is any 'necessity' involved in this development. The increasing role of the state, is the result of bad ideology, they say, and the tendency towards monopoly, is the result of bad policy on the part of the state. A return to something approaching laissez-faire is, therefore, perfectly possible.[12] I think that the liberals are wrong in this contention. As Gunnar Myrdal (1960: 9–13) has pointed out, the development towards central planning has been completely independent of governmental ideology, and often contrary to a declared faith in a free market economy. There is, I believe, indeed, a sense in which the development towards increased central planning is 'inevitable', or, at least, highly imperative.

Historically, central planning, in the form of state-interventionism, has been an answer to the crisis produced by the capitalist economic system, and its inability to cope with some major social problems. The state has made its entrance in every field where the market has failed, or was considered inappropriate from the very beginning: education, health, social welfare, and what is usually summarized under the term 'infrastructure' (roads, railways, electricity, etc.).[13] There was a time when it was thought to be no conflict between private interest and public interest, when it was believed that a system where everybody pursues his own interest would automatically lead to the best solution for all. Today this belief is held only by a small minority of laissez-faire liberals. Today, most economists would agree that what is rational from the point of view of a single enterprise is not always rational from the point of view of society.

One deficiency of the market is its inability to create a demand for *collective goods*, such as roads, parks, museums, children's play gardens and the like. Another deficiency of the market is its 'short-sightedness', the inability of single enterprises to make rational investment-decisions for the distant future. The demand of today is simply no reliable guide for decisions concerning production some 10 or 15 years ahead. As investment-decisions become increasingly long-range, the market will become increasingly irrational as a mechanism of co-ordination. The reason for this is that the market co-ordinates investment-decisions only ex post, while, with central planning, it is possible to achieve such co-ordination ex ante.[14] The most serious deficiency with the free market economy is probably its inability to cope with *external diseconomies*, i.e., such negative effects of an economic agents' activity on others that do not enter his economic calculations. Among the most important external diseconomies may be mentioned pollution of air and water, loss of life and health in traffic and in industries, noise from traffic and industries, overcrowding of our cities, uglification of our cities, and destruction of natural beauty (see Mishan, 1967, part 2).

More generally, I believe that central planning is a 'necessary' outcome of a high level of technology and organization, the productive forces of society. The bigger the organizations and the more technology used, the wider the ramifications of decisions and therefore the need for more planning. The more every part of society depends on every other part, the more need for central planning. When the level of technology becomes high enough, only the state and the biggest corporations can raise the capital needed for investment. When enterprises are large, only the state can handle the negative consequences of their activity. If, for instance, a large enterprise closes down and thousands of men and women lose their jobs, the state has to interfere, at least, if the sitting government wants to win the next election. Private property becomes a public concern because of its public effects on society.

I have argued that the development towards increased central planning is 'necessary'.[15] My contention is, therefore, that the trend towards central planning will continue in the capitalist countries of Western Europe. To lots of people, central planning is the same as socialism. According to Ludwig Mises (1952: 1), 'The term "planning" is mostly used as a synonym for socialism, communism, and authoritarian economic management'. This may be true as a statement about the usage of words, but is this a right usage? Is central planning identical with socialism? If so, the development towards central planning would also be a development towards socialism. I don't think that it is though. Of course, it all depends upon what is to be understood by 'socialism'.

If we go back to Marx, there is not much to be found about the nature of socialism. His negative attitude towards utopian programmes prevented him from saying anything substantial about it (see, for instance, 1871: 73). There are some remarks, however, scattered all over his writings, and they do point in the direction of a centrally planned economy, but certainly not of an authoritarian or totalitarian kind. Properly speaking, the term 'socialism' refers only to a form of ownership. 'Socialism' means social or common ownership of the means of production.[16] Other features of the socialist society do not belong to it by way of definition, but are contingent features. Central planning, then, is not to be equated with socialism, but is a contingent feature of socialist society. Marx, of course, had a wider image of socialist society than might be suggested by the reference to property relations, but most of these other features were supposed to follow by way of causation, once common ownership of production was introduced. But this notion of social or common ownership of production seems to have no implications for the method of production, or does it? Nor does it seem to have any implications for the political organization of society, or does it? I suggest that it is impossible to separate the question of political organization from the question of ownership under socialism.

There are two tendencies to be found in Marx's writings about socialism. On a first account they seem to be contradictory. One tendency might be called the *centralist*, the other the *decentralist*. The centralist tendency is clearly expressed in *The Communist Manifesto* (1848: 104), where Marx and Engels describe the first act of the proletariat after its rise to power. 'The proletariat will use its political supremacy to wrest, by degrees, all capital from the bourgeoisie, to centralize all instruments of production in the hands of the state, i.e., of the proletariat organized as the ruling class.' It is also expressed by the idea that production is to be regulated by a social or common plan. In *The Civil War in France* we find the following passage:

> if united co-operative societies are to regulate national production upon a common plan, thus taking it under their own control, and putting an end to the constant anarchy and periodic convulsions which are the fatality of capitalist production – what else, gentlemen would it be but communism, 'possible' communism? (1871: 73)

The idea that society is to regulate production, is to be found already in the *German Ideology* (1846: 53). Besides this direct mentioning of a social or common plan, we have the hostility against the market, which seems to call for central regulation of production. In the above quotation from *The Civil War in France*, it was said that communism would put an end to the constant anarchy of capitalist production. In *The Critique of the Gotha Programme* we find that

> within the co-operative society based on common ownership of production, the producers do not exchange their products; just as little does the labour employed on the products appear here as the value of these products, as an objective quality possessed by them, since now, in contrast to capitalist society, individual labour no longer exists in an indirect fashion but directly as a component part of total labour. (1875: 14)

This can only mean that under socialism there is no market. It is thus quite clear that Marx conceived the socialist economy as a centrally planned economy. But how centralized, and how much planning we do not know. A wide range of different alternatives are possible.

The decentralist tendency in Marx's writings shows itself most clearly in his hostility against the state. The state, according to Marx and Engels (1848: 82), is primarily an organization for class-rule. 'The executive of the modern State is but a committee for managing the common affairs of the whole bourgeoisie.' The struggle against the bourgeoisie is, therefore, a struggle against the state, and in the classless, i.e., socialist society, the state will disappear. Some functions of the state will remain, however, only the oppressive functions will disappear. 'While the merely repressive organs of the old governmental power were to be amputated, its legitimate functions were to be wrested from an authority usurping pre-eminence over society itself and restored to the responsible agents of society.' (1871: 166) *The Civil War in France* — from which this quotation is taken — is on the whole a fierce attack upon the centralized power of the state and its bureaucracy. The Paris Commune is described as a revolution 'not against this or that...form of state power', but as 'a revolution against the state itself' (p. 166); as 'the reabsorption of the state power by society' (p. 168). This example of a socialist political organization, is, furthermore, described as a highly decentralized organization with self-working and self-governing communes, where politics is not a profession, where the representatives have no privileges and can be recalled at any time, and where the state is turned from a master of society to its servant (p. 171). 'The fact is that, far from bearing any authoritarian imprint, the whole of Marx's work on the state is pervaded by a powerful anti-authoritarian and anti-bureaucratic bias, not only in relation to a distant communist society but also the period of transition which is to precede it.' This judgement of Ralph Miliband (1965: 177) is undoubtedly true. But how then, can it be reconciled with the centralist tendency in Marx's works?

The answer to this question is that Marx makes a distinction between politics and mere administration, a distinction which corresponds to that between social relations and technico-organizational relations.[17] Social relations in Marx's sense are *relations of production*, while technico-organizational relations belong to the *forces of production*. Exploitation is the characteristic of certain relations of production and ends with the introduction of socialist relations of production. The mere technico-organizational administration, on the other hand, lacks political content and can safely be centralized. In the words of Engels (1878: 333), 'the government of persons is replaced by the administration of things, and by the conduct of processes of production'.

Today, when we have experience of countries with a highly centralized economy, and know that in these countries the 'administration of things' is accompanied by the most oppressive 'governing of persons', one may be inclined to regard this idea as naive, or even as a myth (see Kolakowski, 1974: 29, 32-34). I wouldn't go so far. I believe that the distinction is an important one. But, of course, there is no such thing as a 'mere administration of things' in production. The regulation of production necessarily involves the administration of persons. And what is more important: the regulation of production is in no sense 'mere administration'. It involves, or, at least, is preceded by decisions on, what must be characterized as, political questions: What is to be produced and in what quantities? How much is to be consumed and how much reinvested? What is the income-distribution going to look like? These questions are definitely political, and they call for a political organization to decide upon them. I believe that Marx's and Engels' idea of a 'merely administered' economy is embedded in their vision of a future society where general affluence is the prevailing condition, when the productive forces have reached such a level that man's material needs can be satisfied with a minimum of effort, reducing man's material interests to insignificance. In Marx's words:

> Freedom in this field can only consist in socialised man, the associated producers, rationally regulating their interchange with Nature, bringing it under their common control, instead of being ruled by it as by the blind forces of Nature; and achieving this with the least expenditure of energy and under conditions most favourable to, and worthy of their human nature. But it nonetheless still remains a realm of necessity. Beyond it begins that development of human energy which is an end in itself, the true realm of freedom, which, however, can blossom forth only with this realm of necessity as its basis. The shortening of the working-day is its basic prerequisite. (1894: 820)

This untenable idea, that under socialism the state is going to wither away; that socialism means the end to politics, has led to a neglect of the question of political organization under socialism. What, then, is the political organization under socialism? I said above that it is impossible to separate the question of political organization from that of ownership under socialism. I will now try to show that this is indeed the case, and that the political organization must be democratic, since this is the only possible meaning of 'social' or 'common' ownership of the means of production.

The common idea that socialism consists in state ownership of the means of production is wrong.

> The modern state, no matter what its form, is essentially a capitalist machine, the state of the capitalists, the ideal personification of the total national capital. The more it proceeds to the taking over of the productive forces, the more does it actually become the national capitalist, the more citizens does it exploit. The workers remain wage-workers – proletarians. The capitalist relation is not done away with. It is rather brought to a head. But, brought to a head it topples over. State ownership of the productive forces is not the solution of the conflict, but concealed within it are the technical conditions that form the elements of that solution. (Engels, 1878: 330-31)

'Social' or 'common' ownership of the means of production is not to be equated with 'state' ownership of the means of production. A society where the state bureaucracy has all power in its hands, but with no democratic control from below — this is the picture liberals generally give of socialism — is not socialism at all. Socialism is, in fact, inconceivable without democracy. Under socialism, it is impossible to separate the 'political' from the 'economic'. A clear separation of the economic sphere from the political sphere is typical of societies resting on private property, where economic power is separated from political power. This separation is no longer possible when the 'state' is turned into an economic organ, with power over the economy. The difficulty to see the implications of this depends, I believe, upon the tendency to regard the 'political' and the 'economic' as institutions, instead of as functions. With this view, it seems as if the state (the political institution) comes from outside and more or less illegitimately interferes with the activity on the market (the economic institution). This view, of course, is reinforced by the way things appear in capitalist countries, where the economic activity of the state takes the form of intervention in an otherwise unhampered market. This view also lies behind the popular, but entirely mistaken, idea that Marx's economic 'determinism' is falsified by the political mastery over the economy under socialism (cf. Popper, 1945, vol. 2: pp 108-9). Once we recognize that instead of the 'state' determining the economy, the 'state' changes its nature and becomes an economic organ with economic functions, the difficulty disappears. To say that an economic organ determines the economy can falsify nothing, it is a tautology. The difficulty to separate the functions and institutions of the 'political' and 'economic' has also left its imprint on Marxist theory. Take, for instance, the curious proposition that under socialism 'the state as state' will disappear (Engels, 1878: 332).

The argumentation, so far, is insufficient to support my thesis that socialism is inconceivable without democracy. I have only tried to lend some support to my view that the 'political' and the 'economic' must be regarded as functions, so that it is possible for one institution to perform both functions. Now I will argue that when the 'state' is turned into an economic organ, the question of political organization is inseparable from the question of ownership. Social ownership, as distinguished from ownership or property as a judicial category, concerns *the real possibility to control economic resources.*[18] He owns the means of production, who has the power to control them. When the means of production are controlled by political organs, not by private individuals, the nature of social ownership depends upon the nature of the political system. Common or social ownership implies a political system where everyone has the right to participate, it is identical with democracy (cf. Lange, 1964: 36). If, in a centrally planned economy, the control over the means of production and the surplus-product is in the hands of a certain group, this group is a class, and the economy is by definition not socialist. The proper name of an economy where the state bureaucracy owns the means of production is 'state-capitalism' (cf. Bettelheim, 1970: 35).

It may be objected to this analysis that it is merely a play with words and their meanings. In a sense — yes. But words are persuasive and it might be of some importance to attach certain meanings to certain words. I think, for instance, that it is important to argue that socialism is different from state-capitalism and, therefore, an alternative to state-capitalism. I think that this is important, because the development towards increased central planning will — of this I am sure — lead either to state-capitalism or to socialism, and these alternatives are open to choice. Such a choice is partly a matter of persuasion.

NOTES

1. See Hayek, 1944: ch. 1 and 1973: 7-10; Mises, 1952: 32-33 and 173-179; Friedman, 1962: 10-11 and 1970: 86-88; Heilbroner, 1959: 103, 109-112, and 145-146; Myrdal, 1960: part 1; Shonfield, 1965: part 2; Galbraith, 1967: chs. 3-4; and Kidron, 1968: part 1.

2. Large-scale central planning presupposes knowledge about society as a whole. It has been argued by some critics of central planning – notably Karl Popper – that it is impossible to attain such knowledge. Popper illustrates this impossibility thus: 'The term "society" embraces, of course, all social relations, including all personal ones; those of a mother to her child as much as those of a child welfare officer to either of the two. It is for many reasons quite impossible to control all, or "nearly" all, these relationships; if only because with every new control of social relations we create a host of new social relations to be controlled. In short, the impossibility is a logical impossibility' (1957: 79-80). Popper's argument, then, is based upon the assumption that central planning presupposes knowledge of all there is in society in its concrete details, a kind of knowledge which is, of course, not attainable.

3. See Hayek, 1944: ch. IX and 1960: ch. 19; and Friedman, 1962: ch. XI.

4. See Mises, 1947: chs. 1-2 and 1952; Hayek, 1960: part III and 1967: part III; and **Friedman, 1962.**

5. This is the socialist view which goes back to Marx, who held that the 'realm of necessity' is the basis for the 'realm of freedom' (*Capital*, vol. 3; 820).

6. The laissez-faire liberals are of another opinion, of course. Hayek (1960: 44) argues that inequality enriches cultural life since it allows the wealthy to experiment with styles of living which serve as ideals for the many to strive for. Friedman argues (1962: 72-78) that a free market economy is a necessary prerequisite for variety and high quality in cultural life.

7. Friedman's somewhat peculiar conception of property is well illustrated by an example he uses when discussing the difficulties involved in justifying a certain distribution of income. 'Suppose', he says (1962: 165), 'there are four Robinson Crusoes, independently marooned on four islands in the same neighborhood. One happened to land on a large and fruitful island which enables him to live easily and well. The others happened to land on tiny and rather barren islands from which they can barely scratch a living. One day, they discover the existence of one another. Of course, it would be generous of the Crusoe in the large island if he invited the others to join him and share its wealth. But suppose he does not. Would the other three be justified in joining forces and compelling him to share his wealth with them?' Friedman's answer to this question is negative. One may well wonder, how in the first place, he got the idea that the islands may be regarded as the property of the Robinson Crusoes. I can see but two possibilities: in the first case private property is presupposed in the example, which then becomes meaningless since it presupposes what it wants to justify. I do not find this possibility very likely, however, since nothing is said about the purchase of the islands. The other possibility is, as far as I can see, that private property is instituted by some divine power and communicated to the four Crusoes through revelation.

8. The view of democracy as a method has been advanced by, for instance, Joseph Schumpeter (1942: 269–73) and Karl Popper (1945, vol. 2: 160-62).

9. Mises, 1920: 89-110, 1947: 25-34, and 1952: 44-47 and 108-109; Hayek, 1935: 158-60, 1944: ch. V, 1963: 256-59, and 1968: 28-31; and Friedman, 1970: 88.

10. See, for instance, Galbraith, 1958: ch. 11 and 1967: ch. 3; Robinson, 1964; and Mishan, 1967: ch. 10.

11. See, for instance, Schumpeter, 1942: part II; Heilbroner, 1959: 112 and 148; Myrdal, 1960: 36-42; Galbraith, 1958: 35-39; and Kidron, 1968: 24-37.

12. Hayek, 1944: ch. IV and 1949: 178ff.; Mises, 1947: ch. 10 and 1952: 30-35; and Friedman, 1962: chs. 3, 8, and 13.

13. See Heilbroner, 1959: 105-107; Myrdal, 1960: 13-15 and 46-49; Kidron, 1968: 24; and Altvater, 1972.

14. It has 'always' been one of the most important arguments in favour of central planning that it is superior to the market with regard to long-range investment decisions. The chief exponent of this view has been the Marxist economist Maurice Dobb. See, for instance, 1933: 39-41 and 1939a and b, where he criticizes the 'market socialism' proposed by Oskar Lange and Abba Lerner for sharing the vices of capitalism, i.e., instability and unemployment. See also 1951 and 1953: 74-92, where he introduces the distinction between co-ordination ex post and co-ordination ex ante.

15. It may be objected that I have conflated two different senses of the word 'necessary'; the *causal* sense in which something is the *necessary outcome* of something else, and the *teleological* sense in which something is *necessary as a means* to achieve something else. This objection is true, and the only answer is that both forms of 'necessity' are involved, as they must always be in human affairs.

16. In the *Critique of the Gotha Programme* (p. 9), Marx describes socialist society as a 'co-operative society based on common ownership of the means of production'.

17. This distinction originates with the so-called 'utopian socialists' (see, for instance, Henri St. Simon, 1825: 78-79), as witnessed by Marx and Engels in *The Communist Manifesto* (p. 116), where they approve of the idea that the state changes its function so as to become a 'mere superintendence of production'.

18. On the difference between ownership as a *social relation* and as a *legal category*, see Marx's famous preface to *A Contribution to the Critique of Political Economy*. See also Bettelheim (1968: 16-21 and 79-81).

REFERENCES

ALBERT H. (1964) 'Social Science and Moral Philosophy', in M. BUNGE (ed.), *The Critical Approach to Science and Philosophy*. Glencoe: The Free Press of Glencoe.

ALTVATER E. (1972) 'Om nogle problemer ved statsinterventionismen', *Kurasje* 7 (1973).

ARROW K. J. (1951) *Social Choice and Individual Values*. New Haven: Yale University Press, 1963.

BARONE E. (1908) 'The Ministry of Production in the Collectivist State', in A. NOVE and D. M. NUTI (eds.), *Socialist Economics*. Harmondsworth: Penguin Books, 1972.

BERLIN I. (1958) 'Two Concepts of Liberty', in *Four Essays on Liberty*. Oxford: Oxford University Press, 1969.

BETTELHEIM C. (1968) *Övergången till den Socialistiska Ekonomin*. Mölndal: Rene Coeckelberghs Partisanförlag, 1970.

– – (1970) 'More on the Society of Transition', in P. M. SWEEZY and C. BETTELHEIM (eds.), *On the Transition to Socialism*. New York: Monthly Review Press, 1972.

BRUS W. (1972) *The Market in the Socialist Economy*. London: Routledge & Kegan Paul.

BUCHARIN N. and E. PREOBRAZHENSKY (1919) 'The ABC of Communism', in A. NOVE and D. M. NUTI (eds.), *Socialist Economics*. Harmondsworth: Penguin Books, 1972.

DOBB M. (1933) 'Economic Theory and the Problems of a Socialist Economy', in *On Economic Theory and Socialism*. London: Routledge & Kegan Paul, 1955.

– – (1939a) 'Economists and the Economics of Socialism', in *On Economic Theory and Socialism*. London: Routledge & Kegan Paul, 1955.

– – (1939b) 'A Note on Saving and Investment', in *On Economic Theory and Socialism*. London: Routledge & Kegan Paul, 1955.

– – (1951) 'A Note on the Discussion of the Problem of Choice Between Alternative Investment Projects', in *On Economic Theory and Socialism* London: Routledge & Kegan Paul, 1955.

– – (1953) 'A Review of the Discussion Concerning Economic Calculation in a Socialist Economy', in *On Economic Theory and Socialism*. London: Routledge & Kegan Paul, 1955.

– – (1969) *Welfare Economics and the Economics of Socialism*. Cambridge: Cambridge University Press.

ENGELS F. (1878) *Anti-Dühring*. Moscow: Progress Publishers, 1969.

FRIEDMAN M. (1962) *Capitalism and Freedom*. Chicago: Chicago University Press.

– – (1970) 'The Market versus the Bureaucrat', in A. KAPLAN (ed.), *Individuality and the New Society*. Seattle: University of Washington Press.

GALBRAITH J. K. (1958) *The Affluent Society*. Harmondsworth; Penguin Books, 1970.

– – (1967) *The New Industrial State*. Harmondsworth: Penguin Books, 1974.

HAYEK F. A. (1935) 'The Present State of the Debate', in F. A. HAYEK (ed.), *Collectivist Economic Planning*. London: George Routledge & Sons, 1938.

– – (1940) 'Socialist Calculation III: The Competitive "Solution"', in *Individualism and Economic Order*. Chicago: Gateway, 1972.

– – (1944) *The Road to Serfdom*. London: Routledge & Kegan Paul, 1971.

– – (1949) 'The Intellectuals and Socialism', in *Studies in Philosophy, Politics and Economics*. New York: Simon and Schuster, 1969.

——(1960) *The Constitution of Liberty*. Chicago: Gateway, 1972.

——(1963) 'The Economy, Science, and Politics', in *Studies in Philosophy, Politics and Economics*. New York: Simon and Schuster, 1969.

——(1966) 'The Principles of a Liberal Social Order', in *Studies in Philosophy, Politics and Economics*. New York: Simon and Schuster, 1969.

——(1968) *The Confusion of Language in Political Thought*. London: The Institute of Economic Affairs.

——(1973) *Economic Freedom and Representative Government*. London: The Institute of Economic Affairs.

HEILBRONER R. L. (1959) *The Future as History*. New York: Harper Torchbooks, 1968.

KIDRON M. (1968) *Western Capitalism Since the War*. Harmondsworth: Penguin Books, 1970.

KOLAKOWSKI L. (1974) 'The Myth of Human Self-Identity', in L. KOLAKOWSKI and S. HAMPSHIRE (eds.), *The Socialist Idea*. London: Weidenfeld and Nicolson.

LANGE O. (1936–37) 'On the Economic Theory of Socialism', in B. E. LIPPINCOTT (ed.), *On the Economic Theory of Socialism*. New York: McGraw-Hill Book Company, 1964.

——(1964) *Ekonomisk Utveckling och Socialism*. Stockholm: Raben & Sjögren, 1966.

——(1967) 'The Computer and the Market', in A. NOVE and D. M. NUTI (eds.), *Socialist Economics*. Harmondsworth: Penguin Books, 1972.

LENIN V. I. (1918a) 'The State and Revolution', in *Selected Works*, vol. 2. Moscow: Progress Publishers, 1970.

——(1918b) 'Political Report of the Central Committee Delivered at the Extraordinary Seventh Congress of the R. C. P. (B.)', in *Selected Works*, vol. 2. Moscow: Progress Publishers, 1970.

——(1918c) 'The Immediate Tasks of the Soviet Government', in *Selected Works*, vol. 2. Moscow: Progress Publishers, 1970.

——(1918d) 'Left-Wing Childishness and the Petty Bourgeois Mentality', in *Selected Works*, vol. 2. Moscow: Progress Publishers, 1970.

LINNEMAN H., J. P. PRONK and J. TINBERGEN (1967) 'Convergence of Economic Systems in East and West', in E. BENOIT (ed.), *Disarmament and World Economic Dependence*. Oslo: Universitetsförlaget.

MARX K. and F. ENGELS (1846) *The German Ideology*. Moscow: Progress Publishers, 1967.

——and F. ENGELS (1848) *The Communist Manifesto*. Harmondsworth: Penguin Books, 1967.

MARX K. (1859) *A Contribution to the Critique of Political Economy*. Moscow: Progress Publishers, 1970.

——(1867) *Capital*, vol. 1. Moscow: Foreign Languages Publishing House, 1961.

——(1871) *The Civil War in France*. Peking: Foreign Languages Press, 1970.

——(1875) *Critique of the Gotha Programme*. Peking: Foreign Languages Press, 1972.

——(1894) *Capital*, vol. 3. Moscow: Progress Publishers, 1971.

MILIBAND R. (1965) 'Marx and the State', in S. AVINERI (ed.), *Marx's Socialism*. New York: Liber Atherton, 1973.

MISES L. (1920) 'Economic Calculation in the Socialist Commonwealth', in F. A. Hayek (ed.), *Collectivist Economic Planning*. London: George Routledge & Sons, 1938.

— — (1947) *Planned Chaos*. New York: Irvington-on-Hudson.

— — (1952) *Planning for Freedom*. South Holland: Libertarian Press.

MISHAN E. J. (1967) *The Costs of Economic Growth*. Harmondsworth: Penguin Books, 1969.

MYRDAL G. (1932) *The Political Element in the Development of Economic Theory*. London: Routledge & Kegan Paul, 1953.

— — (1960) *Beyond the Welfare State*. New Haven: Yale University Press, 1968.

PETROVIC G. (1967) *Marx in the Mid-twentieth Century*. New York: Doubleday.

POPPER K. (1945) *The Open Society and its Enemies*, vol. 2. London: Routledge & Kegan Paul, 1966.

— — (1957) *The Poverty of Historicism*. London, Routledge & Kegan Paul, 1961.

ROBBINS L. (1932) *The Nature and Significance of Economic Science*. London: Macmillan, 1935.

ROBINSON J. (1964) 'Consumer's Sovereignty in a Planned Economy', in A. NOVE and D. M. NUTI (eds.), *Socialist Economics*. Harmondsworth: Penguin Books, 1972.

SAINT-SIMON H. (1825) 'On Social Organization', in F. MARKHAM (ed.), *Social Organization, the Science of Man and Other Writings*. New York: Harper Torchbooks, 1964.

SCHUMPETER J. A. (1942) *Capitalism, Socialism and Democracy*. London: Unwin University Books, 1954.

SHONFIELD A. (1965) *Modern Capitalism*. New York: Oxford University Press.

TINBERGEN J. (1964) *Central Planning*. New Haven: Yale University Press.

TOCQUEVILLE A. (1835-40) *Democracy in America*, 2 vols. New York: Schocken Books, 1961.

WEBER M. (1922) *The Theory of Social and Economic Organization* (T. PARSONS ed.). New York: The Free Press, 1964.

3

SPONTANEITY AND PARTICIPATION IN WORK AND COMMUNITY: A SOCIOTECHNICAL APPROACH

Albert Cherns
University of Loughborough, UK

1. THE PARADOX OF SPONTANEITY

Play is a fundamental and universal form of expression in man and animal. But play is too frivolous to be accepted as a legitimate activity for adult humans in societies which are dominated by the values of seriousness, 'relevance', 'affective neutrality' and deferment of gratification. In extreme form, puritan values were invoked to condemn play in children as the most powerful instrument in Satan's orchestra. Ironically play has been rescued from disesteem by the demonstration of its service to seriousness; by ranking as 'learning' it has become acceptable but simultaneously invites attention and interference from those who are worthily concerned to ensure that the right values are learned from play: peace not war, tolerance not exclusiveness.

In adult life play becomes 'recreation', is organized and ultimately bureaucratized as society simultaneously legitimizes, defuses and finally domesticates the source of so much energy. Society acts wisely; play is dangerous. It is both anarchic and constructive, individuating and socializing; anything so Protean is inherently unpredictable and unsafe. It is the spontaneity, the unprogrammed and unregulated element that is so dangerous; a regulated, programmed safe society must control, channel and restrict it. Nor is it short of institutions to undertake these requirements; the family, the school, the church, the club, the society, the association, the college are its agents. The job they do is so efficient, so thorough that in our admiration of the pure transparency of the filtered bathwater we are slow to register the absence of the baby. We are not ourselves above these mistakes in our own science as we are graphically reminded by the title of Homans' classic paper, 'Bringing Men Back In' (1971).

Progressive purification of the flour used to bake bread excluded impurities vital to a balanced healthy diet; we now seek to replace them, 'enriching' the flour with the synthetic equivalent of what we have scourged away. The parallel is apt. We bemoan the loss of spontaneity with its valuable ingredients of originality, imagination and inspiration. Having trained them out, we seek to train them in: 'divergent' thinking, 'lateral' thinking, 'non-linear' thinking are now offered as a form of remedial education to correct the deformations of conventional teaching and training.

The way we learn to behave in groups would appear to be equally depressive of spontaneity. We are, of course, all familiar with the classic demonstrations by Sherif of the power of perceived group norms over individual expression if not of perception. To restore the lost ingredients a variety of group training programmes are available, made more or less enticing by titles like 'synectics', 'synergetics' and so on.

What we have done to bread by refining and to the individual's imagination by education we have done to social innovation by planning. It is hard to see how any of the major social innovations of the past could have occurred in a planned society: planning could be the last social innovation! If, under planning, spontaneous innovation is desired, then it has to be carefully planned for; that is the Paradox of Planning. We now talk of spontaneity in planning because we fear that planning has banished spontaneity; we must plan the return of the exile. And after all the synthetic substitute in flour for the lost vitamins is probably no less nutritious, trained lateral thinking is probably no less imaginative, trained synectics no less synergic than their spontaneous counterparts. But if bringing spontaneity back in does not mean the end of planning, it certainly requires that planning undergo a renewal of concepts, goals and methods.

2. PARTICIPATION AND SPONTANEITY

Participation is a necessary but not a sufficient condition for spontaneity in planning. The demands for participation in planning derive from several sources:

(i) planning in democratic societies has been seen to be inherently undemocratic in practice. However democratic, or democratically selected, the ends, it is the means chosen for their attainment that determine the kind of world we experience. If the means are planning and the instrument bureaucracy, then bureaucracy is what we experience. And bureaucracy is the instrument of 'their' will, not 'ours' even though we freely chose 'them'.

(ii) as succinctly expressed by Richard Martin (1977: 1): 'where the individual does not have the responsibility for determining the nature of development that affects him, that development will have a propensity to fail' — i.e. without participation (and the responsibility which full participation implies) planning fails.

(iii) the planning process appears corrupt. It is no accident that some of the most unsavoury public scandals surround planning, especially of land development. And the more flexible the planning process becomes in response to the perceived absurdities of rigid planning, the more it rests on negotiation between public authorities and private developers rather than on legal sanction, the more corruption is suspected and the more powerless, the more alienated the feelings of the private individual.

Planning, then, has become perceived as an instrument of 'them' against 'us'. Under those circumstances there is no moral obligation upon 'us' to respect either the process of planning or the plan. The isolation of the planner from the moral community of the planned is a familiar feature of planning in developing countries. Again the response is the call for participation in planning at the level of the community. But here the argument becomes confused: it is often implied, if not stated, that participation will not only render planning acceptable but will yield truly local and original solutions. But it is not at all clear that these two objectives are compatible, or rather that they are compatible with 'planning'. On the contrary, the probability is very high that such participation will reinforce 'traditional' solutions. The moral community not only excludes outsiders, it also constrains insiders and ensures that solutions shall not threaten to disturb the precarious balances of interests within the community. The emergence of spontaneity depends on other changes occurring within the community itself. How can new patterns of behaviour be stimulated and reinforced? Before people can participate in planning and before they can manifest spontaneity, they will need to acquire competences, a sense of competence and an assurance that their expression will not be punished.

3. THE ROLE OF THE 'EXPERTS'

The circularity of social processes is familiar enough — structures give rise to processes which reinforce them, behaviour validates the assumptions on which it rests. Change involves entering the circle; if you cannot directly assault a structure you may try to modify the process. Participation is a matter of process and of structure. They must be compatible. The first principle of sociotechnical design is the principle of compatibility (see Cherns, 1976 and 1977). A participative organization can be successfully developed only through a participative process of design. We shall not be surprised to find yet another paradox. Designing and planning require special competences and skills beyond the scope of the people for whom the plan or the design is intended; participation in planning also requires new skills and competences. The time honoured mode of incorporating new skills is by acquiring an 'expert'. But acquiring an expert means alienating to him the exercise of the skills and competences in question. And this is the reverse of participation. Before we can participate we have to learn how to participate, how to use the 'expert' by getting him to teach us his skills, to teach us how to use him as a resource not as a specialist expert who does something for us. And this contradicts his own expert training and his own motivation to exercise his expert skills to solve a problem to produce an outcome he can regard as his own. The expert's own training and self-perception, his values and rewards must become those of the facilitator and the coach. We not only have to plan for participation, plan for spontaneity, but plan also for the preparation of new types of expert.

4. FROM INDUSTRY TO COMMUNITY

Even if we have the right kind of 'expert' we still face the question of how and where we can enter the circle. Obviously any occasion when the circle is opened to admit a fundamentally new activity creates an opportunity. That opportunity will not last long; the new activity will soon be assimilated to existing social and cultural patterns or the social and cultural patterns will accommodate themselves to the new activity with as little fundamental change as possible.

We have not far to seek for our fundamentally new activity. The development of a community involves the generation and development of new forms of employment. Most commonly this means the introduction of new industry, not necessarily of a large or sophisticated kind, but certainly one requiring new skills. It is widely accepted that new industry is a force for social change, disrupting existing patterns of relationships, demanding new work disciplines, offering new consumption patterns and so on. It is less often understood that the changes are not deterministic, but entail choices which are not always recognized to exist and frequently made without adequate forethought to their consequences. Thus the *way* in which new industry is introduced may either disrupt or reinforce existing structures of caste or class or race relations (Pocock, 1968; Epstein, 1972). But there are other choices too which go even closer to the heart of industrialization.

If industry is perceived instrumentally solely as a means for producing wealth or material goods and services to the community, the nature of the jobs it provides is a matter of indifference. Faced with the prospects of employing a population lacking in prior industrial skills and unaccustomed to the disciplines of industrial work, designers will follow the line of reasoning adopted by F. W. Taylor (1911). They will design on the assumptions of 'scientific management'. The work provided will do nothing to develop the competences and skills, the social skills, the sense of competence which are the fundamental requirements for participation and spontaneity in planning. On the contrary the work provided is likely to stifle such skills and the methods of supervision and management will impose or reinforce patterns of dominance and subordination inimical to participation and to spontaneity.

Nor need the designers even take explicit decisions about the way in which the work is organized in order to achieve this outcome. The way in which the work is organized is usually *implicit in the technology itself*. In making a choice of technology we willy-nilly choose an organization structure and a set of assumptions about people and machines and their relative importance and functions. We choose a set of values whether we realize it or not; the values are built into the technology. We can, if we understand well enough what we are doing, choose our social system (Trist et al., 1963); we don't *have* to buy our social system with the technology. But that is what we do if we accept without question the implications built into the technology. Even an assembly line technology permits of some choice of organization and of jobs, but the choices are limited once the nature of the line itself has been determined. But even assembly permits a choice of type of line or a choice of no line at all; it all depends what kind of jobs we want; and on what we see to be the end product. The output of industry is jobs and 'the output of jobs is people' (Herbst, 1975). Even a small modification to a technical system can radically alter the nature of the jobs provided (Cherns, 1977).

Let us enunciate three propositions:

(i) Development decisions invariably involve decision to employ technology. We are using 'technology' in a fairly broad sense to include not only the equipment, the 'hardware' but also the methods and procedures for employing it, the 'software'. Thus a budgetary system, for example, is a technology in this sense as is the equipment and methods for processing palm oil. Again the equipment and procedures for the delivery of health care or education are technologies.

(ii) For any purpose or task there is a choice of technology although that is not always recognized; familiar ways of doing things appear inevitable if not 'natural'.

(iii) Underlying the design of any technology are a set of assumptions and a system of values. The assumptions include those about the nature and capabilities of men and of machines; the values include those about the desirable role of man in society and its organizations, the desirability of size per se, the relative priorities of conservation and exploitation and so on. The assumptions and values are implicit and usually unrecognized by those who employ the technology.

Extensive empirical support exists for the theoretical proposition that technology is not simply hardware or a set of procedures, but rather the embodiment of social values and assumptions about people designed into them (Rice, 1958; Davis and Cherns, 1975). For example, technologies of the developed world embody social assumptions and values of that world. This is true not only of the products and their uses, but also the processes by which they are designed and made, and by which these decisions are made. Technology is then a social process. The process of decision making on technology is also a technology – of decision making. This is also not value neutral in its assumptions and consequences. We cannot separate choices from the decision process, nor technological systems from the social process whereby they are chosen. The selection of an appropriate technology then involves 'multivalued choice' (Vickers, 1968). Although the many dimensions of this choice may go unrecognized, they are no less real in their implications.

We can now pose the general issue as follows. In the process of development shall developments in technology oblige society to adapt? Or shall society seek appropriate means (technology) – that embody selected values – to attain desired ends?

5. TECHNOLOGY AS THE OBJECT
OF SOCIAL CHANGE

The existence of social choice in decisions on technology is more often than not unrecognized. Where a response is made to the relationship between technology and development, it tends to take the form of 'technology assessment' (Hetman, 1973: 55). The input is a specific technology and assessment ideally involves examining its total consequences. This is a reactive approach where the initiative is with technology. But if development planning is viewed as a process of multivalued choice, or scenario selection, then a more proactive approach is necessary.

As an alternative, technology may be regarded not as an independent force, but as contingent upon social goals, values and choices. To subordinate technology to social goals involves more than just a shift in emphasis. It requires capabilities for developing and assessing alternative designs to meet social objectives.

However, selecting social goals and searching for appropriate technologies — regarding society as the independent and technology as the dependent variable — is not sufficient. It raises the problem of appropriate technology of choice. Specifically the questions are: (1) Whose preferences shall count? (2) What preferences shall count? (3) How are preferences of different interests to be aggregated? Common planning assumptions are: (i) a public agency — holding a monopoly of power — should articulate for the community collective social goals; or (ii) the planner can assume that the problem disappears if there exists a uniformity of values (and understanding of consequences) in the community which he embodies. Another model of social development requires that the selection of technology be governed by a large number of norms, some of which may not be known. Since the required criteria for choice are not available a priori, choice of appropriate technology then requires in addition to technical analysis a non-formal procedure for dialogue and therefore participation.

The choice of an appropriate technology in a given community then involves all of these dimensions. All are relevant to the process of development. Consider the choice of a given labour-intensive technology for the processing of raw materials. Technology A assigns as much control as possible to machines, employing people as their servants. For reliability it trusts the machine and treats men as inherently unreliable, overcoming this unreliability as far as possible by fragmenting tasks and specifying them rigorously. Control and co-ordination beyond what can be provided by the machine is exercised by supervision and inspection. All planning and decision making are performed at levels removed from the workplace. Technology **A** then provides jobs which require little and encourage less participation in decision making, which emphasize individual tasks rather than group co-operation; and which therefore do not spread the capacity to make informed judgments about future technological developments.

Technology **B** assumes that people are rational, reliable when they understand what is required and why, and are capable of acquiring and exercising a range of skills as they do in life outside the workplace. It is designed to provide jobs in which people can learn and acquire social as well as work skills, can acquire competence to engage with others in decision making, as well as habits of self-discipline. On these assumptions machines are allocated tasks which are needlessly heavy, routine or repetitive to be demanded from people as well as tasks of a computing nature at which machines are far superior. It is designed so that workers are provided with the information and authority they need to get their work done. The choice of technology **B** then trains people in these social skills and enhances the feeling of competence and widens the horizon for the individual and the community.

In point of cost and productivity there may be little to choose between technologies **A** and **B**. But where **A** gives to its community employment and production, **B** provides much more — the skills, competence, sense of competence, social and decision-making skills which represent a major investment in human capital for further social and economic development. To complete the example, the issue must be raised as to what the implications of either alternative are for existing social institutions in the community.

The choice of technology based upon an assessment of its capacity for engendering social development involves what we call *sociotechnical assessment*. Sociotechnical assessment enlarges the focus of (and participation in) the dialogue on the relationship between technology and development at the specific project (and community) level. In addition to questions about resources, infrastructure and environment impacts, it poses questions about social assumptions underlying the type of organization required to operate and maintain a given technology and the technology of decision making required for and implied by it.

The choice of technology is a crucial element in all development decisions. It is vital for the articulation of development in a social as well as economic dimension. This provides an arena for testing the articulation and consistency of micro- with macro-theory through an analysis of assumptions and values underlying both. Finally, it is pervasive as a phenomenon in development process and accessible for intervention.

Hitherto, theories, especially macro-theories, of development have totally ignored these aspects. Treating technology as an exogenous variable whose successful importation involves the appropriate value changes within society, they have failed to observe that technology incorporates values which are a matter of choice. Indeed, the typical industrial design values are those of a society which, as we have said, treats capital as assets and people as costs. But within wide limits, technology can be based on whatever set of values we choose.

The capacity to examine, assess and redesign technology to incorporate human values is beyond a small community — it may be hard to find anywhere. Sociotechnical skills are rare and have been little exercised in relation to community/industrial development. Once again we encounter a dilemma. If widespread diffusion of sociotechnical competence is required, how can this be achieved without treading the path from top to bottom, from centre to periphery which characterize the spread of expertise bringing with it a reinforcement of the control from the top, domination by the centre which stifles spontaneity and reinforces the subordination of local to national?

One solution is to follow Schon's (1971) prescription for the role of the centre. Briefly, it is to encourage the development of networks linking the points on the periphery with one another, encouraging local initiatives by assisting them in acquiring the necessary resources. If the centre can help the peripheral points to learn from one another the spread of sociotechnical competence need not become yet another sort of domination.

But more is required. With the skills, the competences, the resources must go responsibility. The community which plans must have the responsibility for carrying out the plan. Resources have to be provided from above to below, from centre to periphery. And since resources are scarce they have to be competed for. In parting with resources, the centre is therefore obliged to assure itself of the viability of the scheme to which these resources are to be applied. What does this imply for control, for planning, for local initiative and spontaneity? (Of course where local resources only are to be used this question does not arise.) If initiative and spontaneity are to have meaning the recipient of the resources must be free to make mistakes. And if they are to learn from their mistakes they must live with their consequences. Richard Martin (1977) describes how this is achieved without loss of the centre's responsibility to its constituency for the resources it provides. Essentially in his example, which concerns road building in Africa, a dialogue between experts and locals involves not only exchange of information — needs and possibilities — but joint generation of new information which is needed for decision:

> This dialogue need not take long, particularly in the oral society of Africa where written communication is not needed. It is then followed by general agreement on specific routes which must be pegged out by surveyors who thereby indicate the exact houses that are affected by the new roads. There follows a series of follow-ups with all the affected families to see if any object to moving. Some do, but most do not, perceiving, as I explained above, that it is their decision anyway and therefore accepting the consequences. Those that object sometimes do so because they are too old to move. In such cases an exchange of houses can usually be arranged easily so that a young family takes over the 'condemned' house and thereby the right to move. Where such an amicable arrangement is not made there are three options. The householder may simply need a little time to make up his mind (as Festinger would put it, for cognitive dissonance to take its effect, and the extra attractions of moving to come to the fore). The second is that the road should deviate to avoid the house. This is a solution that can simply be made and involves only a few consultations to see if others are willing to move where the original householder is not. The final option, which is one for the community to accept or not, is that the road will not pass there at all. If they do not accept it they will bring social pressure on the reluctant householder, and in the end he will move.
>
> This may seem very longwinded and complex. In practice, however, it takes 2-3 months for a community of 40,000 persons, which in terms of the acceptance of a major proposal from start to finish, is exceptionally quick. As a decision-making process it can be seen to be working from the general to the particular. Neither the technician nor the people start with a fixed position, but rather they are looking forward to coming to an effective solution. (pp. 9-10)

This case study exemplifies some of the processes involved in participation in planning and the relationship needed between centre and periphery. Even in so simple an example the processes are not without difficulty, the strains on the 'expert', the engineer and the surveyor, are considerable. But the process implies a structure of relationships which will in time release rather than stifle spontaneous development. The paradox remains: spontaneity requires meticulous, if imaginative, planning.

REFERENCES

CHERNS, A. B. (1976) 'The Principles of Sociotechnical Design', *Human Relations* 29 (8), August: 783-792.
— — (1977) 'Can Behavioural Science Help Design Organizations?, *Organizational Dynamics*, Spring: 44-64.
DAVIS, L. E. and CHERNS, A. B. (1975) *The Quality of Working Life*, vol. I. New York: Free Press.
EPSTEIN, T. S. (1972) 'Economic Development and Social Change in South India and New Guinea', pp. 131-156 in T. S. EPSTEIN and D. H. PENNY (eds.), *Opportunity and Response*. London: C. Hurst.
HERBST, P. G. (1975) 'The Product of Work is People', pp. 439-443 in L. E. DAVIS and A. B. CHERNS (eds.), *The Quality of Working Life*, vol. I. New York: Free Press.
HETMAN, F. (1973) *Society and the Assessment of Technology*. Paris: OECD.
HOMANS, G. (1971) 'Bringing Man Back In', pp. 403-421 in D. KUBAT (ed.), *Paths of Sociological Imagination*. New York: Gordon and Breach.
MARTIN, R. (1977) 'Development: A Failure Theory', *ITCC Review* 6 (4), October.
POCOCK, D. (1968) 'Social Anthropology: Its Contribution to Planning', pp. 271-292 in P. STREETEN and M. LIPTON (eds.), *The Crisis of Indian Planning*. Oxford: Oxford University Press/Royal Institute of International Affairs.
RICE, A. K. (1958) *The Ahmedabad Experiment*. London: Tavistock.
SCHON, D. A. (1971) *Beyond the Stable State*. London: Temple Smith.
TAYLOR, F. W. (1911) *Scientific Management*. New York: Harper.
TRIST, E. J., G. W. HIGGIN, H. A. MURRAY, and A. B. POLLOCK (1963) *Organizational Choice*. London: Tavistock.
VICKERS, Sir G. (1968) *Value Systems and Social Process*. London: Tavistock.

II
ILLUSTRATIONS AND APPLICATIONS

4

SPONTANEITY AND ORGANIZATION: REVOLUTIONARY PARTY AND MODERNIZATION

Bogdan Denitch
City University of New York, USA

The relationship between spontaneity and organization in revolutionary upheaval has been studied quite extensively, although much of the work has been marred by the ideological predilections of the authors. Theorists of revolutionary parties have tended to place an overwhelming emphasis on the role of the party and its leadership in directing, fanning, and organizing the revolts and rebellions into a consistent programmatic direction aimed at constructing a new revolutionary authority. Liberal and conservative theorists, when not trapped into variants of plot theories, have tended rather to stress the spontaneous nature of revolts and to provide an over sociological explanation for the incidence of revolutionary activity itself.

There are a number of overarching problems which are common to most revolutionary organizations in the process of struggle for power. The first basic problem is the difficulty of making subtle, often unconscious, shifts from an organization of protest and revolt to an organization which poses itself as an alternative authority or rather a potential alternative government. This particular transformation occurs with both revolutionary and reformist transformational movements, and is fundamental, indicating a shift from a struggle to disrupt or destroy the old authority and to replace it with new forms. Many revolutionary organizations, parties and movements never make that first critical transformation. The relationship of this first step to the problem of spontaneity is reasonably clear. At the stage of being an oppositional movement, a revolutionary party or organization may well welcome numerous spontaneous oppositional revolts or actions over which it has no direct control, and for which it does not have to take responsibility. As a matter of fact, it can use such spontaneous acts of rebellion to point to the increasing loss of legitimacy by the old social and political order. On the other hand, once a transformational movement begins to conceive of itself as the alternative authority, it increasingly attempts to channel spontaneous revolts along lines predetermined by itself, and often finds itself clashing with various spontaneous activities which potentially threaten the prospects of the organization to achieve power. Put in another way, once a movement reaches for power and sees itself as a serious contender for authority, local banditry, spontaneous attacks on representatives of the old order, grass-roots attempts at redistribution, assassinations and uncontrolled local tribunals meting out rough-and-ready revolutionary justice can become a problem because they threaten the stability of the new order which is in the process of being created and polarize the population in a way that may well be antagonistic to the new revolutionary authority. Thus, in the stage of transforming itself from an instrument of struggle to an instrument of new order, a revolutionary party is often forced to turn on and crush the spontaneous elements which have struggled alongside it.

There are a number of historical examples of this process. The more familiar ones which come readily to mind come from the Bolshevik Revolution and the crackdown by the Bolsheviks on the anarchist organizations and groups in Moscow and Leningrad, which were continuing a revolutionary ferment at the point when the Bolsheviks were trying to consolidate Soviet authority and provide a minimal political and social order for the society which was emerging from the Revolution. Similarly, some of the more bitter struggles during the Red-White civil war were directed at the anarchist movement in Ukraine, which while opposed to the Whites and quite effective in its opposition, prevented the consolidation of Soviet authority and was crushed by the Bolsheviks. Other examples in Algeria and Yugoslavia can be cited, particularly the attempt in the latter stages of the struggles to eliminate possible future contenders for authority and to consolidate around a single party all authority normally appertaining to a revolutionary government. This process, however, is a delicate one because revolutions, even those led by tightly organized revolutionary parties, represent a large scale attempt at mobilization of spontaneous forces from below, of the previously passive strata and elements of the population on the side of the new order. It is this mobilizational aspect of mass, broad-based support which basically distinguishes *revolutions* from coup d'etats and seizures of power at the center which require that the power later be extended to the countryside.

Again, we can look at a general similarity between the successful revolutionary upheavals of our century. The Bolsheviks, the Chinese communists and the Yugoslav partisans, and to a lesser extent the Algerian FLN. What was characteristic about the Chinese, Yugoslav and Algerian examples was the fact that revolutionary authority was consolidated in the countryside and in the more backward sections of the country before the conquest of the capital. The Bolsheviks on the other hand began by the seizure of power in the center which was then gradually extended to the territory of the Soviet Union. Put most sharply, the difference is that in the first case, the takeover of the capital city represented *the end* process of a victorious struggle, while in the Bolshevik case, the struggle *began* with a takeover of the capital. The city-countryside relationships are reversed in the two cases, and the Bolshevik case therefore involved necessarily a systematic attempt by the modernizing city-based revolutionary party to conquer and transform the countryside which had been the reservoir of its enemies and which continued to resist the revolutionary authority for a good decade after the consolidation of the revolution. The Chinese, Yugoslav and Algerian Revolutions on the other hand, began with the enormous asset that the potential reservoirs of traditionalist opposition to a modernizing revolutionary party were conquered before the seizure of power, and the villages and countryside were themselves transformed into elements of support rather than obstacles to the new revolutionary authority.

The Yugoslav case is particularly intriguing in that there was little about pre-World War II Yugoslavia which could have led an informed observer to suppose that a successful communist-led revolution would have occurred in that country. On the contrary, there were numerous particular specificities in the Yugoslav case which argued against such a prospect. The Yugoslav party was relatively small, numbering around 12,000 members at the time of the German invasion. It had been subject to considerable police repression, and had weak institutional links with other mass organizations. Other than the university students, it was limited to industrial workers, themselves a small minority in the country in a handful of cities, and small town intelligentsia. It had hardly any peasant base to speak of. Further, the party had suffered demoralizing defeats throughout the late twenties and thirties, even while facing a relatively ineffective regime. The country itself was multi-ethnic, and the various national groups had a tradition of considerable hostility against the major group, the Serbs who had dominated the pre-war state. In the early stages of the resistance, the Allies — Great Britain and the Soviet Union and later the United States — recognized the exile government in London as the sole legitimate authority in Yugoslavia, and the nationalist anti-communist Chetnik movement led by Milhailovich as the major organization leading the resistance. The collaboration by local police authorities with the German and Italian occupying authorities led to rapid and effective crackdowns on large sections of the communist party membership in the cities, practically destroying the largest organization of the CP in Zagreb and Belgrade. The communists, to add to their other problems, were in the early stages of the resistance rather ultra-leftists and sought to exacerbate the divisions with the potentially resistant peasant population, attempting even to wage an 'anti-kulak' campaign in the first bitter winter of resistance in 1941. A further underlying difficulty was created by the major victories of the Nazis in the early stages of the war, and the subsequent demoralization of a part of the population which felt that the resistance was therefore futile, particularly given the harsh, almost genocidal reprisals by the Nazis and their supporters against villages which resisted. Overall, a still further problem existed in that large well-armed detachments of collaborators, quislings and 'Whites' were present in the country, receiving considerable armed support from the German and Italian occupiers and certainly outnumbering the communist forces through the first half of the civil war.

Despite all of these problems, in contrast with the much better organized Polish resistance movement and in contrast with resistance movements based on large, well-organized communist parties such as the French, Bulgarian, Italian and Czech parties, the Yugoslav communist-led partisans managed in three short years to become the dominant military force in the countryside. They crushed the remnants of the pro-London government nationalists, driving the few who remained into collaboration with the occupier and thus delegitimating their claims to represent a national resistance. Before the end of the World War II they established revolutionary organs of authority in wide sections of the countryside throughout most of Yugoslavia.

These achievements had clearly required a major mobilization of the peasant masses which had been previously untouched by communist ideology, and involved a stretching out of the remaining communist cadre beyond any possibility of maintaining organizational control over all of the struggles which were occurring in the name of the partisan movement. It is sufficient to note that the Yugoslav party emerged from the civil war with roughly 3,000 members of the pre-war party alive, and that consequently the enormous bulk of the party membership in 1945 when it numbered 150,000, were freshly-recruited peasant and small town workers who entered the party via the armed struggle. With all the best attempts in the world, those recruits drawn in as they were in the middle of a bitter civil war, could hardly be politically educated and socialized in a manner approximating the norms of a 'normal' pre-war communist party.

What clearly took place was the successful assertion of the party's organizational leadership over struggles which were often spontaneous, sporadic and locally based, and the transformation of these spontaneous forces of resistance into a more or less coherent revolutionary movement. Many examples abound of how this process occurred, but two can be used to illustrate it briefly.

In Bosnia, primarily Serbian peasant masses were driven into spontaneous resistance by communal massacres directed at them by the fascist Croat Ustace regime. These village defense guards were often leaderless and when a leadership did arise, at least in the early stages, it tended to rest heavily on the local village notables and reserve officers of the pre-war Yugoslav army. Alongside these volunteer detachments were small, tightly-organized communist led partisan units. In the bitter struggle which resulted for leadership of the resistance movement, the communists in case after case managed to get local units to accept political commissars and a loose control by the party. The process was by no means a one-way road to greater communist consolidation. It see-sawed back and forth. There were numerous cases where the commissars were assassinated by the detachments which they led as a preliminary to making a temporary truce with the occupying authority. The insistence of the party on setting up new revolutionary organs of authority posed it from the very beginning as a challenger to the 'legitimate' pre-war organs of authority which recognized the London government and the King in exile. This conflict was generally won by the party, in those cases, where the mass of the local peasants spontaneously seized the occasion of resistance to destroy tax rolls, court records, and redistribute village stores. Where such processes occurred, a number of unpoliticized peasants found themselves 'compromised' and therefore linked willy-nilly to the future success of the communist-led partisans.

As the war continued, a second phenomenon emerged. A civilian local political support structure had to be developed parallel to that of the military detachments. This is for two reasons. The partisans found it impossible, by and large, to defend liberated territory against major punitive expeditions. As a consequence, the armed resistance bifurcated into local detachments which remained behind and larger partisan units which were mobile, and formed the travelling core of the new authority. This mobile force of 'proletarian brigades' uprooted the peasants who joined in from their local tightly-knit village environment and transformed them, much like in the case of China and Algeria, into a revolutionary army free of local loyalties and therefore more willing to engage in those activities which would provoke enemy reprisals. The reprisals, in turn, drove much of the local population into resistance, and increasingly made impossible the maintenance of traditional authority in the village. The second branch of the resistance rested far more clearly on spontaneous local forces, on local village-based detachments which often lapsed into passivity, and on new grass-root revolutionary organs of authority which counterposed themselves to the traditional village notables and pre-war officials.

These new organs of authority tended to be based on the 'outsiders' from the traditional hierarchy. They were disproportionately young, female and educated. As often as not, they were in conflict not only with the political authorities in the village but with the economically more substantial peasants and the local priests. Thus, in the framework of the larger civil war and war liberation, thousands of local micro-struggles isolated from each other occurred in individual villages between the new and the old authority.

Obviously, whenever an area would be liberated by the large scale partisan detachments, the new revolutionary organs of rule would emerge and assert their authority openly. When the major partisan detachments were forced to withdraw, the dormant traditionalists would seek to reconquer the village. But as the years of the civil war went on, the villages increasingly tipped to the side of the resistance and thus often without thinking of it consciously, to the side of the partisans in the civil war.

The very destructiveness of Axis forces in dealing with the resistance tended to destabilize the villages and thus weaken the bases of traditional authority. The result was that in wide areas, towards the end of World War II, the partisans had won the micro-civil war and held de facto authority over the civilian peasant population. This had numerous consequences, but the most important one we would point to, is that it created local spontaneous village-based organs of authority which were committed to the new regime, which was emerging, and loosely-speaking, committed to a policy of rapid transformation and modernization of Yugoslav society.

Why this would have been so is fairly clear. The equivalent of campaign promises that the party made to its peasant supporters were the promises that a new social order would follow which would be more just, more egalitarian and, above all, more modern. It was the modernizing ideology of the communist party in general, rather than specific political promises, which proved to be enormously attractive to the young people in the villages. Thus, the forces which existed in the countryside, which held de facto authority, were committed to a transformational program, even without spelled-out details, which readily lent itself to the extension of the party rule nationally.

Several processes can be identified here. Clearly, the new revolutionary regime, in sharp distinction with the communist-led regimes in the rest of Eastern Europe, had a massive clientele which felt that it had rewards coming for the sacrifices made during the war. Since the most brutal struggles had occurred by and large in the more undeveloped parts of the country, it meant that the party now had a ready-made reservoir of young peasant men and women who desired nothing as much as to cease to be peasants. It was this wave of former peasants that filled out the social niches which had been made vacant in the cities and economy of Yugoslavia. It was this element which played a major role in the post-World War II reconstruction and as they moved upwards in the emerging new social structure, their advances were clearly linked to the success of the revolution and the maintenance of the party rule. The destruction of the opponents in the civil war meant that vast sections of the state bureaucracy and of new managers of the growing industry had to be staffed de novo. These new men and women were extremely successful agents of modernization, not only in their move to the cities but because they retained personal links with their villages of origin. The maintenance of informal networks of contact with distant relatives and neighbors provided for a continual interaction between a new modernizing elite and the villages. Role models of successful villagers who had properly utilized the new opportunities which arose in a modernizing Yugoslavia tended to bridge the city-countryside gap and provided a beacon for ambitious young men and women from the villages who continued pouring into the ever expanding industries and urban sector of Yugoslavia. The result was a dramatic social transformation, changing a country which had been 85 percent rural to one which is today over 65 percent urban. A further consequence is that the new cities are in good part populated by persons who have made a drastic change in their lives in their own memories. Within a single generation, they have leaped from the countryside into the cities, from peasants to workers or lower officials. While this mobility is not necessarily much greater than the mobility which occurred in advanced industrial countries of Western Europe, it is unprecedented for pre-World War II Eastern Europe, and those who successfully made that transformation remained committed, broadly speaking, to the regime which made this possible.

In the case of Yugoslavia, we have an example where a successful revolutionary party rode on spontaneous waves of support for its broad-gauged modernizing program and turned the successes of that program into new bases for political legitimacy of the regime.

It was *the mix* of spontaneous and organized efforts which made the revolution possible, and it was the element of spontaneity and localism which tended to place far more emphasis on local initiative by previously uninvolved strata, characteristic for a guerrilla war, which created a regime noted for its remarkable self-confidence and tendency to experiment with participatory forms both in industry and local government. Precisely because the party had successfully channeled spontaneous local support during the war into a winning combination, it was more willing to devolve authority from the federal center to local republics, down to county level, and to move into the development of workers self-management in industry. This is the opposite of the practice of the parties which had won power in the center first and then had to attempt to expand out, and consequently had little confidence in their own ability to turn spontaneous local struggles and organs of rule to their own advantage. The result has been that the East European states have remained highly centralized, both in the political and economic spheres, and suspicious of local spontaneous initiatives in general. It is this ability to interact with spontaneous forces for example that has given the Yugoslav party the self-confidence necessary to permit strikes, widening prerogatives to the workers councils, and considerable autonomy to local organs of self-rule. They are, after all, the victors of a struggle which had involved a collaboration between a highly centralized party organization and grass-roots spontaneous upheavals and activists.

A further result of this willingness to decentralize geographically and institutionally in Yugoslavia is that the non-party members are far more willing to participate articulately and actively in the socio-political framework which has been created than is the case with the other one-party modernizing regimes. This has meant in practice that the policy of modernization, by and large, has not had to be imposed from the center but has continually been shored up locally by local activists who are accustomed to functioning without detailed instructions and directions from the center.

In the case of the other major revolutions of this century the mix has worked differently. In China, there seems to be a consensus among experts that the party has been successful in the countryside with its communes to a far greater extent than in the cities and industries.

One way of looking at this is to say that in the countryside, the spontaneous autonomous productive units, while working within broad party directives, have utilized the creative energies of the local peasants to advantage. The industries, however, had in principle remained grossly over-centralized and the spontaneous elements that are seen in the Chinese urban development have tended to be more in the nature of eruptions, sometimes initiated from the center, than an interplay between the party and the spontaneous masses. The balance in China in the latter years of Mao's life was off also in that the organizing element was reduced to the very pinnacle at the top, and therefore was grossly over-centralized and could not assert itself as an organized force over prolonged periods of time.

Algeria represents a different example in that the revolutionary authority of the FLN has tended to rest far too much on the hier-archical structure of the armed forces. While spontaneous elements existed in the mobilization of resistance, during the revolutionary war a highly centralized regime has emerged, giving little vent to local initiative. Perhaps the problem here is the combination of two different but highly centralized traditions, that of the French administration and of the revolutionary army. In any case, Algeria does represent a regime far more stable and legitimate, even with these defects, than are most of the Third World post-revolutionary regimes. This is a continued benefit flowing from the fact that massive mobilization of popular support for the revolution had preceded the victory of the FLN. This still remains a major difference between these revolutions and the one in Cuba where such mobilization as did take place *followed* the establishment of the revolutionary regime.

In the Soviet case, one can observe the consequences of the repression of most elements of non-systemic, spontaneous input into the system and the resultant stagnant immobile bureaucratic regime which shows little self-confidence and ability to interact with non-institutional forces from below. Therefore, in the case of the Soviet Union, as that of the East European countries modelled on it, all such pressures are seen as automatically inimical to the maintenance of the social order. All spontaneous intellectual or popular currents tend to assume an anti-regime and anti-state character. Strikes by the massive new industrial working class may well represent a nemesis of the regime.

The problem of spontaneity and organization is one which haunts mass popular movements. The exact mix has been, after all, the main point of debate between the Bolsheviks and the other Marxist currents in pre-revolutionary Russia, and represented one of the major foci of Rosa Luxemburg's attacks on Lenin's conception of the party. It lies at the heart of Gramsci's conception of a movement as distinct from a party as being essential for the social transformation of an established political and social order. A party organized in a hierarchically structured form may well be the instrumentality indispensable for the coordination of struggles in repressive regimes, and in situations where delicate tactical adaptation is required. A movement, on the other hand, represents more than that and must, ultimately, involve the conscious, voluntary participation of the mass institutions, informal groupings and networks of the populace in the process of change.

The ideal relationship, clearly, is one in which there is a dialogue and interaction between the two, rather than one in which the party assumes that it *alone* has the requisite consciousness and intellect to direct inchoate elemental struggles. Specifically, while the party acts as the institutional transmitter of experiences from former struggles, it is always in danger of imposing the lessons and the patterns of past struggles on living movements. Or, to put it differently, parties tend to learn from their past, movements interact with the present. Consequently, well-structured organizations such as revolutionary or transformational parties, find themselves all too often running after the mass movements which they seek to lead. There are classic examples of this, and the best one is probably the example of the creation of the first workers, soldiers and peasant Soviets in the Russian Revolution of 1905. These spontaneously evolved forms of struggle and potential alternative authority emerged *outside* of the framework of the organized parties and tendencies of Russian Marxism and socialism. It is not an accident that Trotsky, an unaffiliated Marxist, rather than a Bolshevik or Menshevik spokesman, assumed the leadership of the Petrograd Soviet. The first Soviets were a lesson which the masses proceeded to teach the organizations. To be sure, in 1917, when they emerged again, the organization was ready and familiar with this new instrument of struggle. But the critical point here is that it is precisely because the masses did not follow the organization that a framework was created which made it possible for the revolutionary organization to eventually overthrow Czarism.

The organized wisdom of the party and the trade union movements in Germany before World War I rejected the concept of the Mass Strike as an instrument of struggle. Rosa Luxemburg was isolated on this issue within what was then the most advanced workers organization in the world, and yet, in the chaotic period following World War I, when a massive right-wing coup was directed at the fledgling Weimar Republic, the Kapp *putsch*, it was stopped dead in its tracks by a mass strike of the organized German working class. That lesson, however, turned out not to have been learned by the Western labor movement and in part is responsible for the victory of fascism in the thirties.

Similar interactions between the mass and the revolutionary organization have occurred in national liberation struggles and in the example used earlier of the Yugoslav Revolution. It is the sign of a mature, competent, revolutionary leadership that it can channel, use but, above all, learn from, spontaneous struggles of the masses which it seeks to lead.

In conclusion, it is the wide scale organization and coordination of autonomous local struggles that forms not only the most successful basis for revolutionary struggle against an old authority and a foreign occupier, but — and this is crucial — provides the optimal massive base for the early stages of modernization and development of a revolutionary polity. It is the successful breakthrough at the early stages of modernization that forms the most stable basis for the legitimacy of a new revolutionary order.

5

SPONTANEOUS AND PLANNED ACTIONS IN CONFLICT SITUATIONS: THE STATE AND THE LABOUR MOVEMENT IN LATIN AMERICA

Elizabeth Jelin
Cedes, Argentina

This paper deals with the change in the relationship between the state and the labour movement in some Latin American countries during the last forty years. The perspective adopted considers development and change as the result of conflicts and compromises between social groups. By their very nature, capitalist societies imply the existence of conflicting social classes with contradictory interests and social projects.[1] Thus, models of social development vary as much as ideologies do. In this light, the way planned and spontaneous social behaviour are combined in social development ceases to be a technical matter of centralized vs. decentralized decisions. It becomes a political issue, focused on alternative models of development proposed by social groups with different ideologies, located in diverse social positions and with differential access to power and the state apparatus.

Thus, from the vantage point of the ruling or dominant social groups, state planning is the set of policies or measures taken to implement *their* project of development. Other social groups may accept or oppose it. Historical processes of change are the result of such struggles, confrontations, negotiations and alliances, in which spontaneous and planned actions are present, both at the moment of proposing and adopting a given model of development and in its implementation.

These premises should not be understood as invariable in a comparative or historical perspective. Important differences exist in terms of the concentration of power in the state, in the degree of social consensus and acceptance of the mechanisms of access and representation in the political arena, and in the degree and type of participation of the subordinate classes in the process of planning and in its implementation. In that sense, no discussion of spontaneity can be made without the continuous reference to the state — be it when dealing with the 'spontaneous' struggle of social classes and groups to control the state apparatus or with the realm of spontaneity left to — or conquered by — the social groups within the 'normal' functioning of the state apparatus.

In the twentieth century societies the state has a crucial position in the structuring of social relations in civil society. It is never simply an 'emergent' body, grounded purely in social class relations and expressing at the political level the articulation of class relations. Not by chance are expressions such as the 'relative autonomy' of the state so usual in our academic language. Although the state is the agency that has the power to plan for the total society and has a variable but considerable degree of autonomy in relation to the social forces in society, its actions are not independent of the interests of the dominant groups and ruling elites. Social development projects are more likely to be successful when the dominant classes are in a clear hegemonic position. Hegemony implies a considerable degree of social consensus, the acceptance on the part of the subordinate classes of the project as legitimate, and even the integration into the dominant ideological discourse, and a consequent neutralization of important and potentially antagonistic alternative ideological contents (Laclau, 1977). In Western representative democracies this also entails the legitimacy of the state apparatus and of the government officials, the existence of mechanisms of representation, and some degree of accepted participation in public life of the subordinate classes.

Historically, this socio-political arrangement was preceded by important struggles for social and political incorporation of the subordinate classes centered in the struggle for the extension of citizenship rights (Marshall, 1965; Bendix, 1964). In most Third World countries today, however, it is hard to find such legitimate mechanisms of domination and of popular representation and participation. Authoritarian regimes of various sorts, based to a large extent on coercion and on the exclusion from social and political participation of various social groups, are more the rule than the exception. In such contexts, the dynamics of the incorporation of the subordinate classes to full social and political life, the recognition of their rights as human beings and as citizens, constitute the core of the debate and struggle between social classes. Social development projects, and the dynamics of planning and spontaneity involved in them, are set in the context of these major societal issues. Furthermore, the state is in such societies the focal point in the social processes linked to development and in the structuring of class relations (O'Donnell, 1977b; Cardoso and Faletto, 1968).

In this perspective, planning is the attempt, on the part of the state and the ruling classes, to foresee a given course of action for specified social actors (in this case, the subordinate classes) and the mechanisms that will lead to such action. There is always an element of social control in planning, although variations exist in the degree of acceptance and in the nature of the sanctions imposed on the non-conformers.[2] If planning takes place at a time when the issues of incorporation and representation are at the forefront of the political process, then the state and the ruling groups have to react by adapting their projects and plans to the outcome of unregulated spontaneous social processes resulting from the struggle between social forces. A first meaning of 'spontaneity', then, applies to social actions involved in actual struggles between contenders in which, although each one may have a well laid out strategy, the outcome cannot be predicted or planned for. Once a given project is accepted or imposed from above, 'instrumental planning' can take place. Then a second meaning of 'spontaneity' becomes relevant: uncontrolled actions, 'left free' in the plan or taken up by those who have to accept and comply with the plan, are spontaneous without necessarily challenging the project.[3]

In the following pages, the analytical issues presented will be discussed on the basis of the evidence provided by the history of the relationship between the labour movement and the state since the emergence of the mass organizations in the late-nineteen thirties and early forties, in some major Latin American countries, namely Argentina, Brazil and Mexico.

THE STATE AND THE LABOUR MOVEMENT DURING THE STAGE OF IMPORT-SUBSTITUTING INDUSTRIALIZATION
The issue of the incorporation of the subordinate sectors

In the central Western countries, the political and social incorporation of the subordinate classes took place in the context of the process of nation-building and had its main manifestation in the gradual extension of citizenship rights. In this long historical process, through confrontations and compromises, the subordinate classes emerged from estate-like positions into a status of accepted and legitimate political participants. In many Third World countries (and for some minority groups in the central capitalist ones) this incorporation is a recent or a still ongoing process. Fast urbanization and industrialization during the twentieth century are causing a very rapid pace of change in the lives of large masses of the population — involving migration to the cities, entry into urban employment (and underemployment), extension of mass media and education, and so on. The political conditions under which these are taking place imply a complex and varying role of the popular sectors, thus affecting their type of mobilization and socio-political incorporation.

In the larger Latin American countries, the emergence of the urban subordinate sectors as a massive phenomenon and their socio-political incorporation took place during the thirties and forties, at a time when the dynamism of the economies was shifting from primary production for export to the world market to industrial production for the internal market — the so-called import-substituting industrialization (Germani, 1962; Cardoso and Faletto, 1968). Important crises and shifts in the balance of power within the dominant classes were taking place at the same time, and profoundly affected the position of the subordinate sectors in this process.

In economic terms, import-substituting industrialization resulted in a very fast development of the industrial working class. Although the expanding industry could not always absorb the growing urban labour force resulting from natural population growth and from the massive wave of rural migrants attracted by the new urban-industrial structure, there were other opportunities and advantages in the cities: the migrants had access to urban services, to a monetary income, and to educational and health facilities unknown to them in the areas of origin (Hauser, 1959). Occupational opportunities were not absent, insofar as the service sectors, important since the agro-export times, were growing through the expansion of the government bureaucracy, while other labour intensive sectors, like the construction industry, were experiencing a boom. Urban population growth and some redistribution of income in favour of the popular sectors during the forties were congruent with a development project inspired by the industrial sector, which required a growing internal market to keep its production expanding. Thus, the logic of industrial expansion was at the same time creating the urban proletariat and giving the popular sectors a place as consumers in the market of industrial products.

The process of rapid industrialization took place in the midst of a major political crisis: the politically emergent industrial bourgeoisie and middle sectors were strong enough to terminate or seriously question the pre-existing oligarchic rule, but they were not sufficiently powerful to solve the crisis and take full control of the state (Graciarena, 1969 and 1978; Weffort, 1974; Cavarozzi, 1975; González Casanova, 1967; Murmis and Portantiero, 1971). The fragmentation and conflict within the dominant classes, at a time when the international economic scene and the new internally dynamic economic sectors required a clear-cut change in the role of the state, led to diverse and complex political solutions in different countries, all of them based on the total or partial inclusion of the popular sectors in the leading political alliances. Such incorporation into the political system was based on the political needs of the industrial elites, and was geared on the one hand, to an alliance with the growing organized labour movement, and on the other, to an appeal to the unorganized masses, usually embodied in the support of charismatic populist leaders — Perón, Vargas, Cárdenas (Germani, 1962).

The economic participation as producers and as consumers, and the political incorporation as (minor) partners in ruling political alliances is one aspect of the story. The development project based on fast industrialization also required a disciplined and predictable labour force. The new interventionist state that was being built included, among its new 'facilitating' functions, the structuring and controlling of the labour force. This was a double-faced process — on the one hand, the enactment of labour legislation and the promotion of mass unionism responded to long felt demands of the workers, who rightly saw in the state actions towards them good reasons to support the political alliance they had entered; on the other hand, the new institutional channels for the expression of workers' interests and needs provided the state with legitimate mechanisms of control and discipline of the labour force.

In Brazil, after the successful coup of 1930, new labour codes and legislation were enacted. The Ministry of Labour was created in 1930; regulations regarding the *Sindicato unico* (representation by only one union for each productive sector) and a limit to the percentage of foreign-born members allowed in a recognized union were established in 1931. These were followed by other measures designed to outline the role of the state in labour relations. The most significant ones in terms of the future capacity of the state to control the labour movement were the requirement of an official Ministry of Labour recognition of labour unions, and the attribution to the state of the power to decide wage levels, thus banning from the beginning collective bargaining (Vianna, 1976). These regulations are still in effect today.

Brazilian scholars have for long debated the reasons for this massive state intervention in the labour scene during the thirties. Some have emphasized the need for political control of the working class; the precarious nature of the political stability achieved by the rival dominant fractions could not withstand a free labour movement (Rowland, 1974). The strong corporatist state, according to this interpretation, was the solution to the weakness of the political alliance and the cleavages within the dominant sectors. Undoubtedly, such political reasons had some counterparts in the economy of the country. Although the new industrial groups were not controlling the state apparatus from the beginning of the new regime, they were exerting strong economic pressures (Vianna, 1976; Andrade, 1977). The Brazilian labour legislation was a clear way to put under state tutelage the organization and expression of workers' interests, assuring a degree of predictability and of discipline in the labour market and establishing the 'rules of the game' to be followed by the new urban masses (Oliveira, 1975). No doubt many paternalistic elements were present, justifying to some extent the predominant interpretation of the labour legislation as 'a gift from above'. Still, the component of economic rationality was powerful.

> As an analyst of the period concludes, rather than acting in distributive terms, in which case it would have been a hindrance to the process of capitalist accumulation, or even when it would have had a neutral effect in this respect, labour legislation contributed to its expansion. This was due to the discipline it imposed in the factories, where wage workers were politically at the mercy of capital, to the dissolution of independent class organizations and to their channelling inside the corporatist unionism. (Vianna, 1976: 152)

The case of Argentina, under different structural conditions, also points in the same general direction. The need for political support — and the degree to which the popular sectors effectively held some power and potential leverage — were much larger than in Brazil, and the labour market had already a relatively high degree of regulation (Gaudio and Pilone, 1976). Actually, working class actions, including strikes and popular mobilizations in support of long-felt demands, were at the roots of many of the rights and benefits that the popular sectors achieved during the forties (Doyon, 1975; Little, 1972). When compared to Vargas' Brazil, Argentine state-working class relationships during the forties had a much less marked paternalistic and gift-giving character.

The political alliance that supported Perón included in a key position the organized labour movement and the popular masses (Murmis and Portantiero, 1971; Germani, 1973). This support, however, was based on the real gains that the working classes were obtaining, and for which they had been struggling. The resulting legislative and organizational features of the emergent mass labour movement were not very different from the Brazilian ones, including a strong regulatory power of the state through the recognition of the Ministry of Labour. If during the first few years of the Perónist regime that structure of labour relations could channel efficiently the interests of the working classes, later it could also be used by the state to purge emerging opposition groups within the labour movement and to control the working classes politically (Little, 1972). After Perón's demise in 1955, there were various attempts at changing the body of labour legislation. Notwithstanding such efforts, the organized labour movement, now politically outside the government, became a strong autonomous political actor, combining its corporatist-sectoral economic role and the representation of the banned Perónist political movement.

Mexico presents some peculiar features that do not allow placing its history in the same sequence as in the other two countries (Spalding, 1977; Reyna and Miguet, 1976). The Mexican Revolution displaced oligarchic rule earlier, and already in the 1917 Constitution many of the labour rights that were enacted twenty or thirty years later in Brazil or Argentina were formally established. For Mexico, then, the thirties and forties were not a period of legal recognition of the working class but rather of *actual* recognition and incorporation of the labour movement into the political system (Marvan, 1977; Anguiano, 1975; León, 1978).

Also, the very early process of legal recognition faced an extremely weak working class. Only small groups of activists and leaders, many of them not of labour origins, gained access to the political life of the country during the revolutionary period. This was not a mass phenomenon. Until the forties Mexico was predominantly a rural-agrarian society, and the urban labour force was limited, in numbers and in organization, except in some special sectors (railways, oil-workers). The emergence and growth of the mass labour organizations and the establishment of channels of participation were concomitant with the creation of a massive industrial labour force. The sequence was not the classical one of a first stage of emergence of an urban working class and then the growth of its organizations. Both took place together and linked to each other.

To a larger extent than in the other cases, labour organizations in Mexico were not a natural outgrowth of the development of the working class; they emerged as part of an exogenous political process, linked to the designs and needs of other social sectors which attempted to control and co-opt the labour movement. Since very early, attempts at the creation of alternative independent organizations (railway strikes in 1926 and 1948, for example) were not allowed to prosper. The crucial period for the establishment of a pattern of state-labour relations was the Cárdenas government (1934-1940). The Mexican state and political institutions at that time were still in flux, not having been totally reconstructed after the Revolution and its aftermath. Alternatives in terms of political organization, representation mechanisms and even political regime were still being discussed. As a matter of fact, the thirties have to be understood on the basis of the alliances and clashes between personalities — Cárdenas, Calles, Lombardo Toledano — who kept defining their positions and carving out their social bases of support. One such conflict, between Cárdenas and Calles, was resolved by a massive mobilization of the subordinate sectors in support of Cárdenas. His victory led to a process of institutionalization and crystallization of his power base, but since he was in control of the state apparatus, such institutionalization took the form, again, of a direct link of the mass organizations and eventual subordination, to the dominant political arrangement. The creation of the CTM (Confederación de Trabajodores Mexicanos) in 1936, and its fast consolidation as a government and party-linked organization marked the end of a period of political mass mobilization and the beginning of its formal incorporation within the institutionalized channels of the one-party political system (León, 1978).

On another front, the reorganization of the Mexican economy after twenty years of disruption due to the Revolution and regional conflicts could only be accomplished through the integration of a national market and the regulation of labour relations. If political demands were predominant in the Cárdenas period, economic ones became much more pressing during the World War II years, when the real industrial boom took place. At that time, a 'labour pact' that froze wages and disputes, was sponsored and fully accepted by the most important labour organization, the CTM, by then already an integral part of the governing party, the PRI (Contreras, 1977; Medina, 1977; Ortega, 1977).

In summary, in the three cases the industrialization project proposed by the new dominant classes during that period involved the growth of the urban popular sectors. Insofar as the project of industrial development required predictable labour relations, it gave way to the creation of a series of regulations governing labour contracts, working conditions, and union activities. Whether such actions were an explicit part of governmental planning or not, whether they were justified or presented as a 'paternalistic gift' or as a victory of the workers against capital, as a right or as a duty, labour legislation and labour organizations had a clear place within the general developmental project of the period.

These new popular sectors — by the very fact of their concentration in urban areas and the concomitant breakdown of traditional modes of domination — were mobilized in political terms, and consequently were called to play a significant, though subordinated, role in the ruling political alliance. Thus the implications of the labour legislation enacted or implemented were several: such legislation was a response to demands stemming from the needs of the working population, but also a mechanism to increase the discipline, control and predictability of the labour force, as well as part of a political bargaining process designed to gain the support of the subordinate sectors. On the one hand, such mechanisms can be considered part of governmental implicit planning for fast industrialization; on the other, they were part of a struggle for access to political power, and therefore not subject to planning.

Even at the height of the success of this model, when it functioned smoothly, there were expressions of discontent and opposition, giving way to the emergence of alternative, unchannelled or 'spontaneous' working class movements. Protest was expressed mainly in two ways: first, some alternative independent workers organizations, linked to minority or opposition political parties, did survive, legally or not, and were ready for action as soon as the political scene showed even minor signs of opening, or the control over the popular sectors' organizations weakened. Examples of such actions include the emergence and development of working class organizations in Brazil during the 'democratization' of 1945-46 (Weffort, 1973); the upsurge of anti-Perónist labour organizations in Argentina in 1955 (Senén Gonzalez, 1971); and the efforts to develop major labour organizations outside the CTM in Mexico in 1948 and 1958 (Alonso, 1972; Pellicer de Brody and Reyna, 1978). Second, there were spontaneous rank and file movements, at times linked to the alternative organizations, but not necessarily. Thus, in Argentina there was a considerable increase in mobilization and strike actions during the last three years of the Perónist regime, 1952-1955 (Doyon, 1975); the same happened in Brazil in 1945-46; and again in Sao Paulo in 1953 (Moises, 1978); and there was considerable spontaneous mobilization in Mexico in 1958 (Alonso, 1972).

In many cases, the established organizations, the functioning system of labour bargaining and the institutionalized mechanisms of conflict resolution could absorb the discontent manifest in such outbursts. For instance, during the 1952-1955 period, demands in Argentina were for higher wages (Doyon, 1975) and they could be handled within the established mechanisms. Other cases, such as the movements in Mexico in 1958-59, required the use of several mechanisms to cope with the demands — the centralized labour movement incorporated some of the demands accepting the pressures from below; the leadership emerging in the opposition movement was co-opted; and finally, repression was resorted to.

In a historical perspective, the body of labour regulations and the type of labour organizations[4] were created and enacted at a time when the working classes were entering as partners within the populist regimes. The legislative and organizational developments were rightly seen in terms of the integration of the popular sectors into the society, and as one of the mechanisms of their political representation. As the economic and political situation changed, especially when the state acquired a more autonomous position vis à vis these subordinate classes that earlier had supported it, the same body of rules and regulations could be used to control and manipulate workers' organizations. Once a given structure of organizations was established, it became relatively independent of the conditions that gave it birth (Stinchcombe, 1965). Thus, arrangements designed to solve a given conjunctural crisis had historical and structural consequences that conditioned the future developments of the position of the subordinate sectors vis à vis the state.

THE NEW STYLE OF DEVELOPMENT:
EXCLUSION AND PROTEST

During the next decades, the economic conditions of the larger Latin American countries changed considerably. The stage of easy import-substituting industrialization ended (Tavares, 1972) and after some years of readjustment, a new strategy of development was adopted. This new model of economic growth was based upon the production of consumer durables and capital goods. It called for the internationalization of the protected economies and for the massive penetration of multinational corporations (Fajnzylber and Martinez Tarrago, 1976; Sourrouille, 1978; Fajnzylber, 1977). In Argentina and Brazil, this economic change took place within the framework of important political crises of the populist regimes. Mexico achieved a similar economic change without going through such an open political crisis, although there were important social and political changes involved. Actually, each of the cases followed its own historical development, and to a certain degree the social and political processes involved were unique. The attempt made here to review them in a comparative perspective will hopefully substantiate some generalizations and direct attention to areas for further study.

Economically, the new stage in the process of industrialization, characterized by the massive incorporation of transnational capital, was based on a regressive distribution of income and on the displacement of mass consumption from the dynamic focus of the economy. A smaller sector of high income consumers, and the state public works projects, became the main markets for the new dynamic industries. The new productive activities required a relatively limited labour force, at a time when the supply was growing notoriously, both due to natural population growth and the exodus of rural workers. Unless counterbalanced by strong political forces (which was not the case) such changes were bound to produce a growing heterogeneity in income, working conditions and standard of living within the urban popular sector.[5]

Political change was congruent with the economy. International capital became a strong partner in the new ruling alliances (O'Donnell, 1977a; Cardoso, 1975; Reyna, 1975) which ceased to rely on the active support of the subordinate classes. These could then be excluded not only from the ruling alliances, but also from any form of political participation and representation. While in the previous stage the economic and political incorporation of the subordinate sectors had been recognized and accepted, now they began to be seen as superfluous and characterized as a 'social problem'.

The change was drastic in some cases, smooth and gradual in others. In Brazil, the early sixties witnessed a high point of mass mobilization, extensive popular participation and the strengthening of labour organizations in support of the populist regime, which was already in the midst of a deep economic and political crisis (Weffort, 1974; Erickson, 1975). The military authorities that took over with the 1964 coup immediately resorted to repression in order to reverse that situation. In Argentina, working class mobilization in the early sixties was highly controlled by the labour leaders, who were willing and able to engage in economic and political negotiations with whoever was in power, provided that the labour movement would be recognized as a legitimate political actor with a double voice: that of the unions qua labour organizations, and that of Perónism. The latter was banned from direct access to the political arena and had to express itself through the labour movement (Rotondaro, 1971; Cavarozzi, 1979; Torre, 1979). After the 1966 coup, the ruling groups attempted to curtail the political participation of the popular sectors, although they were willing to negotiate economic demands of the unions. A few years later, repression would be used also in labour issues. In Mexico, attempts were made continuously to maintain the labour movement within its bounds — i.e., at the same time limited in its demands to specific labour issues within the established and recognized range *and* maintaining its political dependence and integration within the PRI. The few attempts at independent expression of popular sectors' interests, such as the 1958 wave of strikes and later on the 1968 student movement, ended in repression (Reyna and Miquet, 1976).

Under these circumstances, the long established pattern of labour relations and negotiations with the state could no longer be effective. The unions could no longer deal directly with the state, especially through the labour ministries, expecting to influence wage decisions or to obtain new labour legislation or social services in exchange for political support and control of the masses. Brazil after the coup of 1964 showed the most clear-cut change in policy, although without a significant alteration in labour legislation. The new authorities took action in three basic areas to implement the new policies of exclusion and control. First, the government increased direct control over the labour organizations. Immediately after the military coup many labour leaders were imprisoned, unions were further restrained and the system of *organizaçoes paralelas* was dismantled and forbidden.[6] Second, the control over conditions of employment changed considerably, especially through changes in regulations concerning stability and layoffs (Vianna, 1976). Third, new income policies were followed by which wage increases were severely controlled through a complex mechanism of adjustments to inflation (Humphrey, 1977b). The result was a drastic reduction in real wages. With an ample supply of labour, regular employment became a privilege, not a right.

Argentina did not show such a clear-cut and consistent labour policy. After Perón's downfall in 1955, the organized labour movement re-emerged with full strength to become one of the main political actors (Cavarozzi, 1979; Torre, 1979). Up to the coup of 1966, and even immediately after, the bargaining capacity of the union movement was considerable in economic terms. Politically, being the only de facto channel of expression of Perónism, it had a strong voice in alliances and negotiations with various political parties and with the state. The complexity of such negotiations and the internal conflicts within the Perónist movement led to divisions and strifes within the once centralized labour organization, and to an increasing distance between the leadership, with its style of high-level bargaining, and the rank and file, that was suffering the impact of the new model of economic growth. The return to a Perónist government in 1973 and the new military coup of 1976 are probably the last attempt — and final dismissal — of a type of centralized unionism based on direct integration and negotiation with the state apparatus (Jelin, 1977).

In Mexico, the new stage of economic development was not accompanied by a major political or institutional crisis, although it was not devoid of conflicts. In the aftermath of the 1958-59 movements, which had finished with repression and massive layoffs (Pellicer de Brody and Reyna, 1978), the state's policy toward the working classes was guided by its need to restore stability in order to assure the conditions for fast economic growth. This meant, on the one hand, a flexible wage policy, favouring some skilled workers and workers in some specific strategic sectors, as a way to curb discontent; on the other, a policy of strict control of the labour organizations so as to eliminate all danger of mobilization. The basic tenets of the approach were 'negotiation or repression, no tolerance' (Pellicer de Brody and Reyna, 1978, 218). Renewed attempts were made to create all-inclusive centralized labour confederations such as the Congreso de Trabajo, which, insofar as the independent unions were included, could neutralize potential opposition (Reyna and Miquet, 1976). Governmental action was mainly geared to maintain, without major changes, the structure of labour organizations and labour relations in operation since the early forties.

Thus, in the three cases the significant structural changes in the process of economic growth affecting directly the employment opportunities and working conditions of the subordinate classes were not accompanied by the emergence of new organizations to channel the demands emerging from the new conditions. Rather, they were associated with an excluding and repressive state policy toward the subordinate sectors. In such conditions, protest movements flourished again.

The student movement in Mexico in 1968, the wave of strikes and mass mobilizations in Brazil (Weffort, 1972), and the *'Cordobazo'* in Argentina (Delich, 1974) cannot be taken simply as local manifestation of the generalized Western protest in the years 1968-1969. Each of them was a specific answer to the new economic and political conditions that were being created and an indication of the breakdown of established patterns of expression of interests of the subordinate classes and of the institutional channels of negotiation. These were social movements with a very high degree of spontaneous participation of large sectors of the urban population, and in all cases the immediate governmental reaction was repressive (Jelin, 1974).

In Brazil there was an intensification of repression after 1968. Whatever space existed for the expression of opposition was closed, and there was no pretending on either part that the old channels still were operating and could be used. Strikes were completely banned, unions no longer could function (even in the very limited way they had done before), and no further attempts to establish extra-legal links between sectors of the organized working class were allowed. Control over the labour force was economically achieved through low wages and job insecurity, and politically through repression of any participation in collective actions. The Brazilian 'miracle' was on its way.

Over the next few years, however, a new pattern of labour protest and of organization started to emerge, especially in the most dynamic and highly productive manufacturing sectors of the economy. When workers found channels of political and union expression at a mass or organized level closed, they started to act at the plant level. Very small, isolated, movements developed, through which workers began to present immediate grievances directly to the plant authorities. These were local movements, involving the participation of most plant-workers, and were usually concerned either with wages or with working conditions (Almeida, 1975 and 1978; Humphrey, 1976 and 1977a). On both subjects there were novel developments. Since the early days of industrialization, the Brazilian government took wage decisions as its own responsibility. Now, when governmental wage regulations were in full effect, implying a prohibition of independent wage-settlements, workers in the dynamic industries were asking for special plant-level negotiations and arrangements, linked to their own conditions of employment and to changes in productivity within the plants.

These localized and isolated movements gained momentum during the last few years, within the general context of the political opening in Brazil. Organizationally, there were soon pressures to have plant-level unions recognized as legitimate. From this, a movement asking for free unionism could grow. Economically, the plant level demands for higher wages (usually based on productivity considerations) implied a demand for direct bargaining between workers and entrepreneurs, without the intervention of the state. The scene of action now had to be the factory, and not the offices of the Ministry of Labour, and those acting were the mass of workers rather than salaried union officials. But beyond the basic shift in labour relations and in state-unions structure implied in such developments, up to now restricted to the area of São Paulo, what could not have been predicted is the way in which they were combined with other democratizing forces in the country.[7]

In Argentina, independent labour protest grew after the *Cordobazo* in 1969. They also took the form of a rejection of the centralized direct negotiations between the union bureaucracies and state officials. In many cases, there was also a request for direct plant-level wage negotiations done by local, rather than by national unions. A high level of workers' mobilization, continuous workers' assemblies and meetings, and direct methods of action inside the plants, were characteristic of these movements (Delich, 1974; Jelin, 1974). The political conjuncture of the early seventies that led to the return of Perón and implied a very high political popular mobilization on one hand, and the strengthening of the centralized, established union organizations of the other, blurred the intrinsic trends in this new type of workers' activism (Jelin, 1977).[8]

In Mexico, the struggle for independent unionism is quite old. During the last decade, however, the number and political significance of attempts to achieve it increased, involving some crucial sectors of the working class, such as the electricity workers (Gomez Tagle and Miquet, 1976) and numerous large modern industrial enterprises (Camacho, 1977; Labastida, 1975; Trejo, 1976; Urteaga, 1977). In these cases, the demands expressed were similar to those in the other countries: free unionism, not directed or controlled by the main national union confederations; recognition of plant-level organizations and bargaining at the local level; in short, direct negotiations without state intervention. The pattern of high rank-and-file participation was also similar. Such local movements were taking place at a time when there were governmental attempts to redirect labour policies so as to avoid new confrontations, but within the framework of the established state-labour movement relations (Arriaga et al., 1977; Durand, 1976; Molina, 1977).

Furthermore, other manifestations of class interests have also emerged in these countries. On the one hand, there is a trend toward militant unionization of white collar workers, especially state employees, who are taking advantage of their strategic location and numerical importance in a growing and increasingly powerful state apparatus. On the other hand, there are also new urban movements, geared to defend the level of living and access to public services of the urban popular sectors (Moises and Martinez-Alier, 1977). These movements, although relatively weak and isolated, present an important challenge to the state in one of the conflicting points of the economic model, namely, the role of the state in providing public services required for the maintenance of the labour force within an economic model that assumes the profitability of all economic acti vities and low wages (Castells, 1977).

Both the labour organizations and the state have reacted to these challenges. Within the state apparatus, exclusion and repression are never defined as permanent conditions (O'Donnell, 1978). There is much debate within the ruling groups about the type of union structure, the system of labour relations, and more broadly about the channels of political and economic participation which have to be opened to the subordinate classes. The union movement also is involved in a revision of old tactics and a search for new strategies.[9] The organizational outcome of the present stage is hard to predict, and will probably depend more on the political role that labour organizations will play and on 'spontaneous' developments within the subordinate classes than on decisions based on specific courses of action planned from above within given models of development.

CONCLUDING REMARKS

In this paper I have discussed the issues of planning and spontaneity in the context of power relations, dealing with the struggle of the subordinate sectors of society to increase their autonomy and decrease the control that the dominant classes and the state exert on them. Control can be conceived as the other face of planning, as the way the action of the planner is seen and felt from the perspective of those subject to planning, the subordinated sectors of society, the powerless. Under conditions of clear class hegemony, when there is a basic social consensus about the social organization and the socio-political mechanisms of expression of interests, the subordinate classes may accept the actions of the rulers as legitimate and fully collaborate in the course of development, following the established channels for expressing discontent or remaining politically passive. When the potentially antagonistic ideological contents have been incorporated and/or neutralized in the dominant ideological discourse, social planning may become part of the accepted social order, and even become part of the official ideology, helping in the ideological justification of the type of existing socio-political system of domination (Habermas, 1971). Dissent and opposition will exist, insofar as subordinate class positions create and reproduce oppositional forces and discontent, but they will be expressed through institutionalized channels.

Under conditions of lack (or crisis) of hegemony, the state will either have to base its actions on coercion, or will be the arena of compromises and relatively unstable alliances between social groups (Weffort, 1974; O'Donnell, 1976). Its ability to plan will then be limited by the type of compromise and by the strength with which the various social groups are able to express their interests when bargaining for a place within the political structure of domination or as opposition forces. In the extreme case, implementation of planning is done by resorting to coercion: in such cases the controlling intent becomes totally open and manifest.

How can the forces of opposition, struggling against control from above, find a way to express themselves? Unquestionably their goal will be to obtain or increase their autonomy in relation to the controlling agencies. This quest for autonomy will be spontaneous or organized according to the conditions under which the class movements exist and act. When organizations are weak or subject to repression, protest has to be spontaneous, with no recourse to institutionalized channels. In the Latin American cases discussed here, working class organizations exist, but they have evolved to become in varying degrees part of the state mechanisms of domination. The mass of workers is faced with a complex situation: for some purposes, the existing labour organizations are responsive to their interests (as well as mechanisms to further develop such interests). But they also are large-scale bureaucracies inserted in a network of state-controlled and state-directed organizations. As such, they have to follow rules, enter into negotiations, and in general have their autonomy considerably restricted. Insofar as they were promoted and created by the state, and from the very beginning were placed in such an organizational network, they never had complete autonomy. Furthermore, in these three countries the state and the dominant classes have often used other tactics to deal with working class organizations and leaders, negotiating and bribing, co-opting and threatening. Under such conditions, spontaneous protests may emerge — unorganized at the beginning, and with great difficulties in creating the organizational structures to channel such protests autonomously, given the existence and strength of the established unions. From this perspective, 'spontaneity' as a means of expression becomes relevant when the organizations fail to incorporate and channel the quest for autonomous action of the working class.

A final word of caution about the relationship between the state and the labour movement. Although the state has been influential in the creation of the labour organizations, the state itself is a social creation and subject to change. After the organized labour movement came into being, its actions could not be inconsequential for the development of the state itself. This is one instance of the more general principle that the creation of class organizations is at the same time the recognition of new social and political actors. Once they exist, they may gain their own dynamics and become influential social forces that exert pressure and contribute to shape the state apparatus and the political regime at a later time.

NOTES

1. Socialist societies known up to now also have to face the facts of conflicting interests and differential distribution of power, but this fact cannot be discussed further in this paper.

2. 'Spontaneous' market mechanisms are also based on control, but the fiction of freedom and autonomy can be maintained on the basis of the apparent lack of regulation of human activity.

3. At this point, it is tempting to refer these unsystematic comments on types of spontaneity and planning to Sztompka's very systematic presentation of the subject. However, insofar as his presentation does not include an explicit consideration of power relations and of social conflicts, no real comparison is feasible (Sztompka, 1980).

4. It should be clear by now that the political role of these organizations was directly related to their subordination to the state apparatus. In this, they differ considerably from the European-type union, where the political role is given more by links with political parties and ideological commitments than by a structural incorporation into the state apparatus. A general overview of the Latin American labour movement with comparative notes is presented in Sigal and Torre, 1979.

5. There are almost no systematic studies on this subject, especially those including a temporal comparison that would allow to detect trends. On the heterogeneity of the labour market see Tokman, 1979; also Di Filippo and Jadue, 1977.

6. Brazilian labour law allows for the functioning of labour unions and sectoral federations, but prohibits centralized labour confederations and even inter-sectoral committees (Vianna, 1976). There were many instances in which such prohibitions were disregarded, and formally illegal organizations created and developed. These were extremely important – both from the point of view of their mass appeal and of their political role in support of the Goulart government – during the early sixties. Their unofficial name – *organizaçoes paralelas* – bears witness to their relevance at that time (Weffort, 1973).

7. At the time of writing (April-May 1979) several significant strikes developed in Brazil, including the metal workers in the suburbs of São Paulo, transport and education workers in other cities. Undoubtedly, such movements are a challenge to the government and are to be interpreted within the general context of the political opening, although it is still early to draw conclusions about their consequences.

8. After the coup of 1976, union activities were severely restricted. Many unions, as well as the CGT, were controlled, strikes were banned, wage negotiations suspended. The labour organizations have since fought to retain as much of their previous sphere of action as possible, knowing that the odds were against them. A major yet unresolved issue is the new union law, which, according to unofficial reports, will allow only for first and second grade organizations (unions and sectoral federations, with no centralized confederation). Its effect on the labour movement is still to be seen. During the last three years, several protest movements within the files of labour took place. They are to be interpreted more as a reactive protest to the harsh economic conditions than as a presentation of alternative models.

9. It is impossible at this stage to draw some comparative notes regarding current developments within the labour-movement ranks. Little information is available, and any interpretation is risky. The comparative study of recent developments in the labour movement of the three countries dealt with in this paper and in other Latin American and European cases with a different history of state-labour movement relations will be undertaken shortly (Jelin, 1979).

REFERENCES

ALMEIDA, M. H. T. de (1975) 'O sindicato no Brasil: novos problemas, velhas estruturas', *Debate & Critica* 6, July.
——(1978) 'Desarrollo capitalista y acción sindical', *Revista Mexicana de Sociologia* XL(2), Apr.-June.
ALONSO, A. (1972) *El movimiento ferrocarrilero de Mexico.* Mexico: Era.
ANDRADE, R. de C. (1977) 'Perspectives in the study of Brazilian populism'. University of Glasgow. (Mimeo.)
ANGUIANO, A. (1975) *El estado y la política obrera del cardenismo.* Mexico: Era.
ARRIAGA, M. de la L., E. VELAZCO and E. ZEPEDA (1977) 'Inflación y salarios en el régimen de LEA', *Investigación Económica* XXXVI(3), July-Sept.
BENDIX, R. (1964) *Nation Building and Citizenship.* New York: J. Wiley.
CAMACHO, M. (1977) 'La huelga de Saltillo, un intento de regeneración obrera', in Centro de Estudios Internacionales (ed.), *Lecturas de política mexicana.* Mexico: El Colegio de Mexico.
CARDOSO, F. H. (1975) *Autoritarismo e democratizaçao.* Rio de Janeiro: Paz e Terra.
——and E. FALETTO (1968) *Dependencia y desarrollo en America Latina.* Mexico: Siglo XXI.
CASTELLS, M. (1977) *The Urban Question.* Cambridge, Mass.: MIT Press.
CAVAROZZI, M. (1975) *The Government and the Industrial Bourgeoise in Chile, 1938-1964.* Berkeley, unpublished PhD dissertation.
——(1979) 'Sindicatos y política en Argentia 1955-1958', *Estudios CEDES* 2(1).
CONTRERAS, A. J. (1977) *Mexico 1940: industrialización y crisis política.* Mexico: Siglo XXI.
DELICH, F. (1974) *Crisis y protesta social. Córdoba 1969-1973.* Buenos Aires: Siglo XXI.
DI FILIPPO, A. and S. JADUE (1976) 'La heterogeneidad estructural; concepto y dimensiones', *El Trimestre Economico* 169, Jan.-March.
DOYON, L. M. (1975) 'Conflitos opérarios durante o regime peronista (1946-1955)', *Estudos CEBRAP* 13.
DURAND, V. M. (1976) 'Análisis critico de la política laboral del gobierno de Luis Echeverria Alvarez, 1970-1976', Mexico: ISUNAM (Mimeo.)
ERICKSON, K. P. (1975) 'Political Strikes in Brazil, 1960-1964: Strengths and Weaknesses of Organized Labor', *Occasional Papers* 17. New York University: Ibero-America Language and Area Center.
FAJNZYLBER, F. (1977) 'Oligopolio, empresas transnacionales e estilos de desenvolvimento', *Estudos CEBRAP* 19.
——and T. MARTINEZ TARRAGO (1976) *Las empresas transnacionales. Expansión a nivel mundial y proyección de la industria mexicana.* Mexico: Fondo de Cultura Económica.
GAUDIO, R. and J. PILONE (1976) 'Estado y relaciones obrero-patronales en los orígenes de la negociación colectiva en Argentina', CEDES, *Estudios Sociales* 5.
GERMANI, G. (1962) *Politica y sociedad en una época de transición.* Buenos Aires: Paidos.

——(1973) 'El surgimiento del peronismo: el rol de los obreros y de los migrantes internos', *Desarrollo Economico* 13(51), Oct.-Dec.

GOMEZ TAGLE, S. and M. MIQUET (1976) 'Integración o democracia sindical: el caso de los electricistas', in J. L. REYNA et al., *Tres estudios sobre el movimiento obrero en Mexico*. Mexico: El Colegio de Mexico.

GONZALEZ CASANOVA, P. (1967) *La democracia en Mexico*. Mexico: Era.

GRACIARENA, J. (1969) *Poder y clases sociales en America Latina*. Buenos Aires: Paidos.

——and F. FRANCO (1978) 'Social Formations and Power Structures in Latin America', *Current Sociology* 26(1), Spring.

HABERMAS, J. (1971) *Toward a Rational Society*. Boston: Beacon.

HAUSER, P. M. (ed.) (1950) *Urbanization in Latin America*. Brussels: UNESCO.

HUMPHREY, J. (1976) 'The Brazilian State, the Working Class and the Economic Miracle', *Bulletin, Society for Latin American Studies*, 24.

——(1977a) *The Development of Industry and the Bases for Trade Unionism: A Case Study of Car Workers in Sao Paulo, Brazil*. PhD thesis, University of Sussex.

——(1977b) 'The State and the Working Class in Brazil: Some Aspects of the Post-1964 Period'. University of Liverpool. (Mimeo.)

JELIN, E. (1974) *La protesta obrera*. Buenos Aires: Neuva Visión.

——(1977) 'Conflictos laborales en la Argentina, 1973-1976', CEDES, *Estudios Sociales*, 9.

——(1979) 'El movimiento obrero latinoamericano en la década del setenta. Continuidades históricas y neuvas tendencias', CEDES. (Mimeo.)

LABASTIDA, J.M. (1975) 'Tula: una experiencia proletaria', *Cuadernos Políticos* 5, July-Sept.

LACLAU, E. (1977) *Politics and Ideology in Marxist Theory. Capitalism-Fascism-Populism*. London: NLB.

LEON, S. (1978) 'El comité nacional de defensa proletaria', *Revista Mexicana de Sociologia* XL(2), Apr.-June.

LITTLE, W. (1972) 'Organized Labour and the Peronist State: 1943-1955'. University of Liverpool. (Mimeo.)

MARSHALL, T. H. (1965) *Class, Citizenship and Social Development*. Garden City, NY: Doubleday.

MARVAN, I. (1977) 'El Frente Popular en México durante el cardenismo'. Paper presented at the meeting of CLACSO's Working Group on Labour Movements, Mexico (November).

MEDINA, L. (1977) 'Origen y circunstancia de la idea de unidad nacional', in Centro de Estudios Internacionales (ed.), *Lecturas de política mexicana*. Mexico: El Colegio de Mexico.

MOISES, J. A. (1978) *Greve de massa e crise politica (Estudo da greve dos 300 mil em Sao Paulo, 1953/54)*. Sao Paulo: Editora Polis.

——and V. MARTINEZ-ALIER (1977) 'A revolta dos suburbanos ou "Patrao, o trem atrasou"', in J. A. MOISES et al., *Contradiços urbanas e movimientos sociais*. Rio de Janeiro: Paz e Terra/CEDEC.

MOLINA, D. (1977) 'Notas sobre el estado y el movimiento obrero', *Cuadernos Politicos* 12, Apr.-June.

MURMIS, M. and J. C. PORTANTIERO (1971) *Estudios sobre los origenes del peronismo/1*. Buenos Aires: Siglo XXI.

O'DONNELL, G. (1976) 'Reflexiones sobre las tendencias generales del cambio del estado burocrático-autoritario'. CEDES, Documento de Trabajo 1.

— — (1977a) 'Estado y alianzas en la Argentina, 1956-1976', *Desarrollo Economico* 16(64), Jan.-March.

— — (1977b) 'Apuntes para una teoria del estado'. CEDES, Documento de Trabajo 9.

— — (1978) 'Tensiones en el estado burocrático autoritario y la cuestión de la democracia'. CEDES, Documento de Trabajo 11.

OLIVEIRA, F. (1975) 'A economia brasileira: critica e razão dualista', in *Seleçoes CEBRAP* 1.

ORTEGA AGUIRRE, M. (1977) 'Estado y movimiento obrero (1940-1959)', in *Coloquio Regional de Historia Obrera. 1., Ciudad de Jalapa, Veracruz, 1977. Memoria.* Mexico: CEHSMO.

PELLICER DE BRODY, O. and J. L. REYNA (1978) 'El afianzamiento de la estabilidad política', in *Historia de la revolución mexicana, v. 8, Periodo 1952-1960, t. 22.* Mexico: El Colegio de Mexico.

REYNA, J. L. (1975) 'Redefining the Established Authoritarian Regime. Perspectives in the Mexican Polity', New York: Center of Inter American Relations. (Mimeo.)

— — and M. MIQUET (1976) 'Introducción a la historia de las organizaciones obreras en México: 1912-1966', in J. L. REYNA et al., *Tres estudios sobre el movimiento obrero en Mexico.* Mexico: El Colegio de Mexico.

ROTONDARO, R. (1971) *Realidad y cambio en el sindicalismo.* Buenos Aires: Pleamar.

ROWLAND, R. (1974) 'Classe opéraria e estado de compromisso', *Estudos CEBRAP* 8.

SENEN GONZALEZ, S. (1971) *El sindicalismo después de Perón.* Buenos Aires: Galerna.

SIGAL, S. and J. C. TORRE (1979) 'Una reflexión en torno a los movimientos laborales en América Latina', in R. KAZTMAN and J. L. REYNA (eds.), *Fuerza de trabajo y movimientos laborales an America Latina.* Mexico: El Colegio de Mexico.

SOURROUILLE, J. V. (1978) 'La presencia y el comportamiento de la empresas extranjeras en el sector industrial argentino', *Estudios CEDES* 1(2).

SPALDING, H. A. Jr. (1977) *Organized Labor in Latin America; Historical Case Studies of Urban Workers in Dependent Societies.* New York: Harper.

STINCHCOMBE, A. L. (1965) 'Social structure and organizations', in J. G. MARCH (ed.), *Handbook of Organizations.* Chicago: Rand McNally.

SZTOMPKA, P. (1980) 'The Dialectics of Spontaneity and Planning in Sociological Theory', pp. 15-27 in this volume.

TAVARES, M. da C. (1972) *Da sustituçao de importaçoes ao capitalismo financeiro.* Rio de Janeiro: Zahar.

TOKMAN, V. E. (1979) 'Dinámica del mercado de trabajo urbano: el sector informal en América Latina', in R. KAZTMAN and J. L. REYNA (eds.), *Fuerza de trabajo y movimientos laborales en America Latina.* Mexico: El Colegio de Mexico.

TORRE, J. C. (1979) 'El movimiento sindical en la Argentina'. Oxford: St. Antony's College. (Mimeo.)

TREJO, R. (1976) 'Lucha sindical y política: el movimiento de Spicer', *Cuader-*

nos Políticos 8, Apr.-June.

URTEAGA, A. (1977) 'Los esclavos del lugo: trabajadores de confianza y conflicto sindical', *Cuadernos Políticos* 22, Jan.-March.

VIANNA, L. W. (1976) *Liberalismo e sindicato no Brasil*. Rio de Janeiro: Paz e Terra.

WEFFORT, F. C. (1972) 'Participacao e conflito industrial: Contagem e Osasco, 1968', *Cadernos CEBRAP* 5.

— —(1973) 'Origens do sindicalismo populista no Brasil — a conjuntura do pós-guerra', *Estudos CEBRAP* 4.

— —(1974) 'Los sindicatos en la política (Brasil 1955-1964)', in CEIL, *Movimiento obrero, sindicatos y poder en América Latina*. Buenos Aires: El Coloquio.

6

FREE-ENTERPRISE STRATEGY AND THE PERSISTENCE OF SOCIAL UNDERDEVELOPMENT

E. O. Akeredolu-Ale
University of Ibadan, Nigeria

I. INTRODUCTION

Planning has two essential functions. The first is the specification of collective goals. The second is the specification of those roles which, in their dynamic interaction, are calculated to bring about the fulfilment of those collective goals. Thus, planning — even comprehensive social planning — is only an application of the principle of division of labour to the management of public affairs and the social theory of planning, therefore, belongs primarily in the realm of organizational theory.

With particular reference to developing countries, the social theory of planning must be seen as part of the broader effort to create some general explanatory model of the change from different types of non-industrial society to more modern society, the latter being invariably technologically more advanced and usually involving industrial organization and production. But even when the ideal of political democracy (as variously conceived) is posed as an important element of the culture of the mature industrial society, the social theory of planning need not thereby become coterminous (the way it seems to have done in certain traditions) with the social theory of democracy.

The social theory of development and underdevelopment emanating from the West has, especially during the last two decades, attempted to interpret the historical process in the developing countries and, thereby, to make itself more truly comparative. But, increasingly, that theory has shown and maintained a strong anti-planning and anti-state-intervention bias which, notwithstanding tactical disavowals on the part of the proponents, reflects an enduring commitment (presumably, on pragmatic-ideological grounds) to primitive evolutionism.

Yet, true comparative analysis of historical change must attempt a closer approximation to historical evidence than would be possible if one subscribed so inflexibly to the assumptions of evolutionism, even of reformed and reconditioned evolutionism. From the error of intellect which opposes planning to spontaneity and which equates the former to control and the latter to freedom, it is but a short step to that a-historical social theory of democracy which opposes socialism to freedom, which denies the possibility of individual liberty within the context of the planned society (especially the more comprehensively planned society), which sees free enterprise strategy as a suitable means of coping with the challenge of social development without limit as to space and time and which sees the capitalist modernization generated by that strategy as the only form of modernization that is consistent with democratic principles and practice.

There has been a tendency to confuse 'social planning' which is really only a technique with the content of particular social plans and, in condemning the orientations of the latter, to also condemn (rather uncritically, I think) the former, usually on the basis of the presumed inevitable consequences of certain types of social planning and social plans for the political culture, especially, for the principle of individual liberty. The anti-planning and anti-state-intervention bias raises important issues concerning not only the mundane question of the choice of an historically appropriate strategy for social development and for the institutionalization of genuine political democracy but also the epistemological question of the nature and purpose of social theory. Some of such issues are identified and examined in the rest of this paper. But before I go any further, I wish to state and underline one observation which I consider fundamental to the position of this paper, namely, that the whole question of whether any country (developing or not) *should* adopt the unalloyed free-enterprise strategy or any degree of central planning is not a scientific problem. As Max Weber once remarked apropos of the adoption of the planned economy,

> On scientific grounds it is possible only to inquire what would probably be the results of any given specific proposal, and thus what unforseen or undesired consequences would have to be accepted if the attempt were made. Honesty requires that all parties should admit that, while some of the factors are known, many of those which would be important are only very partially understood.[1]

This observation highlights the need to base one's conclusions concerning the probable implications or the appropriateness or otherwise of the adoption of any particular development strategy in any given case, not merely on the general principles of economic and social analysis but even more particularly on the specifics of the historical case being considered. One particular factor in the historical situation of today's developing countries which I consider very relevant to the question of choice of development strategy but one which, in my view, has not been given due weight in the discussion of this problem in the literature, is the nature of the challenge of development, as conceived by the developing countries themselves.

The specific challenges of development as they are perceived by the policy makers in any given developing country and the national development objectives in which such challenges are expressed reflect more or less accurately the society's prevailing common social purpose or what one may call its prevailing 'revolutionary social conscience'. National development objectives, therefore, invariably relate not only to a rate of growth of income (though this concern has usually tended to be dominant) but also to other social goals and, while all developing countries share the commitment to the objective of income-growth, they often differ remarkably among themselves and from most of the early developers in terms of both the specific package of social goals they have adopted and the particular sets of obstacles they would have to tackle in pursuing those goals.

If the social theory of planning is to be of any use in interpreting and understanding the experiences of the developing countries, therefore, it must abandon or at least transcend its evolutionist conception of development objectives. It must reconcile itself to history. The reflections and views expressed in section III below are based mainly on the experiences of Nigeria in the period since 1960. That background case study is presented in the next section.

II. PLANNING, FREE-ENTERPRISE AND
SELECTED DEVELOPMENT OBJECTIVES:
THE CASE OF NIGERIA

Planning, at national (and regional/state) levels, has been a long-standing aspect of Nigeria's development strategy, dating back to 1946 when the colonial administration launched the *Ten-Year Plan of Development and Welfare*. That first plan has been followed by four others: 1955-60/61, 1962-68, 1970-74 and the current one, 1975-80. Neither the 1955-60/61 Development Plan nor the one of 1962-68 contained any significant statement on the country's overall philosophy of development. However, it was possible to see in the 1970-74 Plan the beginnings of such a statement.[2] That Plan also enunciated a number of development values and goals which planning in Nigeria was being geared to pursue. Most prominent among such values and goals were self-reliance, dynamism, egalitarianism and social justice, freedom and democracy.

Self-reliance and dynamism refer principally to the improvements required in the capacity of the national economy to generate adequate opportunities in productive employment for the population and to insure the standard of living of the people against disruptions from within but, even more particularly, from outside the national economy (such as the vagaries of financial aid and technical assistance, foreign private investment and sudden changes in the prices of her exports and imports). Egalitarianism, social justice, freedom and democracy are social goals concerned with the implications of national economic gains for the quality of life of the people. The architects of the Plan also saw Nigeria as having the resources 'to lay a solid foundation for a socio-economic revolution in black Africa'.[3] There is a transnational aspect to this particular objective but it ties in strongly with the historic role which has fallen to Nigeria in the development of black Africa and, for that reason, has to be regarded as one vital element of the challenge of development in the Nigerian case. Thus we find that, for Nigeria, the overriding objective of planning transcends the acceleration of the role of economic growth and includes the correction of those aspects of the country's social and political structure and relations which conflict with the principal social goals enunciated above.

An examination of the various development plans reveals a set of even more specific social development objectives, the ones to which the basic policies, programmes and projects of the plans were directly addressed. Among the most important of such more specific objectives are acceleration of the growth of gross domestic product; expansion of the industrial/manufacturing capacity of the Nigerian economy; modernization of agricultural organization and production with a view to enhancing productivity and output in the sector; expansion of *indigenous* entrepreneurial capacity, especially in industry; development of national technological dynamism; reduction of inequality in the distribution of income, wealth and opportunities as between individuals, groups and regions; eradication of mass poverty and its associated cultural conditions; and institutionalization of democracy and social justice.

In pursuing these public objectives, Nigeria has relied heavily on the spontaneous activities of a dominant private sector which, for most of the period since 1960, has remained firmly under the control of foreign investors. Thus, the situation has been one in which the Nigerian government was enunciating and 'planning' for the attainment of certain major economic and social development objectives but the wherewithal for pursuing such objectives was under the control of a free-enterprise system dominated by non-Nigerian firms. The commitment, conscious or otherwise, of the political class to the philosophy of an open free-enterprise economy was upheld in the 1962-68 Development Plan. Towards the end of that Plan, however, more direct governmental measures began to be introduced to control the working of the industrial sector. Even though these measures were necessitated specifically by the disjuncture between the activities and orientations of foreign firms on the one hand and the national objectives on the other, they were also the beginnings of pressures to re-examine the workings of the *private* sector of the economy as a whole in relation to *public* social development objectives.

The inherent problems were raised and highlighted, perhaps for the first time, in the 1970-74 Development Plan which made a strong case for integrating the private sector into the national planning framework 'through a set of mutually consistent policies that induce or compel functional units within the national economy to conform to the pattern of economic behaviour postulated by the objectives and priorities (of the country)' so that the private sector (which, in the Nigerian case, accounts for more than 80 percent of both gross domestic product and employment) can begin to function as part of the country's instrument 'for economic and social transformation'.[4]

It is significant that the private modern sector of the Nigerian economy has consisted mainly of foreign firms and this has often meant that measures intended to control foreign firms did not necessarily have anything to do with the question of the role which a private sector (assuming that it became mainly indigenous) should play in the Nigerian economy. Both the 1970-74 and the 1975-80 plans were full of praise for the dynamism of the private sector. But then, the evaluation in both documents was concerned with the investment and capital formation performance of the sector,[5] i.e. with economic growth and not with the relationship between the dynamics of the sector on the one hand and the other major specific social development objectives on the other.

Among the other social development objectives not covered by this evaluation of the private sector in the plans are expansion of the industrial capacity of the Nigerian economy, development of national technological dynamism, reduction in inequality in the distribution of income, wealth and opportunities, eradication of poverty, and institutionalization of democracy and social justice. However and, as I hope to show in the following subsections, it is in relation to these other social development objectives that one sees most clearly the conflict between the dynamics of spontaneous private enterprise, as it has been experienced in Nigeria, and the pursuit of public purpose.

Expansion of national industrial capacity

The potential for profitable investment in manufacturing in Nigeria has been great for quite some time and some notable attempts have been made to analyse the dynamics of the ongoing transition from importation to local manufacture.[6] For example, one author (Kilby, 1969) has attributed the onset of the ongoing expansion of manufacturing capacity in Nigeria to the coming of the 'competitive threshold' when the market, as mapped out by imports, had reached or had closely approached that size which will support a plant of optimum or near-optimum efficiency.

In my review of Kilby's book,[7] I have challenged that author's view that in Nigeria's 'open economy' — which Kilby saw as being characterized by, among other things, a conservative monetary policy, avoidance of foreign exchange restrictions, 'an unusual degree' of openness to international trade, free entry to foreign capital, foreign entrepreneurship and foreign technical skills, and the absence of extensive state intervention[8] — the ordinary market forces manifested in the heightening of competition in import trade have sufficed to change the orientation of investing firms from an emphasis on import distribution to one on local manufacturing. In my opinion, one critical factor and the one which, more than any other, actually sparked off the transition to manufacturing was neither the technological threshold nor the competitive threshold but what could be called 'the political threshold' — a point marked by the arrival of the aggressive intervention policies of a government committed to the industrialization of the Nigerian economy. I had suggested the existence of 'a triangular interaction process between political factors (especially as crystallized in government intervention), market forces and adaptive entrepreneurial behaviour' but it seems to me that the political factors had proved decisive in this case. Of course, whereas Kilby's interpretation had led him to counsel a liberal-conservative strategy of industrialization in Nigeria, my modification of that interpretation seems to me to show that state-intervention in this case was indeed a structural necessity.

The mild intervention which began in the late fifties has since become a more important factor in terms of both its scope and character and its implications for the pace and pattern of industrialization in Nigeria. The lethargy of the private sector in embarking on the course of industrialization showed the Nigerian government the inherent conflict between free enterprise and public purpose. Since 1968, beginning from the promulgation of the Companies' Decree of that year,[9] the government had demonstrated through its policies an awareness that the unguarded application of the orthodox principle of the free-enterprise economy could retard national development and has therefore adopted new orientations not only in dealing with foreign private investors as a special category but also in managing the dynamics of the whole private sector and in defining the role of the state sector. The 1972 Indigenization Decree, as revised in the Nigerian Enterprises Promotion Decree, 1977,[10] represents a summation of these policy changes in respect of foreign private investors. These policy changes amount to a cautious attempt to enforce a programme of phased and cumulative withdrawal for foreign private investment, the first and current phase consisting mainly of provisions to re-channel rather than to do away with such investment altogether.

In view of (1) the fact that to rest the national economy on the spontaneous activities of the private sector is to rest it on the activities of *foreign* private investors and entrepreneurs (since indigenous private entrepreneurship in the modern sector remains so badly underdeveloped), (2) the inherent conflict already noted between public purpose and private enterprise and (3) the dominant position which the private sector at present occupies in the national economy, the whole question of the role which the private sector could meaningfully (in terms of the industrialization objective) be expected to continue to play is under serious review. So also, by implication, is the role and scope of planning and of the state sector. And two important developments in this regard are worth noting, namely, (1) the integration of the private sector in national planning and (2) the expansion of the state sector, both implying more centralized direction of the economy.

The original idea in (1) was simply to align the goals and objectives of the private and public sectors by 'influencing the quantum and composition of investments undertaken in the private sector in order to ensure that such investment activities are in consonance with national objectives and priorities',[11] the private sector being defined to include the activities of both incorporated and non-incorporated ('household') businesses. The private sector was projected to achieve a gross investment of £816 million and for consumption of the order of £6,840.8 million during the 1970-74 Plan period. This meant that the private sector was projected to account for 53 percent of planned gross investment, 91 percent of planned consumption and 85 percent of total planned resource use.[12] In the 1975-80 Plan, however, projected effective private sector investment was N10.0 million which, though far bigger than the 1970-74 figure in absolute terms, was only 33.3 percent of total projected effective gross investment.[13] A detailed study of the sectoral distribution of planned gross fixed-capital formation for the 1975-80 period shows that the state sector accounted for substantially higher projected investment than the private sector not only in the usual infrastructural sectors such as Electricity and Water, Transport and Communication, Education, Health and other services but also in Agriculture, Livestock, Forestry and Fishing, Mining and Quarrying, Manufacturing and Crafts. This illustrates the second development noted above, i.e. the expansion of the state sector and of direct governmental participation in actual production. The list below shows the wide range of industrial production activities in which the Nigerian government at present participates more or less directly.

Thus we find that mostly as a result of the tendency of the private sector's spontaneous orientations and activities to produce results which conflict with important national social development objectives (the particular one already considered was the expansion of national industrial capacity) and, despite the fact that the private sector has usually fulfilled its projected gross investment in previous plans, there has occurred in the Nigerian case an unmistakable progression toward more direct state participation in actual production activities, more decisive state initiative in setting the course of economic transformation and more comprehensive planning (see Table).

TABLE
Company Shares Held by the Nigerian Federal Government

Name of Company	%
1. Petroleum Refining Company Limited, Lagos	49
2. North Brewery Limited, Kano	100
3. Nigerian Paper Mills Limited, Jebba	90
4. Bauchi Meat Products Company Limited, Bauchi	100
5. Nigerian Sugar Company Limited, Bacita	50
6. Nigerian External Tele-Communications, Lagos	100
7. The Nigerian Security Printing & Minting Company Limited, Lagos	100
8. West African Distillers Limited, Apapa	100
9. National Supply Company Limited, Lagos	100
10. Opobo Boatyard Limited, Opobo, Cross River	88
11. Nigerian National Shipping Line, Apapa	100
12. Aba Textile Mills Limited, Aba	70
13. Savannah Sugar Company Limited, Numan	85
14. Cargo Handling Company Limited, Lagos	100
15. Nigerian Gas Products Company Limited, c/o Federal Ministry of Petroleum Resources	60
16. Nigerian Yeast and Alcohol Manufacturing Company Limited, Kwara	60
17. New Nigeria Salt Company Limited, Sapele	55
18. National Salt Company of Nigeria, Ijoko	55
19. Federal Superphosphate Fertilizer Company Limited, Kaduna	100
20. Nigerian National Fish Company Limited, c/o Federal Ministry of Industries	90
21. Nigerian National Shrimp Company Limited, Lagos	65
22. Volkswagen of Nigeria Limited, Lagos	60
23. Peugeot Automobile Nigeria Limited, Lagos	60
24. Road Construction Company of Nigeria Limited, Apapa	60
25. Impresit Bakolori (Nigeria) Limited	40
26. Nigerian Engineering & Construction Company, Lagos	60
27. Galambi Ranching Company, Bauchi	100
28. National Grains Production Company Limited, Kaduna	60
29. National Root Crop Production Company Limited, Enugu	60
30. Daily Times of Nigeria Limited, Lagos	60
31. Nigeria Beverages Company Limited	50
32. Calabar Cement Factory Limited, Calabar	20
33. Portland Cement Company Limited, Ewekoro	85
34. Sunti Sugar Company Limited, Sunti	90
35. Lafiaji Sugar Company Limited, Lafiaji, Kwara	90

Development of national
technological dynamism

There are three important areas in which the private sector could have contributed towards this objective. One area is the development of scientific and technical manpower. Another is the prosecution, as much as possible locally, of research and development activities. Such activities will be concerned mainly with the processing and utilization of local raw materials in industrial activities, modernization of traditional processing and production methods and local production of tools and equipment. And the third area is the more direct transfer of technology to local scientists, technologists, technicians and entrepreneurs through operational arrangements which actively involve appropriate local personnel in the research, development, production and overall management activities of the transnational firms which invariably dominate the private sector.

With particular reference to the transfer of technology to indigenous entrepreneurs the main conduit could have been a subcontracting system which links the small firms (mostly Nigerian) to the bigger ones (mostly non-Nigerian) within the national industrial system. This would require that the bigger firms buy components from and subcontract various operations to the small firms. However, these requirements have not been met and are unlikely to be met in the Nigerian situation since the operations of the bigger firms are planned outside the country in pursuit of a different set of free-enterprise objectives and on the basis of a different logic of costs and efficiency to neither of which the creation of an interwoven local network is an important consideration.[14]

Thus, the contribution of private sector firms to the development of technological dynamism in Nigeria has been very little indeed, even after 20 years of deliberate government measures (mostly in the form of incentives which many consider to be over-generous) to induce them to align their operations with national objectives in this respect.[15] According to an official source, the present total stock of scientific manpower in Nigeria was estimated at 20,000 by 1975.[16] On the basis of the target of 2,000 scientific personnel per million of population recommended for developing countries in Africa in the United Nations' *World Plan of Action for the Application of Science and Technology to Development*, Nigeria's target can be put at about 150,000 scientific/technological personnel and the estimated figure of 20,000 represents 87 percent target underfulfilment, even when the need for middle-level technicians has not been taken into consideration!

One implication of this shortfall is, of course, continuing techno-logical dependence. Outside of agriculture, the trend has in fact been towards greater technological dependence on the rest of the world, most especially in manufacturing and in the building of infrastructure. The technology required in these areas tends to be obtained and im-ported from abroad under the R and D programmes of multi-national firms. Nor has the investment by private firms usually involved the local 'unpackaging' of the technology of their production and this has meant that little or nothing gets transferred regarding ability to innovate, to improvise and to conduct the research needed to bend the technology to maximize the use of local resources.

Apart from the delay of the development of national technological dynamism which it implies, continuing technological dependence is a serious drain on Nigeria's limited foreign exchange due to the payment for foreign technology, the corruption-induced inflation of the contract terms underlying such payments, the payment for imported inputs for externally derived products and production techniques and for im-ported finished goods. Finally, technological dependence tends to breed addiction to foreign products and, thereby, to create a vicious circle which frustrates the whole self-reliance objective in many ways. Yet, there is reason to believe that the intensification of inter-governmental activities in this sphere (which would require more decisive state initia-tive, more direct state involvement and long-term programmatic national planning, at least on the part of the recipient developing country) is likely to yield more satisfactory results.

The other major social-development objectives mentioned above, namely, reduction of inequality, reduction of poverty and the institu-tionalization of genuine democracy, are very closely interrelated and, in the next subsection, we examine briefly how these distributive equity objectives have been affected by the working of Nigeria's free-enterprise sector.

Distributive-equity objectives

The objective concerned with reducing inequality and that concerned with reducing poverty overlap to a very large extent and are both intended to improve the quality of life of the lower strata of society through a strategy of development which ensures, in a more or less automatic way, that existing resources and increases in them are more equitably distributed among individuals, groups and regions of the country. Free-enterprise economics does not have a satisfactory theory of economic inequality and has no theory of poverty at all. The hypothesis that impersonal market forces fix the prices of all productive factors and their marginal productivities at a level that corresponds to maximum economic efficiency and that this explains economic inequalities in society is rather naive. With particular reference to the returns to labour, for instance, even if one granted for purposes of argument that the pseudo-scientific exercise called job-evaluation determines the relative contents of jobs objectively, it must still be admitted that science plays very little part, if any, in fixing the floor wage, the differential between the floor wage and the highest salary and the specific income differentials existing between levels of the job-hierarchy in the national economy. Therefore, a satisfactory theory of inequality and poverty must concern itself with identifying the political forces which govern and determine the pattern of ownership of the factors of production since it is that pattern which, in turn, determines the structure of interpersonal and inter-group differentials in income, wealth and other opportunities in society.

Free-enterprise economics and sociology, both developed in relation to capitalist entrepreneurial theory, give the impression that the evolution of inequalities and of the poor classes in society is a normal development in the early stages of industrialization. In fact, increased inequality and the crude exploitation of the poor are often named as the conditions that made possible the rise in savings and the aggressive entrepreneurship that gave momentum to the industrial revolution. Almost naturally, the proponents of and the principal agents in a free-enterprise economy tend not to regard large income inequalities as a social problem (at least, not before it actually gives rise to severe industrial conflict) and, even then, they tend to consider only welfarist solutions rather than major structural reforms which may lead to income redistribution. In its working, Nigeria's free-enterprise sector has not only displayed this typical indifference; it has also vitiated important measures aimed at achieving even a limited degree of distributive equity. Two particular sets of measures in the implementation of which this antagonism between the inherent logic of the free-enterprise strategy and the distributive-equity objectives shows clearly are those on indigenization and on price control. Nigeria's experience in industrial location illustrates the same conflict.

In the implementation of the Indigenization Decree, the shares went mainly, perhaps exclusively, to those Nigerians who either had personal savings or had effective access to money from institutional lenders or had both. The great extent to which those who have acquired the shares have relied on the institutional sources of funds is shown in the fact that of some N40 million which backed up the transfer exercises (up to late 1975), as much as N15 million (37.5 percent) had come from the Nigerian Bank for Commerce and Industry alone. In addition, many of those who acquired a large number of shares in Schedule-2 firms or who took over and paid for enterprises in Schedule 1 made use of loans obtained from the commercial banks, sometimes on the strength of what one of them (who was at that time a Federal Commissioner) had ingenuously called 'technical securities'.

Of course, those who have acquired most of the shares are, by and large, the elite (persons already in business as proprietors or hired executives, in the higher echelons of the civil service, the universities and the armed forces and private practitioners of the more lucrative professions such as medicine, law, architecture, engineering, quantity surveying, and so on). And those who have not are the teeming thousands of poor urban workers and the millions of peasants and other rural persons. Thus, there have been two kinds of concentration (departures from the distributive equity objective) in the pattern of share acquisition, namely, concentration among the urban population, as compared with the rural population and concentration (within the urban area) among the higher-income elite and sub-elite categories, as compared with the lower-income population, the general run of urban dwellers.

It is significant that money for buying the shares came, to a very large extent, not from the personal savings of those acquiring the shares but from sources which are, by and large, public: the Nigerian Investment Development Bank (NIDB), the Nigerian Bank for Commerce and Industry (NBCI), even the major commercial banks in which the government has substantial or controlling shareholding. I have often doubted the propriety of this strategy whereby, in the name of ensuring the survival of private enterprise, 'public funds' have been made available to finance private acquisitions, especially in such a way as to enhance existing inequalities.

The price control measures were similarly frustrated by the spontaneous dynamics of the private sector. The genius of the traders devised all kinds of escapes from the provisions of the price control regulations and produced a run-away inflation which has depressed the standard of living of most people and made it virtually impossible for persons with low income to ensure themselves even of subsistence provision. There may be some truth in the argument of some economists that the price escalation was in fact due to the price control measures and that the latter's removal would produce necessary reductions in the price level as a result of the operation of market forces. But one is not sure that this could apply to all commodities. It should be noted that the distortions noted in respect of the indigenization and price control measures were due mainly to the dynamics of the indigenous part of the private sector. It is therefore an indictment not of foreign private enterprise but of the free-enterprise strategy itself.

With respect to industrial location, this has been one area where, according to one author, 'there is an apparent lack of coordination, planning and control of foreign industrial investments, making it possible to leave everything to market forces and little to national aim or strategy.'[17] And the spontaneous operations of private sector firms have tended to exacerbate income and opportunity differentials as between regions of the country and to give rise to unwholesome industrial concentrations which, if the situation of Lagos is anything to go by, threaten to choke off further growth.

I have classified the goal of institutionalizing democracy with the distributive-equity objectives because, essentially, it is concerned with the establishment of an economic and social structure which, in its internal dynamics, reflects and guarantees an equitable distribution of political power and, hence, of other valued resources in society. The economic and social structure in Nigeria and the social relations which it sustains have become increasingly polarized and less egalitarian than they were about the time of independence, due largely to the inherently undemocratic character of the free-enterprise economy.

More recently, there have been some policies to enforce a measure of equity in the administration of public affairs. I refer to attempts to regulate and control urban rent, land acquisition and use and private practice by professionals. Notwithstanding these policies and other similar ones, however, Nigeria's economic and social structure remains basically inegalitarian. The power structure has continued to protect the interests of the controlling classes, i.e. the political class (now civil, now military), the 'econocrats' (to use Peter Self's term),[18] the educated classes and professionals, the emerging capitalist class and the propertied classes, at the expense of traders, industrial workers, peasants and the other teeming millions who share the culture of poverty to which most of these belong. It has made possible the situation whereby Nigeria's indigenous capitalist class has risen on the farmers' surplus (initially) and now on collectively-owned oil revenue — a pattern which deviates from older traditional models implied in Weber's venturesomeness and frugality theory, Schumpeter's creativity and innovation theory or even Karl Marx's theory of systematic labour exploitation (as applied to the operation of individual capitalist enterprises). It has made possible the exploitative relationships in which Nigeria's rural sector was pillaged for the benefit of the urban sector in general and of the exploiting and affluent urban classes in particular to such an extent that rural inertia and decay now constitutes a serious national social problem.

The implications of the free-enterprise strategy and of the working of the free-enterprise economy for the distributive-equity objectives highlight the fundamental questions concerning the politics of social development and underdevelopment in Nigeria. The free-enterprise system generates political and economic inequalities as part of its normal output and, therefore, necessarily conflicts with both the distributive-equity and the democratic objectives. This conflict has been strongly confirmed in the Nigerian experience. The same antagonism between the free-enterprise strategy and social development had earlier in this paper been discussed in relation to the specific objectives concerning the development of national industrial capacity and national technological dynamism. The attempt has been to show that, in the Nigerian case, the trend towards more decisive state intervention and towards more programmatic planning has arisen not from mere doctrinaire commitment to any particular ideology nor from mere fanatical opposition to others but from historical exigencies. And one suspects that similar exigencies are at work in many other developing countries.

III. A-HISTORICITY, INERTIA AND THE UNDERDEVELOPMENT OF THE SOCIAL THEORY OF PLANNING

There are two main levels of conflict between the free-enterprise strategy and social development objectives in most developing societies. At one level, conflict arises from the particular historical circumstances of such societies in the international economy and society of the late twentieth century, from the fact of dependency. At the second level, conflict arises from the inherently inequitable and anti-democratic nature of the *historical* market economy, whether the dominant actors in such an economy be indigenous or foreign, or both. It is the conflict at the second level which illustrates most clearly that the choice open to developing countries is not the simple one between the free-enterprise economy (which is presumed to entail maximum possibility for individual liberty and choice) on the one hand and the planned economy run mainly on the basis of state initiative and direction (which is presumed to entail minimum possibility for individual liberty and choice) on the other but the more difficult one between the Scylla of control by state monopolies and the Charybdis of control by private monopolies.

Lessons from American history

In the last two hundred years or so, the United States has been the scene of the most spectacular growth of the free-enterprise business system in modern history. Until the 1850s, the American economy was still, very largely, pre-industrial. Total population was 25 million; businesses were still, for the most part, very small; 80 percent of the population still lived on farms, largely engaged in subsistence agriculture; working conditions in the few large factories were quite bad, a situation condoned by the courts on the strength of the common law doctrine which viewed unions as 'conspiracies against the state'; and there was very little institutional regulation of business processes.

After the American Civil War of 1861 (and largely as a result of it too) the erstwhile predominantly mercantile America rapidly gave way to the beginnings of industrial America that we know today. In particular, the period 1870-1920 (the so-called Gilded Age) witnessed the true beginning of 'big business' in America. That was the era of the industrial tycoons, the business titans, the captains of industry — the industrial pioneers who forged ahead against odds which most of their contemporaries regarded as overwhelming. These were the men who founded business dynasties in large-scale manufacturing, large-scale financing, large-scale marketing, and so on — the entrepreneurs and capitalists par excellence.

Two important final features of the free-enterprise industrial American economy which emerged from the Gilded Age and which are of particular significance for the topic of this paper were the increase in monopolistic tendencies and the constraining regulations of business which such tendencies attracted from the government. Thus we find that, as the system grew, it did become clearer that the American society could not afford a pure laissez-faire business system, at least not the way it was unfolding in their experience. It became clear that free-enterprise business activities would have to be controlled in the interest of the public good, that they would have to be brought in line with some social purpose. The motives underlying the control measures which government has introduced in the period since the 1870s[19] were the enlarging contradictions between the logic of the free-enterprise business system on the one hand and the American dream of a democratic society on the other.

By the 1950s, the pattern of 'big business' was firmly established in America. But government interference with the 'unseen guiding hand' had also become a fact of the situation and, to those who deprecate all state intervention in the economy, the economic functions of the American government had reached offending proportions. Apart from the wielding of fiscal and monetary controls to insure dynamic stability and full employment, the American government now participates directly in a number of vital industries, shares the management of certain other industries (especially public utilities and financial institutions) through regulations and continues to struggle to reduce the ever-widening gap between private profit and the public good. Now, what has been the impact of America's free-enterprise business system upon the American society during the period which I have considered?

At least one thing is clear — that the free-enterprise business system succeeded in producing enormous wealth in America: real per capita income has been multiplied more than threefold since 1850 and the standard of living has increased significantly even for the masses. But there has also been another less palatable side to the story of free-enterprise business system in America. Inequality of incomes has remained at a high level. Secondly, even though differences in living standards between rich and poor have become smaller, the pattern of income distribution over the years has produced many instances of disgraceful poverty — mostly among the blacks, Puerto Ricans and other minorities but also among white Americans too.[20] Thirdly, even though opportunities for making it have increased enormously, such opportunities are far from being equitably distributed among groups in the society. Fourthly, the concentration of economic power and hence of political power in a few hands has given rise to the tyranny of business and managerial power which makes a huge joke of the American claim to being a democratic system.[21] Because of those major ill-effects, one must conclude that the vast growth of the American economy through the free-enterprise business system has been accompanied by major departures from the professed ultimate American social purpose — the democratic ideal. Many of the contemporary economic and social problems of America must also be attributed, in a large measure, to the working of the free-enterprise business system as it has crystallized in the American experience.

In view of the negative social effects of the free-enterprise business system, it is not surprising that the whole world (including the giant free-enterprise nations) is gravitating toward greater planning and state capitalism, toward the so-called 'mixed enterprise' system. These modifications in the orientations of the West raise important questions. Is the mixed-enterprise business system likely to prove a stable alternative to free-enterprise capitalism or is it bound to give way, in the long run, to the socialist economy? In these respects I am not rushing to any conclusions. The free-enterprise business system has survived major crises before – e.g. the Depression and the damages and destructions of the Second World War. Keynesian economics did the trick. And economists in the West have thereafter synthesized Smith, Marshall and Keynes into what, until current troubles, must have seemed adequate theory of social economy. But the truth is that the mixed-enterprise business system is presently on trial not only in America but elsewhere. And many economists, even American economists, now realise that the Marshall-Keynes synthesis is not foolproof after all and that they must intensify their search for a new, perhaps a different theory of social economy. As Galbraith puts it 'the main body of neoclassical or textbook doctrine is in the process of being replaced now: the sun is setting on that whole structure of thought.'[22]

As the American experience also confirms, the resolution of the conflict between the dynamics of the free-enterprise system and the democratic ideal tends to call forth state intervention and the resort to planning as an instrument of public administration. The fact of dependency which further complicates the numerous imperfections of the market system, the obligations of government to accelerate the modernization process even within the context of that dependency, the 'democratic revolution' (à la Barbara Ward) and the structural legitimation which it lends to the pressures upon government, the dependence of the international system of assistance on the initiative and leadership of national governments and on their programmes of action, and so on – all these have made the progression to greater state intervention and to more direct and programmatic national planning in developing countries even more historically necessary than it has ever been. These historical pressures and constraints have tended to invest the challenge of social development with all the attributes of a national emergency, such as war, famine, etc.

To plan or not to plan:
that is not the question

It is not possible to establish through objective scientific reasoning, however rigorous, the general superiority of the strategy which avoids planning over that which does not, or the other way round. Once we transcend that limited conception according to which development merely entails 'rapid economic growth' and incorporate in a general social-equilibrium analysis those development objectives with which the apparatus of free-enterprise economics cannot cope, it becomes not only hazardous but dishonest for social scientists, qua scientists, to insist on prescribing those models and methods of change for which they have a predilection.

Like most of the major objectives of a plan, the decision to adopt or not to adopt the strategy which entails less or more comprehensive planning is a political value and, as such, must be treated as given by social scientists interested in building a social theory of planning. As will become clear in the next subsection, this is not to say that the implications of planning for the political order, and vice-versa, should be neglected.

Social theory of planning:
Science or evangelism?

The social theory of planning is primarily an aspect of organizational theory and only as such is it a part of the general theory of social development and underdevelopment. There are many ways in which the social theory of planning could enhance the understanding of social transformation: deriving from historical evidence (past and current) a comprehensive typology of planning; clarifying and documenting the empirical relationships between different types of planning and particular social development objectives; exploring, on the basis of historical evidence, the political implications of planning as an instrument of change.

The question, 'What type of planning?' when asked and explored in relation to particular development objectives, is an organizational-theory question and is quite relevant for both development practice and democratic theory. For there is, invariably, a class angle to the use of state power and planning in developing countries as in developed ones. And for this reason, the extension of state initiative, of state control in economic and social affairs and of national planning does not necessarily or automatically solve the problem of distributive-equity, of democracy or even of economic underdevelopment.

In fact, with particular reference to most developing countries, most of the benefits from planning policies have not reached the poor, even if such was the raison d'etre. And there is no reason why the social theory of planning, as part of organizational theory, should not systematically investigate the social processes which produce such divergence between the major objectives of planning and the outcomes of plans in so many countries.

Viewed in terms of these possibilities, the social theory of planning is very underdeveloped indeed for it neither elucidates planning in the latter's role as a near-universal instrument of social transformation nor provides a scientific guide to development policy and administration. And I would attribute this underdevelopment, above all, to that political evangelism which has continued to tie social science to evolutionist dogmas (from the West and from the East) and to reinforce the partition between it and the facts and lessons of comparative history.

NOTES

1. M. Weber, *The Theory of Social and Economic Organization.* Trans. by A. M. Henderson, and T. Parsons, 1947, New York: The Free Press, paperback ed., 1964, pp. 216-217.

2. Federal Republic of Nigeria, *Second National Development Plan, 1970-74,* Lagos: Federal Ministry of Information, 1970; especially, Chapter 4.

3. Ibid., p. 32.

4. Ibid., p. 279.

5. Ibid., Chapter 28 and *Third National Development Plan, 1975-80,* Chapter 30.

6. For example, P. Kilby, *Industrialization in an Open Economy: Nigeria, 1945-1966,* London: Cambridge University Press, 1969; T. A. Oyejide, *Tariff Policy and Industrialization in Nigeria,* Ibadan: Ibadan University Press, 1975.

7. E. O. Akeredolu-Ale, 'The "Competitive Threshold" Hypothesis and Nigeria's Industrialization Process: A Review Article', *Nigerian Journal of Economic and Social Studies* 14 (1) (March 1972): 109-120.

8. Kilby, op. cit., p. 1 for a fuller statement of his 'open economy' concept.

9. The Nigerian Companies' Decree of 1968 was designed to bring local subsidiaries of multinational corporations under more effective local control.

10. Federal Republic of Nigeria, *Nigerian Enterprises Promotion Decree, 1977*, Lagos, 1977.

11. *Second National Development Plan, 1970-74*, p. 280.

12. Ibid., p. 58, Table 16.

13. *Third National Development Plan, 1975-80*, p. 53, Table 5.10.

14. The absence of a subcontracting system as well as its implications for technological development was also noted in W. A. Lewis, *Reflections on Nigeria's Economic Growth*, Paris: OECD, 1967.

15. For an outline of the various incentives see P. Asiodu, 'Industrial Policy and Incentives in Nigeria', *Nigerian Journal of Economic and Social Studies* 9 (2) (July 1967): 161-174. For useful critiques, see A. O. Phillips in the same journal, November 1967, March 1968 and July 1969 issues.

16. National Council for Science and Technology, *National Policies for Research in Science and Technology*, Lagos: Cabinet Office, December 1975, esp. p. 15.

17. A. N. Hakam, 'The Locational Pattern of Foreign Private Industrial Investors in Nigeria', *Nigerian Journal of Economic and Social Studies* 8 (1) (March 1966).

18. P. Self, *Econocrats and the Policy Process*, London: The Macmillan Press Limited, 1975.

19. There were Antitrust Laws from many States, beginning from the 1870s and the famous Sherman Antitrust Act came in 1890.

20. The subject of Mike Harrington's *The Other America*. New York, 1962.

21. The subject of many books, among them James Burnham's *The Managerial Revolution* (New York, 1941), C. Wright Mill's *Power Elite* (New York, 1956).

22. Interview with John K. Galbraith on his book, *Economics and the Public Purpose*, reported in *Dialogue* 6 (4) (1973): 52. For other neo-radical critiques of economic analysis as related to the social purpose, see the feature 'Does Economics Ignore You?' in *Saturday Review*, 22 January 1972, especially the comments by Leonard Silk and by Daniel Fusfeld.

7

SPONTANEITY AND PLANNING IN CLASS FORMATION: THE ASCENDANCY OF THE BUREAUCRAT BOURGEOISIE IN MALAYSIA

K. S. Jomo
National University of Malaysia

This paper deals with the themes of spontaneity and planning in the context of a particular social phenomenon. Specifically, we are interested in the elements contributing to the consolidation of what we term the 'bureaucrat capitalist class' in Malaysia, a post-colonial society. We argue that it is necessary to understand this development in relation to class conflict and the specific nature of the post-colonial state. Spontaneity and planning are situated in this context.

In the first part of this paper, we briefly discuss the nature of the post-colonial state in relation to class and class conflict. We shall then identify the conditions for the emergence of bureaucrat bourgeoisies in post-colonial societies. In Part II, we shall briefly survey the specific conditions giving rise to the emergence and consolidation of a bureaucrat capitalist class in Malaysia and then identify some major contradictions which have accompanied this. Finally, we discuss the significance of the elements of spontaneity and planning in the ascendancy of the Malaysian bureaucrat capitalist class.

I

Several key concepts employed in the following discussion need to be defined as they are used in this paper. We begin with the concept of social class. Class relations are defined with reference to social relations of production though the two are not identical. Every social class is defined by political and ideological as well as economic criteria (Poulantzas, 1973a), though it is the economic aspect which is ultimately determinant. Classes exist when non-producers exploit producers, principally by appropriating a share of the product of the latter. This portion is termed social surplus or surplus labor or simply, the surplus. Appropriation of surplus by the exploiting class is ultimately ensured — directly or indirectly — by coercion (exercised by the appropriating class). In other words, class relations involve the exploitation of a producing class by a non-producing appropriating class. Hence, the interests of the two classes united in a particular system of production are necessarily opposed.

After drawing these broad lines of class demarcation, we can further distinguish class fractions. 'Fractions are distinct from simple strata since they coincide with important economic differentiations and as such, can even take on an important role as social forces, a role relatively distinct from that of other fractions of their class' (Poulantzas, 1973a: 38). Members of a class fraction share common interests which put it in contradiction with other fractions of the same class. Despite the significant contradictions that may exist among different class fractions, they are also united by shared class commonalities. Nevertheless, identification of such contradictions is important for understanding social change.

Class conflict involves more than the overt aspects of conflict between classes. The term also refers to the always extant contradictory relations among classes as well as class fractions. In general, contradictory class as well as fractional interests give rise to class conflict and hence to social change. Class conflict occurs not only between the exploiting class or classes on the one hand, and the exploited class or classes on the other, but also among exploited classes as well as among exploiting classes. This is to be expected since neither the dominant classes nor the dominated classes have entirely identical or homogeneous interests. In other words, class relations in general are contradictory and where there is class contradiction there is bound to be class conflict.

Social change and development demand explanation and class

dialectics are crucial in this regard. It is in this sense then that the histories of class societies are essentially histories of class conflict. It is only at specific historical conjunctures, usually when collective consciousness as well as organization coincide with common class location that class conflict becomes more apparent. Such historical conjunctures may give rise to radically new class configurations, especially when the protagonist class or classes are sufficiently organized and powerful as well as effectively guided by an ideology capable of inspiring and guiding the social movements seeking the transcendence of the existing social order.

However, it should not be forgotten that the class structure of society is always, though usually less dramatically, subject to the forces of social change. Class relations are never reproduced identically without change. Reproduction of the social relations of production involves the dynamic reproduction — i.e. the growth (or expansion), replication (or conservation) and dissolution — of the social classes, or in other words, class formation. Class formation not only defines the contradictions underlying class conflict, but is in turn also subject to the outcome of conflict among classes and class fractions.

It is not possible here to discuss the nature of the capitalist state (see Esping-Anderson et al., 1976; Miliband, 1969; Poulantzas, 1973b) or even more specifically, the character of the post-colonial state (see Alavi, 1972; Leys, 1975, 1976; Mamdani, 1976; Meillasoux, 1970; Murray, 1967; Saul, 1974). However, we shall outline our perspective on the state particularly with regard to class relations. The state has three basic aspects: first, state structure is always an *outcome* of past class conflict; second, the activities and role of the state are a *determinant* of class conflict; third, political power, especially control of the state, is also an *object* of class conflict.

Because of its contradictory composition, the capitalist class has generally been incapable of holding political power on a completely unified basis. The existence of capitalist class fractions — e.g. comprador capital, national capital (see Poulantzas, 1973a; Jomo, 1977) — undermines such class unity. Intra-class conflict contention is, of course, not confined to the capitalist class alone. Struggles by other dominant classes as well as those waged by exploited classes also undermine the unified hegemony of the capitalist class.

In such circumstances, the existence of a relatively autonomous state structure, not under the complete and direct control of any single capitalist class fraction, can ensure the hegemony of the capitalist class as a whole (Poulantzas, 1973b; Bamat, 1977). Hence, the relative autonomy of the state from particular dominant class interests may be viewed as a consequence of the inability of the fractions of the dominant class or classes to hold and exercise state power on a consolidated and coherent basis. The realization of capitalist class interests is not contingent on direct exercise of state power, i.e. capitalists do not need to govern directly. In fact, the concept of relative state autonomy can imply the hegemony of the capitalist class without its direct exercise of state power.

The state in capitalist society is not relatively autonomous in all circumstances. Further, relative autonomy has varied manifestations and implications in different societal and historical conditions. The relatively autonomous character of the state enables it to make compromises among capitalist class fractions and other competing dominant class interests. It also enables the state to more effectively legitimate itself as the embodiment of the 'national interest'.

In the study of post-colonial societies, the concept of relative state autonomy is especially applicable because of the implications of the colonial class configuration for class relations and political hegemony in the post-colonial era. The incomplete generalization of capitalist relations of production under colonialism and since independence, as well as the external economic domination of most post-colonial economies which has stifled the development of local bourgeoisies, have both accentuated this absence of coherent dominant class unity in these societies. This has enhanced the relative autonomy of post-colonial states, allowing the governing stratum even greater freedom from other specific dominant class interests.

In colonial societies, the development of the local capitalist class was subject to and conditioned by the dominance of foreign capital. Consequently, the local bourgeoisie has typically been weak in relation to the colonial capitalists. Many local capitalists tend to be tied into the world market and are often subservient to the interests of foreign capital. The usually weak fraction of the local bourgeoisie which developed independently of and in opposition to colonial capital has rarely drawn strong support from the local members of the colonial bureaucracy. As a result of colonial policies, ethnic divisions tend to coincide with the colonial class configuration in multi-ethnic colonial societies.

In the colonial era, bureaucrats were made to serve the interests of colonial capital, while in the post-colonial era they have often been oriented to serve the interests of international capital in general and particularly its dominant segments.[1] Hence, the local bureaucracy spawned by colonialism has an essentially comprador orientation. It will therefore tend to promote national development along an essentially 'dependent capitalist' path. Depending on its relations with the local comprador capitalists, this bureaucracy may serve this class faithfully. Alternatively, it may organize itself to compete with the dependent bourgeoisie for the gains of collaboration with foreign capital. Usually, however, the actual relationship reflects the unresolved contradiction between these two tendencies.

Hegemony by an 'absent' bourgeoisie (foreign capital) and the relative weakness of the local bourgeoisie (including its comprador component) enhance the degree of autonomy enjoyed by the post-colonial state. Other elements often also provide the governing class with a greater measure of independence and relative strength.[2] The higher degree of relative autonomy of most post-colonial states allows the government a greater range of manoeuvrability and initiative. In certain circumstances, this has led to the self-conscious reorganization of the bureaucratic governing class into a bureaucrat capitalist class. However, the emergence of a bureaucrat bourgeoisie is not an inevitable outcome of the extent of relative autonomy enjoyed by post-colonial states, and their governing classes. Nevertheless, evidence from several countries suggests that the nature of the state in several post-colonial societies has given rise to bureaucrat capitalist classes (e.g. Shivji, 1976).

Control of the state by the bureaucrat bourgeoisie is necessary for its development. Deprived of state power, the bureaucrat capitalist class cannot survive. This class accumulates through the state, i.e. it is the state that undertakes the main financial and other responsibilities for capital accumulation. Hence, the typical organizational form employed is the state-owned (public) enterprise, though the growth of private firms owned by bureaucrats and politicians also reflects this tendency. The bureaucrat bourgeoisie gains pecuniary benefits from such development in various forms, including high salaries, expenses as well as other allowances, nepotism, bribery, other forms of corruption and so on. Since the primary responsibility for capital accumulation rests with the state, lucrative incomes for the bureaucrat capitalists tend to encourage extravagant life styles, though private capital accumulation should not be discounted altogether.

II

To illustrate the argument in the preceding part, we shall now briefly discuss the ascendance of the bureaucrat capitalist class in Malaysia. This should illustrate how the particular circumstances of the relative autonomy of the post-colonial state in Malaysia allowed the governing bureaucratic petty bourgeoisie to create conditions for its own transformation into a bureaucrat capitalist class. Yet this very development has engendered new contradictions which have changed the terrain of class conflict and which in turn implies new constraints to the ascendance of the bureaucrat bourgeoisie. Hence, the relative autonomy of the post-colonial state is clearly contradictory. While providing an important condition for bureaucrat capitalist ascendance, it has also imposed certain structural limitations to this tendency.

It is necessary to look at the historical conditions which have given rise to the recent ascendance of a bureaucrat capitalist class in the post-colonial period. The configuration of social classes in the post-colonial period may be traced to the class relations existing under British rule.

After almost a century of confining direct rule to a few key ports, from the last quarter of the nineteenth century, the British government extended its colonial realm to the rest of the Malayan peninsula. The expanded colonial order in Malaya involved a complex mix of 'direct' and 'indirect' governing arrangements. Initial resistance from sections of the pre-colonial Malay ruling class (who had been deprived of most of their usual sources of income by colonial rule) was eliminated by a combination of carrot and stick policies. While those who actively opposed the British imperialists were severely punished, the colonialists sought to co-opt other members of the pre-colonial Malay ruling class. The grooming of an administrative stratum of Malays from royal and aristocratic families was also expected to legitimize colonial rule in the eyes of the Malay peasant masses. Hence, most indigenous administrators who served British officials and colonial dictates can usually trace their social origins to the pre-colonial ruling class.

In the colonial order, the indigenous population were no longer subject to most pre-colonial systems of exploitation, such as slavery, debt-bondage (peonage), corvee labor, taxes on traded goods and other items. (Some such forms were perpetuated — at least temporarily — in the service of the new colonial masters, e.g. corvee labor.) Instead, they were subordinated to the colonial state and hence, to its laws, policies and taxation. As colonialism accelerated the growth of commerce and the accumulation of capital, the peasantry became increasingly subject to exploitation by merchant and usury capital. Perhaps most significantly, the conditions accompanying British rule engendered new tendencies differentiating the peasantry. Unlike in the pre-colonial order when peasants comprised a relatively undifferentiated mass in relation to the ruling class, new tendencies in colonial Malayan society resulted in peasant stratification. The differentiation of peasant strata was especially crucial in relation to land owned and land cultivated, land being the peasantry's primary means of production. Land hunger is manifest today in various forms of landlessness, including inadequate land holdings and rural unemployment as well as underemployment. Rural landlordism or its flip side, tenancy, is also very much a product of the colonial order.

While the Malay peasantry was undoubtedly transformed in the colonial economy, they remained peasants largely divorced from wage labor relations while the pre-colonial Malay ruling class served as an administrative salariat in the colonial bureaucracy. Hence, most Malays were divorced from capitalist relations of production, defined here essentially by the wage-labor relationship. Instead, the capitalist sector in the colonial economy mainly involved the non-Malay Malayan population, as well as expatriate capital. Expansion of capital in the colonial economy did not only involve the sphere of circulation (i.e. usury and merchant capital), but also the sphere of production. The profitable opportunities offered by mineral (especially tin) extraction and cash cropping (most notably rubber) did not pass the early merchant capitalists unheeded. Such production — which was mainly export-oriented — was initially organized with various involuntary forms of immigrant labor (e.g. indenture) from China, India and what is now Indonesia. This was necessitated by the absence of a local proletariat readily available for wage employment due to colonial efforts to preserve a Malay yeoman peasantry in the interests of political stability. However, with the gradual emergence of a local wage labor force — initially recruited primarily from settled immigrants and their offspring — and also as a result of struggles waged from early this century by workers and others opposed to forms of involuntary labor, free wage labor increasingly became the mode of employment used by capital.

While the colonial economy was dominated by British capital, Chinese and other businessmen were allowed to play a largely auxiliary role. In the colonial economy, whenever the development of Chinese business interests threatened British capital, the colonial state generally intervened to curb the former and to promote the interests of the latter. The predominantly Chinese local capitalists were, of course, not homogeneous. They may be differentiated by several different criteria which do not necessarily coincide with one another. (These criteria include enterprise size, degree of monopoly power, relationship to foreign capital, relationship to the state, nature of business activities and so on.) Such differences are important to recognise if we are to correctly understand the response of local capitalist interests to certain aspects of post-colonial development, particularly the rise of the predominantly Malay bureaucrat bourgeoisie.

When British rule in Malaya ended in 1957, the departing colonialists had paved the way for the predominantly Malay bureaucratic stratum to govern in the post-colonial era. As we noted earlier, this stratum was recruited largely from the families of the pre-colonial Malay ruling class. They derived their incomes from salaries and other pecuniary benefits provided by the colonial state. Except for some important ties with the comprador fraction there were few links with the predominantly Chinese local bourgeoisie. Hence, it is not surprising that the new governing class could not even be expected to lead or to participate in any *bourgeois-based* opposition to economic domination by foreign capital, let alone anything more radical.

The post-colonial ruling coalition, known as the Alliance, involved three political parties. The UMNO (United Malays National Organization) was led by Malays with close ties to the pre-colonial ruling class and the Malay administrators; the MCA (Malayan Chinese Association) was capitalist dominated and the MIC (Malayan Indian Congress) was headed by bourgeois and petty-bourgeois Indians. The Alliance arrangement lasted until 1969. For the first dozen years after independence in 1957, the class interests that it represented were faithfully reflected by political and economic policy. The key features of rule by this class coalition, for the purposes of this discussion, were its laisser faire policies towards accumulation by foreign capital and the predominantly Chinese local bourgeoisie, and the free hand given to the predominantly-Malay bureaucratic petty bourgeoisie to expand and consolidate itself. This uneasy class compromise continued to define the role of the post-colonial state until the late sixties.

Few Malay capitalists emerged during the colonial period. Even today, many ostensibly Malay capitalists are actually of Indonesian, Arab or Indian descent. With the pre-colonial Malay ruling class co-opted into the colonial bureaucracy and the Malay peasantry left with land to cultivate, mobility into the bourgeois world was neither attractive nor easy for most Malays. Government efforts to promote Malay capitalists began in the twilight of the colonial era, in the early fifties, in response to charges — by the leader of the ascending Malay bureaucratic stratum — of previous government neglect in this matter. Promotion of Malay capitalists was limited not only by weak financial support from the colonial government. Though financial support increased with independence and grew thereafter, the post-colonial government's espoused commitment to the creation of a Malay bourgeoisie continued to be circumscribed by the state's longstanding commitment to facilitate capital accumulation by the longer established and more powerful capitalist interests. This continued for the first dozen years after independence, i.e. until the late sixties. New interests unassociated with the colonial economy, also thrived. Industrial development became more significant, largely as the outcome of new alliances involving local and foreign capitalist interests.

After independence, the efforts to create and consolidate a Malay capitalist class steadily grew. These mainly took the form of provision of special amenities and various kinds of subsidy. Various measures increased the ranks of the Malay petty bourgeoisie, especially the bureaucratic petty bourgeoisie who took over the government with the exit of the British. By the provision of scholarships, the stipulation of ethnic employment quotas and other similar measures, this class grew rapidly. Benefiting from state policies, it provided important support for the then nascent bureaucratic bourgeoisie.

By the mid-sixties, the emerging Malay bourgeoisie began to make its presence felt. In 1965, the first Bumiputra[3] Economic Congress was held. Significantly, it was organized by bureaucrats and politicians and not by the few established private Malay capitalists. In the same year, two other major developments further boosted the emerging Malay capitalist class. The Rural and Industrial Development Authority (RIDA), first established in the early fifties, was reorganized and greatly expanded in the form of MARA (Majlis Amanah Rakyat or the Council of Trust for the People). MARA has since played a very significant role in the expansion and development of the Malay bourgeoisie and petty bourgeoisie in various fields. The other important event was the establishment of Bank Bumiputra, designed to serve as a key financial base for Malay capital expansion.

Nevertheless, the development of Malay capitalist interests through the sixties continued to be constrained by the class compromise underlying the post-colonial Alliance arrangement. Firstly, this involved perpetuation — as well as extension into new spheres such as industry — of the hegemony of foreign capital, and also the preservation of the interests of that fraction of the domestic bourgeoisie aligned with it. Secondly, existing local capitalist and other propertied interests were consolidated after the attainment of independence. The pattern of capital accumulation in the colonial period meant that the bulk of this local bourgeoisie was ethnically Chinese, represented in the Alliance through the MCA. With accumulation by capitalist interests established in the colonial era continuing unhindered and, in fact, encouraged by the state in the post-colonial era, there was not much room for the creation of a viable Malay bourgeoisie.

This does not mean that no Malay capitalists emerged in the first dozen years after independence. On the contrary, several dozen influential politicians, powerful civil servants and other similarly well-connected Malays lucratively cooperated with foreign and local capitalists in need of political or bureaucratic links. Compared to the other ethnic groups, Malay capitalist interests grew fastest in the first dozen years after independence. Yet, only 1.5 percent of total share capital in public limited companies in 1969 was owned by Malays,[4] compared to 22.5 percent in Chinese hands and 62.1 percent being foreign owned. While, highly remunerative for the individual Malay partners concerned, limited Malay participation in post-colonial business arrangements could not possibly satiate the rising expectations of the rapidly growing Malay petty bourgeoisie. Frustrated ambitions in such quarters fueled the apparently 'extremist' challenge by 'Young Turks' against the established UMNO leadership. The latter were depicted as having 'sold out Malay interests' to non-Malays, especially to the Chinese. While undoubtedly a politically expedient caricature, this nonetheless reflected — even if only in a distorted fashion — some of the ethnic dimensions of the class compromise underlying the post-colonial Alliance formula.

Several different but simultaneous trends culminated in the events of May 1969 which put the Alliance arrangement to an end. Statistical data show that economic conditions for poorer sections of the entire population deteriorated despite the impressive economic growth record after independence. For example, evidence on income distribution for 1957 and 1970 suggests growing inequality in the distribution pattern for all three major ethnic groups, as well as absolute declines in real household incomes for the poorer sections of the population (e.g. see Treasury, 1974). With much of post-war Malayan politics marked by ethnic ideologies and mobilization along racial lines, and given the effective restriction of the parliamentary left, popular sentiments critical of the Alliance government were channeled mainly into support for ethnically-based opposition parties. While the MCA fared worst among the Alliance partners in the 1969 general elections, even the UMNO failed to capture half the Malay vote. However, the Alliance-constructed electoral framework continued to ensure an Alliance majority in Parliament even after the MCA's temporary withdrawal. Within days of the elections, a racial conflagration broke out.

With the dominant Alliance partner UMNO firmly in command, parliamentary rule was suspended for about two years. Slowly but surely, the country's first prime minister and those closely associated with him were eased out of power and replaced with a generally younger group from within the UMNO headed by the previous deputy prime minister. A broader coalition — involving an increased number of political parties, many of which were formerly in the opposition — was slowly forged with a combination of coercion and enticement; under the name National Front, it contested its first general elections in 1974. In this expanded arrangement, the preeminence of UMNO was further enhanced in relation to its partners.

This transition was of great significance for the development of the bureaucrat bourgeoisie. Government economic policy became increasingly influenced by the UMNO 'Young Turks' of the late sixties, many of whom were frustrated products of the Malay 'special rights' policies of the earlier years of post-colonial government. In 1972, the government declared the New Economic Policy (NEP) in conjunction with the announcement of the Second Malaysia Plan for 1971-1975. In its Outline Perspective Plan for the period 1971-1990, the government projected dramatic changes in the percentages of corporate share ownership by ethnicity and citizenship along the lines shown in Table 1. While the New Economic Policy's two declared 'prongs' are poverty eradication and the 'restructuring of society', emphasis — particularly in terms of actual policy and implementation — has clearly been on the latter. To 'restructure society', special attention has been given to the creation of a Malay 'commercial and industrial' entrepreneurial class. Achieving the goals of the NEP has involved a greatly enlarged role for the state. In fact, three quarters of the targeted 30 percent of total share ownership to be held by Malays in 1990 are to be held in the form of public enterprises, whereas only the remaining quarter has been projected for Malay individuals. Thus, by its policy and practice, the government acknowledged that state forms of ownership — i.e. in the form of public enterprises — are compatible with building a Malay bourgeoisie.

In a dramatic break with past policy, the NEP has involved direct participation by the state in capital accumulation. This has entailed not only an expanded use of the fiscal and monetary tools available to government, but also the ploughing back of returns — if any[5] —

TABLE 1
Peninsular Malaysia: Ownership of Share Capital in Limited Companies, 1970-90

	1970[1]		1975[2]		Average annual growth rate(%) 1971-75	1980[3]		1990[3]		Average annual growth rate(%) 1976-90
	$million[4]	%	$million	%		$million	%	$million	%	
Malays and Malay interests	125.6	2.4	768.1	7.8	43.6	3,284.3	16.0	24,009.7	30.0	25.8
Malay individuals[5]	84.4	1.6	227.1	2.3	21.9	695.4	3.4	5,914.2	7.4	24.3
Malay interests[6]	41.2	0.8	541.0	5.5	67.4	2,588.9	12.6	18,095.5	22.6	26.4
Other Malaysians[7]	1,826.5	34.3	3,687.3	37.3	15.1	8,290.5	40.4	32,012.9	40.0	15.5
Foreign[8]	3,377.1	63.3	5,434.7	54.9	10.0	8,952.2	43.6	24,009.7	30.0	10.4
Total private sector[9]	5,329.2	100.0	9,890.1	100.0	13.2	20,527.0	100.0	80,032.3	100.0	15.0
Gross domestic product (in 1970 prices)	9,038.0		12,914.0		7.4	19,487.0		42,462.0		8.3

1. Actual.
2. Estimated.
3. Targets.
4. Totals for 1970 differ from those presented in the SMP and its Mid-Term Review because of the exclusion of the Government, the re-classification of the trust agencies as Malay interests and the re-allocation of most of the shares previously categorized as 'held by other companies' to the shareholders of these companies.
5. Includes institutions channelling private Malay funds such as Amanah Saham MARA and Lembaga Urusan dan Tabung Haji.
6. Shares considered to be held in trust by agencies such as MARA (excluding Amanah Saham MARA), PERNAS, UDA, SEDCs, Bank Bumiputra and Bank Pembangunan.
7. Includes nominee companies and third-company minority holdings.
8. Non-residents.
9. Excludes the government and its agencies except trust agencies.

Source: Third Malaysia Plan, 1976-1980, p. 86.

from previous investments, and perhaps most significantly, increased reliance on debt financing, both from domestic as well as foreign sources.[6] While the burden of capital accumulation has been shared by those contributing to the national product, the primary beneficiaries have been none other than the rapidly emerging bureaucrat bourgeoisie.

The bureaucrat bourgeoisie today is mainly drawn from the ranks of leading politicians with business connections, businessmen with strong political or bureaucratic ties, as well as present and former high level bureaucrats (including military, police and other government officers) in direct and indirect control of those enterprises set up or otherwise controlled by the state. Hence, this class straddles both public and private sectors. While this distinction (between the two sectors) is quite blurred in reality, it is useful in so far as it provides some insights into various issues, such as possible contradictions within the bureaucrat bourgeoisie. Also, though there are different modes of private appropriation practised by individual bureaucrat capitalists — such as salaries, expense and other allowances, honoraria, graft, directorships, partnerships and so on — they may all be considered as belonging to a single class fraction.

While its political dominance has been clearly established for the moment, the bureaucrat bourgeoisie continues to be involved — to varying degrees — in conflict with other classes and class fractions. As these have affected and will continue to impinge on the course of its future development, it is important to indicate what some of these contradictions are, though space limitations do not permit a fuller discussion in this paper.

The bureaucrat bourgeoisie is hardly capable and is, in general, unwilling to break fundamentally with continued domination of the national economy by international capital. Even the projected decline in the proportion of foreign shareholdings (see Table 1) is not necessarily antagonistic to the interests of foreign capital. First, no absolute decline in foreign-owned assets is envisaged. Second, the projection will actually only involve an acceleration of an already existing tendency for the proportion of foreign share ownership to decline. Given the growing trend for technological, managerial and indirect financial ties to supercede the importance of stock ownership in ensuring control and outflow of surplus, the envisaged decline in the proportion of foreign stock ownership is not all that significant as far as continued foreign dominance of the economy is concerned.

The essentially comprador character of the bureaucrat bourgeoisie has already been mentioned. However, the bureaucrat bourgeoisie is not unanimously reconciled to the total subordination of colonial days. Enjoying direct exercise of state power has encouraged what foreign capital views as 'excessive' behavior. Hence, within the continued framework of domination by international capital, there has actually been some significant contention. This was most dramatic with the legislation of the Petroleum Development Act (1975) and other similar 'nationalistic' enactments. International capital responded with a virtual 'investment boycott', retarding the accumulation process so key to the viability of the NEP.[7] This was largely achieved by publication, in the international business media, of criticisms and doubts regarding government policy towards foreign capital. Confronted by such formidable opposition and unwilling as well as unable to break with international capitalist control, the Malaysian government soon relented, though not without trying to obscure the real character of the concessions with face-saving measures. Since then, it has worked hard to restore 'investment confidence' (especially with foreign capital), through a variety of measures such as investment promotion missions and the offer of additional investment incentives.

The dependent nature of the largely ethnically Malay based bureaucrat bourgeoisie has also brought it into rivalry with more established, predominantly Chinese compradors. To preserve their positions, the older compradors have generally been successful in constructing mutually beneficial inter-racial business partnerships. While these have been somewhat satisfactory to the Malay partners involved, they have — quite understandably — become the object of resentment to those aspiring to, but left out of the picture. This of course, refers to much of the Malay bourgeoisie and petty bourgeoisie.

The current arrangement of establishing public enterprises[8] — ostensibly on behalf of the Malay community — temporarily postpones the problem of intra-class asset distribution among bureaucrat capitalists. Nonetheless, it has not failed to raise questions as to how this will eventually be settled.

While the existence of state-owned enterprises is not antithetical to capitalism, their recent proliferation has often threatened particular businesses in the private sector. It appears that even the established comprador bourgeoisie's endorsement of government policy has diminished as government intervention and activity against its favor increases; nevertheless, it is far from withdrawing its support for the state.

In view of the essentially comprador nature of the bureaucrat bourgeoisie, it is not surprising that national capitalists — i.e. those with an interest in breaking foreign domination to further 'autonomous' indigenous economic entrepreneurship — have not fared much better in the post-colonial era compared to pre-independence times. Comprising mainly of small and politically less influential non-Malay businessmen, they continue to be in ambiguous opposition to imperialism and to the state in Malaysia, though not to capitalism per se.

The attitudes of the petty bourgeoisie to the bureaucrat bourgeoisie are largely determined by their respective relationships to the state. In so far as the dominant ethnic ideology is somewhat reflected in government policy and practice, it has affected the petty bourgeoisie unevenly, with the main differences apparently being along ethnic lines. On the one hand, the bulk of the large non-Malay petty bourgeoisie sees the state acting very much against its interests in its various efforts to consolidate and expand the Malay bourgeoisie and petty bourgeoisie.

On the other hand, the Malay petty bourgeoisie has, in the main, been an important beneficiary of post-colonial state policies and thus far remained quite loyal to the bureaucrat bourgeoisie. However, several recent developments[9] have caused growing disenchantment with the state and hence with the bureaucrat bourgeoisie. This is already manifest in the growth of a significant Islamic revivalist movement with rhetoric against materialistic acquisitiveness, a feature associated with the bureaucrat bourgeoisie.

To preserve and consolidate its support among the Malay peasant masses, the government has expanded its rural development programs ostensibly 'to eradicate poverty'. Constrained by the class character of its support at the village as well as at the national level, it cannot undertake a thoroughgoing land reform against the established landed interests. Hence, the main thrust of rural development programs has been to raise productivity. However, such efforts have had mixed outcomes, often resulting in widening rather than narrowing income disparities, in favor of the bureaucrat bourgeoisie and their rural petty-bourgeois counterparts. These are connected to changes in class relations which have accompanied government-encouraged technical changes. In rice farming and fishing, for example, there has been a significant expansion in the extent of wage-labor employment with the spread of 'modern' technology.

To end our brief survey of some of the significant new class contradictions emerging with the consolidation of the bureaucrat bourgeoisie, a short comment needs to be made on the working class. Our earlier survey of the socio-economic history of Malaya indicated some of the major reasons why an ethnic identification with class location developed in the colonial period and for some time thereafter. The NEP's stated goal of 'restructuring society' includes an attempt to partially dissociate ethnicity from class and occupation. This has been most rapidly achieved in the working class, especially in the unskilled labor categories. The accelerated integration of Malays into the wage-labor force has many important implications for the future of ethnic as well as class relations and already appears to be redefining the character and contours of class conflict in post-colonial Malaysia.[10]

III

In this concluding section, we would like to relate the preceding discussion to the issue of 'Spontaneity and Planning in Social Development'. The above argument implicitly maintains that the historical unfolding of class contradictions is best understood dialectically in terms of the contradictory relationship between spontaneity and planning. This is crucial for the theoretical and empirical elaboration of the position that it is class conflict that moves history. Class contradictions give rise to conflict which may in turn stimulate planned endeavors in dealing with them. As contradictions get resolved or merely displaced, fresh ones spontaneously emerge which in turn generate more class conflict, albeit on different terrain.

Here, we may note that class conflict cannot be completely planned though it may be anticipated. The element of spontaneity in class contention is strong indeed. The development and outcome of class contradictions are essentially spontaneous in so far as they are not completely subject to planning by any one side alone despite planned activity by any of the contending classes or class fractions. In other words, the outcome of class conflict cannot be completely planned by any party to it. The unfolding of class contradictions and the results of class conflict are essentially spontaneous in so far as they are not completely subject to planning by any one side alone, whatever the intentions and efforts of any of the contending classes or class fractions.

As Charles Bettelheim has argued in a different context, it is not the contradiction between state planning and the market which is crucial in itself (Bettelheim and Sweezy, 1971). Rather, it is more important to identify the underlying class relations. Hence, he argued, state interference in otherwise spontaneous market mechanisms and the spread of planning are in themselves no guarantee of either the abolition of capitalist relations of production or the irreversibility of the transition beyond capitalism.

In the Malaysian context, the specific issues are obviously different, though the essential argument remains tenable. Increased state intervention and planning in the Malaysian economy with the promulgation of the NEP has not involved any break with capitalism or even with foreign economic domination. While government planning undoubtedly affects the processes of capital accumulation and commodity exchange, such interference is generally intended to better serve the dominant fractions of capital rather than to undermine continued development along capitalist lines. The expanded use of planning instruments by the post-colonial Malaysian government is primarily a consequence of the specific characteristics of the bureaucrat capitalist class, particularly the necessity for it to directly use the state apparatus for the purpose of capital accumulation.

Hence, planning in this instance tends to support and encourage selected elements in the otherwise more spontaneous capitalist development process. Planning in such a context becomes primarily a tool for the dominant class interests to interfere to their own advantage with more spontaneous tendencies in the capital accumulation process. Yet, the very logic of capitalism ensures that spontaneous forces retain the upper hand, thus perpetuating the essential anarchy of the system. Within this context then, planning by the state only has limited significance. Hence, Malaysian social development in the seventies reflects planned as well as spontaneous displacement of certain class contradictions and the spontaneous emergence of new ones.

NOTES

1. See Ngun and Siegel (1976) for examples from the Malaysian case.

2. For example, these may include effective control of repressive state machinery such as the military. Alternatively, the governing class may be able to mobilize some mass support, e.g. in the form of corporatist or even fascist movements.

3. *Bumiputra* literally meaning 'princes of the soil' is the official term used to refer to what is collectively referred to as the 'indigenous people', of which the Malays are by far the most important.

4. As late as 1974, the Singapore and Kuala Lumpur Stock Exchange Handbooks showed only 30 Malay directors of public limited companies, though many of these had very impressive strings of directorships.

5. The business record of most public enterprises in Malaysia has been disappointing, at least in terms of profits and losses.

6. The resulting inflationary situation was further compounded by changes in the international economy as well.

7. For example, there are two important kinds of public enterprises in Malaysia. The 'public corporation' is generally established by statute and is hence subject to relevant legislation. The government has also financed the establishment of 'government enterprises' which are subject to ordinary company laws like private companies. The latter have much in common with private companies established by businessmen enjoying government credit facilities and other privileges due either to state policy or to political connections.

8. For example, total investment in government-approved industrial projects has declined dramatically from a 1974 peak of 759.1 million Malaysian *ringgit* to 357.9 million *ringgit* in 1977 — a drop of more than half (see Jamil Jan, 1978). Of course, other factors — including depressed international economic conditions — have contributed to this decline.

9. For instance, the government's Third Malaysia Plan for 1976-80 projects that an estimated one-third of university graduates in the humanities and social sciences can expect to be unemployed at the end of the plan period. Most students in these fields in Malaysian universities are Malays.

10. For example, no longer can the powers that be simply dismiss worker demands as being 'non-Malay'. Also, Malay workers are generally less intimidated by the state — which is ostensibly serving the 'Malay interest' — and are hence emerging as those most likely to be openly militant in confronting capital and management.

REFERENCES

ALAVI, H. (1972) 'The State in Postcolonial Societies: Pakistan and Bangladesh', *New Left Review*, 74.

BAMAT, T. (1977) 'Relative State Autonomy and Capitalism in Brazil and Peru', *The Insurgent Sociologist* 7(2): 74-84.

BETTELHEIM , C. and P. SWEEZY (1971) *On the Transition to Socialism*. New York: Monthly Review Press.

ESPING-ANDERSON, G., R. FRIEDLAND and E. O. WRIGHT (1976) 'Modes of Class Struggle and the Capitalist State', *Kapitalistate*, 5.

JAMIL JAN (1978) Penyertaan dan Pencapaian Bumiputra dalam Perindustrian. Paper presented at the Bumiputra Economic Convention, National University of Malaysia (12 March).

JOMO, K. S. (1977) 'Class Formation in Malaya: Capital, the State and Uneven Development'. PhD thesis, Harvard University.

LEYS, C. (1975) *Underdevelopment in Kenya*. Berkeley, Ca.: University of California Press.

— — (1976) 'The Overdeveloped Post-Colonial State: a Re-evaluation, *Review of African Political Economy*, 5.

MAMDANI, M. (1976) *Politics and Class Formation in Uganda*. New York: Monthly Review Press.

MEILLASOUX, C. (1970) 'A Class Analysis of the Bureaucratic Process in Mali', *Journal of Development Studies* (January).

MILIBAND, R. (1969) *The State in Capitalist Society*. New York: Basic Books.

MURRAY, R. (1967) 'Second Thoughts on Ghana', *New Left Review* 42.

NGUN, B. A. and L. SIEGEL (1976) 'The U.S. in Malaysia', *Pacific Research* (May-June).

POULANTZAS, N. (1973a) 'On Social Classes', *New Left Review* 77.

— — (1973b) *Political Power and Social Classes*. London: New Left Books.

SAUL, J. S. (1974) 'The State in Post-Colonial Societies: Tanzania', *The Socialist Register 1974*.

SHIVJI, I. (1976) *Class Struggles in Tanzania*. New York: Monthly Review Press.

STENSON, M. (1976) 'Class and Race in West Malaysia', *Bulletin of Concerned Asian Scholars* (April-June).

VON FREYHOLD, M. (1977) 'The Post-Colonial State and Its Tanzanian Version', *Review of African Political Economy* 8 (January-April).

TREASURY (Malaysia) (1974) *Economic Report, 1974-75*.

ZIEMAN, W. and M. LANZENDORFER (1977) 'The State in Peripheral Societies', *The Socialist Register 1977*.

8

SOCIALIST PLANNING: THE PROBLEM OF CO-ORDINATION AND AUTONOMY

Branko Horvat
University of Zagreb, Yugoslavia

It is still generally believed, both in the East and in the West, and also both by experts and laymen, that 'planning' and 'market' represent two incompatible forms of organization. In this respect the neoclassical position is well presented by English liberal economist Lionel Robbins:

> The alleged advantage of economic 'planning' — namely that it offers certainty with regard to the future — depends upon the assumption that under 'planning' the present controlling forces, the choices of individual spenders and savers, are themselves brought under the control of the planners. Therefore, the paradox presents itself: either planner is destitute of the instruments of calculating the ends of the community he intends to serve, or if he restores the instruments, he removes the raison d'être of the 'plan'.[1]

In its vulgar Marxist version the same statement will assert that the private market implies anarchy in production and generates capitalist relationships and ought to be replaced by state planning. Private property can only — and, therefore, must — be replaced by state property whereby autonomous individual decisions are replaced by central, hierarchically structured decisions of the state.[2]

As we proceed, it will become clear that the paradox and anarchy belong to ideology and apologetics and not to scientific thinking.

I. MARKET FAILURES

If consumers are sovereign in their choices, they will spend their incomes on such assortments of goods and services which maximally satisfy their needs. If producers are free in their economic activities, they will combine purchased inputs in such a way as to minimize cost and will produce outputs which will maximize profits. Most profitable outputs will turn out to be exactly those which are most valuable for the consumers. Thus by furthering their individual interests, by maximizing their *private* gains, the actors in the market automatically maximize *social* welfare. This laissez-faire vision of the market, defined by Adam Smith as the 'invisible hand', is the basic market model of classical and neoclassical economics.

We know that actual capitalist economies widely diverge from this model. The reasons for the divergence of the reality from the model are analytically rather simple. In order to work, the model requires an environment of certainty, full information available to the actors, instantaneous adjustments and divisibility of all commodities. The real world is different; decisions must be made under uncertainty, information is costly, adjustments occur with considerable lags and investment is often bumpy. As a result, production is subject to business cycles, many people are unemployed, monopolies and advertisements distort price and output structures and economic welfare is obviously substantially lower than it could objectively be otherwise.

What is the reason that such a misleading model has existed for so long a time? There are at least three reasons. First, it serves well the ideological needs. It 'proves' that capitalist systems maximize economic welfare. Secondly, it served a useful purpose as a methodological device. Economic reality is so complex that it must be drastically simplified to be analytically tractable. The construction of the model and the study of the conditions under which it might be valid have helped to build an ingenious economic science. Thirdly, the model may be used as a standard of comparison. This is the use I am going to make of it. We shall then encounter a paradox somewhat different from that of Robbins. It will turn out that an efficient operation of the market is possible only in a planned socialist economy! Let us proceed by examining the imperfections and the failures of the ordinary market.

1. Consumer choices are not correct

Consumers' choices are often irrational, shaped by habit and custom and lack of knowledge. Use of narcotic drugs and liquors, conspicuous consumption and purchasing foods of little nutritive value in proportion to the money paid out by the housewives of the poor are examples frequently quoted. If medical service is to be paid, health is frequently neglected in favor of some trivial consumption item. Books are bought and read, and theater performances watched only by those introduced to them. Education is appreciated only by those educated. As Maurice Dobbs points out:

> the consumer and his wants are a social product, moulded both by the commodities which enter into his experience and by the social standards and customs amongst which he has been reared. Thus, in shaping the course of development, economic policy inevitably shapes the changing pattern of consumers' wants....[3]

If our choices are socially determined, then we had better consider how to control the forces responsible for this determination and not flatter ourselves how sovereign we are individually.

2. Producers' choices are not correct

Uncertainty and lack of knowledge generate windfall gains and losses. The concentration of market power generates monopolies with concomitant exploitation of consumers and other producers. As Moore and Keynes have shown, the sum of individual gains may result in a societal loss. This happens when, for instance, aggregate saving is greater than aggregate investment. Since demand does not match available supply, production falls and workers are rendered unemployed. The only cure against unemployment and periodic slumps is social planning.

3. Money prices do not exist
or are not applicable

Even in a universal market economy not everything has a money price. If I cultivate a beautiful garden, my neighbor will enjoy it too. If I produce unpleasant noise in my garden, my neighbor's satisfaction will be reduced. Since we live in a society, our activities affect our fellow citizens and these effects can often not be appropriated. Occasionally considerable differences arise between real social cost and money cost and between real social benefit and price. Air pollution, professional diseases and depletion of aesthetic values may appear on the cost side, while enjoyment of economic and social equality, security from disease and employment security will appear on the benefit side. The so-called public good also comes under this heading. The cost of providing a public good does not increase at all or does not increase appreciably if the number of consumers increases. Alternatively, no individual must reduce his consumption of the good because of consumption of an additional consumer. Clean air, a lighthouse and national defense are examples. In such cases the ordinary market mechanism with transactions between buyers and sellers breaks down.

4. Technological and pecuniary externalities

Here prices are in principle applicable, but the production does not react properly and an uncontrolled price system leads to uneconomic production solutions. Static externalities are to be found in external economies and diseconomies in current production which the profit maximizing firms do not take into account and in uncaptured effects of new industrial locations. Examples are familiar. If an industry supplier operates under the conditions of economies of scale (say, the steel industry), its expanded operations will benefit the industrial purchases (say, the coal industry) in terms of lower costs. A hydro-electric power station may help farmers by increasing the supply of water, or may cause damage by changing the climate. An oil refinery may spoil tourism, a chemical factory may kill fish. Two complementary factories at one location are likely to be more efficient than just one at each of the two different locations. In all such cases, market and prices do not generate rational solutions; the intervention of a planning authority is necessary. One particular, dynamic, externality has so far eluded the attention of the market theorists. It is a consequence of limited capacity of any economy to absorb investment. Marginal efficiency of an additional unity of investment to a particular firm may be high and positive, while at the same time being negative for the economy as a whole. This happens when organizational strains and resource scarcities reduce the aggregate output of all other firms more than is the increase in output in the investing firm. There exists no market signal for the communication of that information.[4]

5. Social decisions by their nature replace individual decisions

There remain two vitally important decisions which ought to be made in every economy and which in a socialist economy cannot be left to a free play of market forces. Every price system will also produce *a certain* distribution of income among the members of the community and *a certain* division of social product as between the investment and consumption parts. In a socialist economy the *optimum* is required in both cases.

The above analysis leads to the conclusion: (a) the price mechanism operates rather inefficiently; (b) it occasionally breaks down in the sphere of production (wrong signals); (c) it most definitely breaks down in the sphere of distribution (since distribution decisions are in principle social, while market organization presupposes decentralized individualist decisions). This is a rather formidable list of shortcomings. The market seems hardly acceptable for socialism. When the market goes wrong all we can do is to introduce planning. If so, shouldn't we opt for planning right away and forget about the market?

The answer is: No! First of all, the choice is not either-or. Secondly, (central) planning can be shown to be rather inefficient as well. Then, perhaps, a combination of the two, a sort of mixed economy? That would imply an eclecticism for which there is no justification. We wish to preserve essential consumers' sovereignty because socialism is based on the preferences of individuals who constitute the society. We also wish to preserve the autonomy of producers since this is the precondition for self-management. Taken both together, we need a market. But not a laissez-faire market. We need a market which will perform the two functions just stated, neither less nor more. In other words, we need the *market as a planning device* in a strictly defined sphere of priorities. In order to make it work properly, the five imperfections of the market ought to be corrected by planning interventions. This, in turn, means that we need *planning as a precondition for an efficient market*. Planning means perfection of market choices in order to increase the economic welfare of the community. Far from being incompatible or contradictory, market and planning appear complementary as two sides of the same coin. Neither is a goal in itself. Both are means for an appropriate organization of a socialist economy. How such an organization can be achieved, will be explored in the following sections.

II. FUNCTIONS OF PLANNING

It is obvious that economic actions must be planned at all levels. For the purpose at hand, we shall concern ourselves with planning on the national level. In doing so, we set out from the assumption that in self-management market economy, the basic economic decision-making units — the enterprises — are completely autonomous in making their economic decisions. This, of course, does not mean a laissez-faire economy, it does not mean haphazardness and it does not mean naive belief in the efficiency of the 'invisible hand'. We dealt with that in the preceding section. But it does mean that in coordinating the initiatives of work collectives, planning and economic policy organs can only exceptionally use administrative, physical control measures, and that it is considered normal only to use economic instruments, providing relevant information if needed. We proceed also on the assumption that social plans have their expert and social components which are equally important. Plans prepared with insufficient expertise, with erroneous forecasts and mistaken analyses — only too often all around the world — cannot be transformed into an effective instrument of guidance by any sort of democratic self-management action. On the other hand, even with the use of the most modern techniques of resource allocation and econometric forecasting models, the plan will remain without effect if it lacks a social base, which in our case means that it should be adopted in a consistently self-management fashion. The planning itself ought to be participatory. By this I mean that plans are worked out at all levels and are then gradually integrated into an overall plan by an iterative process of consultation and negotiation. Surviving disagreements are eventually ironed out through political processes in the assembly.

Attention should be called to the fact that planning does not reduce to the elaboration of plans, which is only one, and moreover the easiest part of the work, but also includes the follow up and carrying out of plans. In this way planning and economic policy comprise a unified whole.

A social plan has four basic functions:

1. The plan is above all a *forecasting instrument*. In addition to the normative part the document of the plan must also contain a detailed analysis of economic trends with equally detailed forecasts. The purpose of every detailed publication of planning forecasts is to provide producers with insights into the most probable economic changes and to provide all the information necessary for formulating their own

business policy. The planning bureau that prepares these forecasts bears full professional responsibility for the realism of the elaborated forecasts.

2. The plan as a forecasting instrument is at the same time an instrument for the coordination of economic decisions. The plan is compulsory only in that part of it which relates to state organs and only for those organs. For everybody else it provides only economic guidance. However, the social plan is worked out in a participatory fashion, which implies prior harmonization of the development progress of various regions, economic associations and firms. Once the plan is finished, it represents not only a projection of probable change but also a projection of the agreed upon change. The more successful this preliminary harmonization is, the greater is the probability that the plan will be fulfilled.

3. On the basis of forecasts of possible development and of coordination of the existing initiatives of the basic economic decision-making units, application of modern methods of economic analysis, along with consultation of all relevant social factors, should determine which economic changes would be optimal from the standpoint of the country as a whole. When this is determined, the economic instruments are chosen, their effects quantified and their application adjusted to attain the adopted social goals most efficiently. Both one and the other comprise another basic function of the social plan, the function in which the plan appears as an instrument for guiding economic development.

4. As an elaboration of economic policy, the plan represents an obligation for the body that has adopted it and a directive for its organs. In so far as it is a question of the social plan, it is the obligation of the federal assembly and a directive to the federal executive council and the state organs subordinate to it.[5] These organs are obliged to carry out the economic policy formulated in the assembly or agreed upon by work organizations, states and consumers. They are responsible for the attainment of the adopted goals — increased production, increased employment, foreign trade balance, stability of prices, rising standard of living etc. For the realization of these targets a set of efficient economic instruments is at the disposal of the planning organs. The non-fulfillment of targets in normal conditions incurs full political and professional responsibility.

Let me add one technical point. Plan requires continuity. As new information comes along, plans ought to be revised so as to make best use of available opportunities. This makes for the so-called rolling plans. If medium-term plans require a period of five years, and long-range plans a period of twenty years, then every year the planning horizon will be shifted one more year in the future preserving a five-year planning horizon at every moment. At the end of the original five-year plan, the long-range planning horizon will be shifted five years in the future thus preserving a twenty-year planning horizon for executive decisions.

Traditional election practices are not consistent with these requirements. Continual planning requires continual government. Every year, or every second year, part of the assembly retires and a corresponding number of new representatives are elected. In this way the 'revolving' assembly keeps track of all planning activities. The executive council can be fitted into the game at any time.

Social planning not only improves macro-economic efficiency but also adds a new quality to the economic process. Liberal-capitalist economy, based on the uncontrolled market, is a competitive economy. Yet, a cut-throat competition is not quite consistent with socialism based on cooperation and solidarity. Both these dimensions are introduced by social planning. Competition is not eliminated, but it is directed towards improving the quality of commodities and reducing costs of production, not to driving competitors out of the market. The competitive firm cannot be bought or subordinated in other ways, it is highly unlikely that it will become bankrupt, monopolistic behavior is not possible, financial power is of no great avail since the market is organized and sound projects will always receive necessary finance. Besides, full employment, relative uncertainty and fast growth provide sufficient elbow space for everybody. Thus there will be a strong tendency for cooperation and division of labor. And this, in itself, is not only socially desirable but, usually, is likely to be also economically more efficient, particularly when coupled with the intra-firm cooperation inherent in workers' self-management. Empirical research in comparative group behavior has indicated that,

> the cooperative groups met the puzzle problem more efficiently and contributed in more detail to the analysis of the human-relations problem.... Within the cooperative groups there was more differentiation of individual function, that is, more division of labour; in the competitive groups, on the other hand, duplication of effort was considerable, for all were equally on their own to do all that was required. Communication was smoother in the cooperative group....Such experiments as Sherif's and Deutch's give micro-economic sanction to what...has long been clear: that the most effective

way of reducing intergroup tensions lies in mobilizing individuals into activities where cooperation is absolutely vital to success – where, in short, it is functional.[6]

Social planning makes cooperation functional and integrates workers' management into a consistent macro-economic system.

III. FIVE TYPES OF REGULATORY MECHANISMS

An economy is a large system involving a multitude of feedbacks with delayed effects and subject to oscillations. Stabilization of that system and the attainment of optimal performance require the building in of automatic stabilizers and the application of certain regulative techniques. The former means the construction of a system of institutions and norms of behavior; we shall discuss this problem later. The latter means economic policy. The regulatory mechanisms which can be used for purposes of economic policy are the subject matter of the present section.

In contrast to engineering systems, an economy is a much more complicated system, and hence the possibilities of completely automatic regulation are limited. The importance of economic policy is then all the greater. Citing of the systems analogy has the purpose of emphasizing that the solution of a problem, after decisions have been made about several basic social dilemmas, is objectively constrained and that little room remains for political bargaining.

By the nature of the matter, it is the functioning of the system as a whole that should be regulated. Accordingly, the economies of constituent states and communes cannot develop efficiently if the basic macro-economic decisions are not made at the level of the federation. As a consequence of participatory planning, the economic policy of the federation ought to be based on interstate agreements. These agreements, if they are to be effective, should be institutionalized. One of the most important instruments for the institutionalization of interstate agreements is the social plan.

So far we have been discussing the market and the plan as the only two coordinating and regulatory mechanisms. However, they are just two among five. A brief, historically interpreted, description of these five mechanisms follows. It will turn out that economic systems can be classified according to the dominant type of mechanism by which the coordination of economic activity is achieved.

1. Historically, the first form of economic coordination (in modern economies) was the laissez-faire market. The free market served as the means for integrating the earlier fragmented feudal economy into the unified national economy. In principle the state is outside the economy and its role is to protect property and permit unlimited private initiative. Since one can sell only what someone wishes to buy, everyone who wants to make a profit must orient his activity so that he satisfies social needs as well as possible. It is for such reasoning that Adam Smith derived his theory of the 'invisible hand': every individual 'intends only his own gain, as he is in this, as in many other cases, led by an invisible hand to promote an end which was no part of his intention'.[7] Motivated exclusively by their personal interests, private producers nevertheless produce precisely those commodities that are necessary, and at the lowest costs of production.

2. The 'invisible hand' did not prove to be especially efficient. We have already mentioned why. Periodic crises of overproduction and unemployment alternated for an entire century and a half. Growth was relatively slow (about 2 percent annually, compared to the world average today of 5 percent and to 10 percent in the most rapidly growing contemporary economies). In addition, the effective (backed by money) demand is not at all identical with the true social demand — it can greatly differ from social needs. Consequently, the socialist critics of the capitalist market oriented themselves toward the *visible hand* as the instrument of coordination. State initiative replaced private initiative, and *central planning* replaced the market.

3. The great economic crisis at the beginning of the 1930s brought the capitalist type of economic coordination to the verge of complete collapse. Central planning and expropriation of private property were obviously not an acceptable alternative in the capitalist countries. Besides, central planning had severe defects when conceived and implemented as administrative planning. An escape was found in introducing the state only partially into the economy, as an organ of *economic policy*. We may call this solution the *indirect hand*.

4. The development of economic statistics, economic analysis and the technology of gathering, processing and distributing information enabled economic decision-makers to obtain incomparably more relevant information than hitherto. In so far as the market represented an information system, this technological progress meant perfecting of the market. The improvement had two aspects: (a) up-to-date and comprehensive economic statistics offer economic decision-makers

complete information about the economic situation and without a delay (whereas the old market gave partial information belatedly); and (b) modern forecasting methods permit the reduction of uncertainty about future wants, and thereby the former ex-post decisions are elevated into ex-ante decisions. Both mean that economic decision-makers obtain a rather complete collection of the parameters important in making correct decisions, i.e. those that will lead to the production of precisely those commodities which can be sold. We can call such improvement of the operation of the market by *organized information diffusion* among economic decision-makers an improvement of the 'invisible hand'. The enormously increased speed and precision of information gathering and processing, made possible by electronic computers, has also substantially improved the 'visible hand'.

5. Finally, the 'visible hand' is capable of a further major improvement similar to that of the 'invisible hand' complemented by economic policy. It consists in various across-the-nation agreements, consultation and arbitration. They constitute a non-market means of coordination which, however, is fundamentally different from administrative orders of the state.

These five types of economic coordination — laissez faire, administrative planning, economic policy, production of information, non-market/non-state coordination — developed in the order just stated. But historical sequence does not mean either hierarchical order or evolution in the biological sense. Individual types are complementary and the main problem is to attain the organizational optimum. Different socio-economic systems allow different degrees of efficiency of economic organization.

Liberal capitalism was based on the free market, which means that laissez faire was the dominant principle of macro-economic organization. Administrative planning is the basis for *élitism* in which state bureaucrats replace individual entrepreneurs as organizers of production. The Keynesian revolution in the theory of economic policy made possible the submission of market instability to the relatively efficient control by the state as an organ of economic policy. Together with the creation of state (public) corporations and the ever-greater use of ex-post and ex-ante information systems, this led to the so-called *mixed economies* (or 'welfare states') characteristic of the contemporary highly-developed capitalist countries. Finally, a *socialist economy* should be characterized by optimal use of all five types of coordinating mechanisms in order to maximize the welfare of the members of the social community.

NOTES

1. L. Robbins, *An Essay on the Nature and Significance of Economic Science*. London: Roemiller, 1932, p. 113.

2. K. V. Ortrovitianov et al., *Politicheskaja Ekonomiija*. Moscow: Gospolitizdat, 1955, Chapters XXIX and XXX.

3. M. Dobb, *On Economic Theory and Socialism*. London: Routledge and Kegan Paul, 1955, p. 79.

4. Cf. B. Horvat, 'The Rule of Accumulation in a Planned Economy', *Kyklos*, 1968: 239-68.

5. The references to a *federal* structure are motivated by the fact that the author has Yugoslavia in mind (editor's comment).

6. R. A. Nisbet, 'Cooperation', *International Encyclopedia of the Social Sciences*. London: Macmillan, 1968. Vol. 3, pp. 388-90.

7. A. Smith, *The Wealth of Nations*. New York: Modern Library, 1937, p. 423.

9

NOTES ON COUNTER CULTURE
AND SOCIETAL CHANGE

Britta Jonsson
University of Uppsala, Sweden

INTRODUCTION

Coming back to your own country after having been far abroad for quite some time could be almost like visiting another new country. You see some changes more clearly when you are not present and participating in the changes.

Coming back from India in 1967 it seemed to me that everybody was suddenly well aware of the reasons for the problems of the Third World and that everybody had strong opinions on how to solve all

---

Editor's note: While all other contributions to this book treat more or less dominant trends and features of various societies, or concepts relating to such trends and features, as they concern the interplay of spontaneity and planning, the following paper gives scope to something seemingly much more ephemeral: counter-cultural movements which spontaneously emerged in a number of advanced industrial societies in the late sixties and early seventies. It seemed to the editor that a book with the term spontaneity in its title would be incomplete without touching on that fountain of unplanned spontaneity, and on the opposition to planned rationality finding an expression in such various counter-cultural movements or groups. Originally this paper was written for the session on 'Counter Culture and Protest' at the Ninth World Congress of Sociology in Uppsala 1978. Britta Jonsson, the author, is presently involved in an empirical research project on various groups and communes trying out alternative life styles in Sweden.

these problems. The whole situation, the political involvement among the students and all the initiatives taken to demonstrate student demands were so different from what I had noticed when I left Sweden two years earlier. Another remarkable thing that happened in 1967 was the visit of Maharishi Mahesh, the Indian yogi, to Sweden. The University Hall in Lund, where I studied at that time, was completely full when he made his speech on Transcendental Meditation. The big hotel in Falsterbo where he introduced and initiated people into his technique of meditation was booked to the last place.

When I then returned from Colombia in 1972 after another two years abroad the situation in Sweden seemed to have changed again. Now the main concern seemed to be ecology and the risks of pollution. Everybody seemed to know a lot about bio-dynamic cultivation and health food. Devotees moved away from the cities into the countryside with the intention of growing their own food and to live a simple and healthy life close to nature. This was all called 'the green wave' (*gröna vågen*) in Sweden. Another wave, a wave of occultism, was also easy to notice.

By that time a lot of literature on 'counter culture' had emerged, mainly from the USA. The concept of 'counter culture' is not widely known in Sweden, nor is the Swedish equivalent '*motkultur*'. In my research I have found almost nothing written on 'counter culture' in Sweden or in Scandinavia, though similar phenomena obviously exist or existed here as well as in other industrialized countries. As I got interested in these phenomena I felt it was important to first find out the conceptual and empirical status of the term 'counter culture' and see if it was a scientifically fruitful concept. Finally, I wished to find out if it would be possible to do empirical research on the phenomenon labelled 'counter culture' today.

A NEW PHENOMENON IN THE SIXTIES

In the mid-sixties remarkable events took place, especially among the the youth in the big university towns of the Western industrialized nations. The most visible outcomes of the events were the radical political activities, deviant life-styles of long hair, loose clothing, an attraction to the irrational with a disdain for the fruit of systematic ambitions. The prelude to these emerging phenomena could be traced back as far as the middle of the nineteenth century in the shape of different subcultures. Anti-rationalist elements within society were nothing new. What made the incidents in the sixties seem like a *new* phenomenon was the fact that the radical rejection of science and technological values appeared so close to the center of society, rather than at the negligible margin. It was middle class youth who were conducting this politics of consciousness, and it all appeared in a relatively large scale in many places of the Western world at about the same time.

REVIEW OF THE USE OF THE CONCEPT OF COUNTER CULTURE

A phenomenon regarded as something new may need a new concept. Already in the end of the sixties articles and books were published which described the events among the youth of the mid-sixties and gave them different labels.

As far as I have found, the first one to introduce the concept of 'counter culture' was Roszak in 1968. What he aimed at was mainly two varieties of youthful dissent. On one side he pointed out 'the mind-blown bohemianism of beats and hippies', and on the other side 'the hard-headed political activism of the student New Left' (Roszak, 1968: 56). At first glance these two manifestations could be regarded as so completely distinct and independent that the only thing they had in common was their appearance at about the same time. As that would have been too much of a coincidence Roszak recognized them as varieties of only *one* phenomenon and eagerly pointed out uniting characteristics. The underlying unity of the counter-cultural variety then was, according to Roszak, the effort of the beat-hip bohemianism to work out the personality structure and total life-style that follow from New Left criticism. When for instance the New Left calls for peace and offers a 'heavy' analysis of what is what in Vietnam, the hippie quickly translates all this into 'shantih', the peace that passes all understanding, and fills in the psychic dimension of the ideal (ibid., p. 66).

The reason for Roszak to give the phenomenon the all-embracing label of 'counter culture' was that he saw as one uniting characteristic that it was all 'counter' to the 'technocracy':

> It will be enough to define the technocracy as that society in which those who govern justify themselves by appeal to technical experts who, in turn, justify themselves by appeal to scientific forms of knowledge. And beyond the authority of science, there is no appeal. (Ibid., p. 8)

Also he saw it as a cultural phenomenon:

> What makes the youthful disaffiliation of our time a cultural phenomenon, rather than merely a political movement, is the fact that it strikes beyond ideology to the level of consciousness, seeking to transform our deepest sense of the self, the other, the environment. (Ibid., p. 49)

In contrast to Roszak other early writers on the events of the mid-sixties clearly separated the two manifestations. For instance Keen published a short article in 1969 where he separates the 'hard' and the 'soft' revolution. The hard revolution he describes as 'explosive and political, primarily concerned with redistribution of political power and committed to a strategy of direct confrontation'. The soft revolution is 'implosive and religious primarily concerned with the alternation of consciousness, with erotic and mystic experience and with the re-sacralization of intimate relationships'. Keen further points out that the soft revolution is diffuse and without organizational manifestations, but its visible outposts are the 'growth centers' (Keen, 1969: 1667).

Another early writer on the topic, Reich (1970), mainly describes the non-activist variety of the counter culture and calls it 'Consciousness III'. Consciousness III is liberation 'from automatic acceptance of the imperatives of society and the false consciousness which society imposes' (Reich, 1970: 190). As far as I have understood, the Consciousness III concept as described by Reich, closely corresponds to Roszak's counter culture except that the radical New Left strategy is excluded from Consciousness III.

Among competing labels of the events in the sixties, it seems that 'counter culture' is the one most frequently adopted at least in American literature. Not all include both manifestations mentioned above though. For instance Flacks in 1971 makes a distinction between 'the movement' by which he refers to the student revolt and political activity at the university campus, and 'the counter culture', which he describes as 'a definite challenge to the values and norms that are officially proclaimed and institutionalized in the larger society' (Flacks, 1971: 17). The only thing they had in common according to Flacks was their emergence from intellectual youth as expressions of a generational revolt. And, as he puts it, certain tension within the youth culture persisted between 'politicoes' and 'hippies', although the radicalization of the latter and the hair of the former were evidently growing (ibid., p. 87).

Curle in 1972 made a distinction between 'mystics' and 'militants'.

The militants tend to be interested in the reshaping of economic and political institutions. The mystics are concerned rather with interpersonal structures which depend directly on the nature of the individuals concerned. According to him the counter-culture builders belong to the mystics though many of them are what Curle calls 'failed militants'. By 'failed militants', Curle means people who have made serious efforts at activism, but who have come to believe that nothing remains except a mystical approach.

According to Curle the counter culture is an approach to living quite different from, though not necessarily in open conflict with, current conventions. To Curle it is all a question of degree of awareness. The militants have a 'higher natural' or 'self-conscious awareness' according to his classification, while for instance the counter-culture builders have what he calls a 'higher supraliminal awareness'. If there is no shift to supraliminal awareness there is a growing compulsion to do something about society, to be involved. The shift to supraliminal awareness leads on the other hand to a compulsion to do something *about oneself* (Curle, 1972: 67).

About the counter-culture builders he further says that they live together in communes, earning their living, or in some sense literally making it, with a minimum of compromise with the world of the market. They run their community affairs as well as their interpersonal relationships on principles that are most seriously intended to preserve and increase individual autonomy and to promote the fullest realization of the human spirit. The counter culture, as manifested in these attempts to create new social forms based on higher awareness of a supraliminal type, blends the objective and the subjective (ibid., p. 67-68). Curle mentions what I find important, that many advocates of the counter culture are attempting so far as this is possible, to exemplify their ideals.

In 1973 Berger, Berger and Kellner make another classification of the counter culture. They mention two movements counter-defining themselves as against functional rationality. One is the ecology movement, which both expresses and legitimates the profoundly anti-technological, 'naturalistic' animus of the counter culture. At least in the more radical branches of the movement, modern urban, techno-logical society is viewed as a planetary cancer. The other movement mentioned is the resurgence of occultism, magic and mystical religion. This has taken a bewildering variety of forms but whatever may divide these movements and groups, they have in common their profound opposition to the definitions of reality that pertain to functional rationality. By 'functional rationality' the authors mean 'the imposition of rational controls over the material universe, over social relations and finally over the self'. The youth culture is in rebellion against all three forms. Feeling is given priority over rational thought (Berger, Berger & Kellner, 1973: 181-183).

As a concluding remark a change in use of the concept 'counter culture' could be noticed during the period 1968-1973. When the concept originally was founded it included two manifestations, the political activism of the students and the bohemianism of hippies and beats. Later the political activism was excluded from the concept, and the emphasis was laid on attempts to build as alternative culture with self-actualization, ecology and also occultism as main concerns. Still the phenomenon was regarded as something rebelling against mainstream society.

EXPLAINING THE EMERGENCE OF
COUNTER CULTURE

Having recognized a phenomenon as new, attempts are made to explain how it could take place. What circumstances caused the counter culture of the sixties or what made it possible? This question has been answered from different angles.

What caused the phenomenon to be regarded as a *new* one was that middle class youth in the most affluent countries of the world by their own initiative conducted the protests and experiments with different life-styles. This presupposes among other things a middle class youth available to do this. 'Youth' could be defined as the stage of life coming after adolescence but prior to full-time participation in work roles. Youth as a stage of life is a rather new phenomenon as such. Not long ago the individual had to meet the demands of an adult 'straight' after childhood. As the need for universal discipline, literacy, specialized training widened in industrialized societies the stage of youth was prolonged. The number of persons in such societies who can be defined as youth has been increasing steadily.

Another point is that the majority of the students of the sixties were brought up after the Second World War. They had benefitted from the particularly permissive child-rearing habits that were a feature of the post-war society. In short the ambitions of the older generation were to give their children economic security, good education and a happy childhood and youth, with a margin of irresponsibility. The parents wished their children to be able to afford to enjoy life in ways that previous generations could not. After the war the number of children who obtained these opportunities quickly increased.

Having sketched the background of the students in the mid-sixties the emergence of counter culture could be explained in different ways. One way is to start from a psychological level. I just wish to mention Maslow's theory which states that there are five levels of individual needs: physiological, safety, love, esteem and self-actualization, and as one becomes satisfied, another takes over. (Maslow, 1970: 35-47). One way of explaining the emergence of the counter culture in the sixties then is to point out that the two first levels in this Maslowian hierarchy of needs were well satisfied. Most students could take safety and economic security for granted. Higher needs then emerged and the counter culture was one way of satisfying them. The movements reflected a broad shift in emphasis from economic issues to life-style issues.

Another way of explanation is to start out from societal needs. Prolonged education and economic security for the children were certainly the desired goals of ambitious parents, but in addition there were other trends emanating from child-rearing practices and changes in the consumption styles of contemporary capitalism. The permissiveness of post-war child-rearing with the idea of not postponing the satisfaction of any desires might have become so popular because of changes in the spirit of capitalism, from the emphasis on saving to that on spending, from self-frustration as a means for economic success to consumption as the basis for an ever-widening market. Youth was expected to become good consumers, but to stay out of production, not to compete on the labour market. As Christie concludes youth had become useless as members of the labour force in contemporary society, and then education was prolonged to keep the youth occupied somewhere (Christie, 1971).

In the mid-sixties the schools and universities were not yet prepared for this increasing demand for education and university towns were overcrowded with students. Musgrove has drawn attention to the possible effects of 'overcrowding' in a historical-comparative study. He found that the core characteristic of all counter cultures appeared to be irrationality, and its invariable accompaniment was technological advance, economic development, but above all population growth (Musgrove, 1974: 14).

> Population movement and growth appeared to underlie and promote great
> periods of economic development and opportunity; and together they pro-
> mote social dislocation and uncertainty, a sense of 'normlessness' and anomie.
> Traditional social rules and expectations are questioned, or lose their useful-
> ness. (Ibid., p. 64.)

The way Flacks puts it the revolt of the youth was a *symptom* of a
fundamental sociocultural crisis. The cultural crisis was experienced as
a crisis of identity — an inability to define the meaning of one's life
and to accept the meanings and models of adulthood offered by parents
and other elders (Flacks, 1971: 6). In general terms, the crisis involved
a substantial conflict between the emergent technological potentialities
of a society to establish social order and cultural system. The young
became increasingly aware of the enormous gap between their acquired
ideals and prevailing social and political conditions (ibid., p. 13).
Flacks points out three changes causing this gap: the first was the
change from individual entrepreneurship to large corporate organizations, the second from free market competition to bureaucratic
co-ordination and planning and the third from accumulation and scarcity to consumption and affluence (ibid., p. 21). In this situation
increasing numbers of youth regarded the culture as incoherent and
the future as undesirable and chaotic. Cultural break-down has reached
the point of no return when the process of socialization no longer
provides the new generation with coherent reasons to be enthusiastic
about becoming adult members of the society (ibid., p. 22).

Reich argued that the new consciousness is the product of two interacting forces:

> the promise of life that is made to young Americans by all of our affluence,
> technology, liberation and ideals, and the threat to that promise posed by
> everything from neon ugliness and boring jobs to the Vietnam War and the
> shadow of nuclear holocaust. Neither the promise nor the threat is the cause
> by itself, but the two together have done it. (Reich, 1970: 184)

Reich used the concept of Consciousness III instead of counter culture.
This choice of concept was meant to point out the contrast to Consciousness I, which was capitalistic, individualistic and puritan, and
Consciousness II which was said to have created the Corporate State
phenomenon of the post-Second World War years.

As counter culture originally was recognized as a phenomenon
opposed to the dominant culture, the final starting-point for explaining
the emergence of the phenomenon then was to specify what main

characteristics of society were rejected by the youth. As already mentioned the main target of the counter culture according to Roszak was 'the technocracy', 'the regime of the experts'. An expert is then defined as 'the one to whom we turn because he is in control of reliable knowledge, one who really knows what is what, because he cultivates an objective consciousness' (Roszak, 1968: 208). Since science is the dominant authority in producing reliable knowledge the scientific explication of reality was questioned and objective consciousness regarded as a myth. When the New Left rebelled against technocratic manipulation the beatniks and hippies pressed the critique even further in their instinctive fascination with magic and ritual, tribal lore and psychedelic experiences. Many students were hungry for new cultural perspectives.

Although counter culture was a reaction to some undesirable consequences of rapid economic and technological development, this development could also serve as explanations for the emergence of counter culture. First, the enormous development of mass media like TV, film, wireless, newspapers, magazines and paperbacks made possible a great flow of information between different countries and classes of the society. Second, the vastly increased speeds and extensions of communication available to youth with more money in their purses than ever before, made it possible for them to move around the world and get in touch with different cultures.

In short, counter culture was regarded as a symptom of a cultural crisis. It was a reaction to technocracy and to the threats of a future society. At the same time technological development, and a prolonged youth with economic security made counter culture a viable enterprise.

EARLY PREDICTIONS OF SOCIETAL
EFFECTS OF COUNTER CULTURE

As counter culture from its very beginning was contrasted and related to the societal development, soon attitudes, hopes and fears implied by counter culture lead to predictions about possible effects of counter culture back on the dominant society. From a consideration of the causes of counter culture we may thus turn to its effects on society.

One prediction made by many of the early writers was that the phenomenon was not likely to pass over in a few years like teenage expressions of generational conflicts known as 'youth cultures'. If the events of the sixties were to be understood as a *symptom* of a fundamental sociocultural crisis it would be the young who would react first as they are more sensitive and future-oriented and, as Roszak puts it, 'because they act against a background of nearly pathological passivity on the part of the adult generation' (Roszak, 1968: 22). But as hopes were tied to these events it was not only regarded as a symptom, but also as a possible solution, 'the saving vision our endangered civilization required' (ibid., p. 1).

It makes sense to look at the counter culture also in terms of its 'function' of keeping many individuals out of the labour market. One can also try to understand counter culture as an escapist response to the frustrations of political conflict. Some of the early writers paradoxically took a very optimistic view of counter culture precisely for such reasons.

According to Roszak technocracy has grown without resistance primarily because its potential critics try to cope with the antiquated categories of the established political system, which only result in quarrels between technocrats or between factions who subscribe to technocratic values. But according to Roszak technocracy is not generally perceived as a political phenomenon. It holds the place, rather, of a grand cultural imperative which is beyond question, beyond discussion (ibid., p. 9). The great task that Roszak believes counter culture will accomplish is to alter the total cultural context within which our daily politics take place (ibid., p. 5f).

As regards the function of relieving the labour-market and the self-chosen poverty of the counter culture life-style, I will first refer to Christie. He regards the counter culture as an answer to the future needs of society. The counter-culture builders try new solutions and forms of common life which can prove useful when society has yet taken another step toward technocracy and automatization. When still less jobs are available for ordinary people and there is still less fresh air and soil available it might prove a good thing that long-haired, barefoot young people have tried to work out some kind of balance between distress and abundance, between bondage and uselessness (Christie, 1971: 41).

Reich's thesis is that the more Consciousness III spreads, the more difficult will it be to sell things to satisfy anything but 'real' needs, which means that the consumer will regain power over what is pro-duced. Furthermore, society can no longer get anyone to work except for 'real' satisfactions which means that the status system is at an end, and people within organizations will regain power over the organizations and structures of society. The new consciousness seeks to transcend science and technology, to restore them to their proper place as tools of man rather than as determinants of man's existence (Reich, 1970: 293). The most important *means* of conversion is and will continue to be, simply living one's own life according to one's own needs (ibid., p. 247).

Flack points out conditions for the counter culture to have any such effect. 'A counter culture is not a cultural alternative until it can embody a way of life that will be appropriate to an individual throughout his lifecycle' (Flacks, 1971: 105). But his analysis is optimistic: 'A society in deep historical crisis has reached the point where fundamental social and cultural transformation is necessary. That society, quite unwittingly has produced a generation capable of making that transformation' (ibid., p. 131).

Clearly many of the early writers made very optimistic predictions. The phenomenon was recognized as a counter culture in the sense that it would develop an alternative culture and society based on a new consciousness and shaped to real human needs. For these reasons it was regarded as superior and capable of transforming the existing dominant society without violence or actual confrontations.

SOME CHANGES IN
DOMINANT CULTURE AND
SOCIETY IN SWEDEN
SINCE THE SIXTIES

It is hard to discover any really profound changes in society since the sixties but still I will mention a few aspects of change in order to show that counter culture hardly could be observed as a distinct counter-phenomenon today but rather as an attribute partly absorbed by dominant society and culture.

The sixties was a period of affluence but since the early seventies there has been a long period of economic recession in the industrialized world. Possibilities for individual increases in consumption have been weakened. The unemployment rate has increased though it has been kept low by administrative solutions like retraining schemes, early retirement, etc.

But at the same time attitudes toward work and consumption

have changed. A recent sample survey reported by Ahrne (1976) presents findings indicating that an overwhelming majority of full-time employees in Sweden consider a transfer of national income to solving environmental and social problems equal or more important than a pay rise or an increase of private consumption. Another point is that workers do not accept the ideal of leisure time consumption as a compensation for the tediousness and strain of work (Korpi, 1972). Work itself must be considered meaningful, and integrated, with any consideration of the quality of life.

Furthermore, the threats felt by the young in the sixties would seem to be recognized by a considerable part of the society today (Himmelstrand et al., 1981: chapter 14). After 44 years of social democratic (SAP) government in Sweden, there was a shift in the last election in 1976 because of the policy of nuclear power. The Centre Party had promised to prohibit the expansion of this energy supply until all safety risks were eliminated. Somewhat more than half of those voters who shifted their allegiance from SAP to the Centre Party are likely to have done so because of the negative attitude toward nuclear power. Other issues were also involved, like negative attitudes to state bureaucracy (Pettersson, 1977: 214 ff.). The leader of the party is a farmer and maybe an increasing attitude of 'nature-worship' was an additional factor in the Center Party gaining more votes.

The interest in mysticism and oriental religions has widened. The most evident sign of this interest is the increased output of literature, and the emergence of bookstores that specialize in this area. Many of the oriental classics are translated into English — and even Swedish. Along with the demand for books of this type we find an increasing demand for spiritual teachers and gurus. The concern about personal health, mental as well as physical, and the possibilities of preventing diseases on one's own instead of relying on medical experts has also increased. This could be noticed for instance in the growing demand for health food, fasting cures, and also courses in yoga, meditation and new types of therapy.

The long hair and simple loose clothing of the hippies became a fashion. In 1960 behaviour and clothing was age-graded. Today age can hardly be judged by clothes, nor behaviour.

What was regarded as new and sensational in the sixties has been spread and embraced by an increasing number of 'ordinary' people in society. However, technocratic development is still dominant.

CHANGES IN THE PHENOMENON
OF COUNTER CULTURE

In a previous section I followed up the use of the concept counter culture in publications from 1968 till 1973. The changing content of the concept might have corresponded to changes in the phenomenon observed. Counter culture never was regarded as a disciplined static or stable phenomenon. On the contrary its essence was constant change, an openness to any and all experience to find ways for constant growth of each individual.

Out of the two manifestations originally included in the concept of counter culture, the activist variety declined after a few years. Already Flacks (1971) points out an observable withdrawal of many from active political participation, a decline in dramatic protest activity, and a shift away from action to introspection, self-expression and privatism. According to Flacks the era of *campus* confrontation and *student* rebellion ended not because it failed, but because it reached the limit of its possibilities. But they did succeed, he maintains, in transforming the consciousness of an entire generation (Flacks, 1971: 101).

The so-called mystic variety has developed in a slightly different way. The general inclination for oriental religions and practices in pursuing an expansion of consciousness has become more and more specific. Early practitioners of this variety of consciousness were mainly characterized by their openness rather than by any direct opposition to the dominant culture. They just wanted to 'do their own thing', and tried different ways of building alternative communes corresponding to the new consciousness or 'supraliminal awareness' as Curle puts it.

Already in 1975 Musgrove made the remark that the communes were changing, becoming more organized and engaged in more purposeful activity than formerly. They also had established good relationships with the local communities: they interacted with them, influenced them, and were increasingly supported by them. According to Musgrove the relationship between culture and counter culture was dialectical, but still not standing as polar opposites. As he puts it, the counter culture changed and 'straight' society with it (Musgrove, 1974: 202-206).

In a later publication, from 1977, Musgrove talks about counter culture as something past, as belonging to the sixties and early seventies. In this book he presents an inquiry into the 'transformation of consciousness'. The main question for which he sought an answer was:

Can adults really change? For this purpose he studied seven margina-
lised groups in England, among them a Sufi commune and Hare Krishna
devotees. In both these communes he found obvious continuities with
the earlier counter culture, but also sharp discontinuities and reversals.
Already the earlier counter culture had been influenced by Eastern
religions. But in the sixties, counter culture emphasized personal freedom and rejected all hierarchies. What Musgrove found as remarkable
for the two religious communes mentioned was the personal discipline
they enjoined and the ordered routines of their days.

Musgrove concludes that new identities were being fashioned not
only in relation to 'straight' orthodox secularized society, but in
relation to earlier phases of the counter culture itself (Musgrove, 1977:
170). The hippie counter culture seemed to have been a prelude to
entering the commune. If the counter culture was examined as self-
initiated desocialization and disengagement from ordinary institutions,
it could be considered as a preceding phase of resocialization in a
commune involving a different cultural context. Instead of 'doing your
own thing' the life in the communes mentioned involved a closely
rule-regulated life (ibid., p. 212).

Hare Krishna and Sufi are only two examples of the kind of groups
that exist and get an increasing number of devotees today, a good
decade after the counter culture came into being both as a phenomenon
and as a concept. One could conclude, that the mystic variety of
counter culture did not decline or die out, but it changed and developed into something else which no longer fits the term 'counter
culture'.

TOWARDS A CLARIFICATION OF THE CONCEPT
OF COUNTER CULTURE TODAY

It could be argued that counter culture was not merely a label, but an
early interpretation of a rather divergent and disorganized phenomenon
that caught attention in the mid-sixties. In view of what has been said
about the changes of this phenomenon one might ask if counter culture
is or ever was a scientifically fruitful concept.

Bash (1972) in particular has carefully discussed problems relating
to the concept of counter culture. Scientific concepts are usefully
ordered into either empirical or theoretical concepts. If a concept
is to be used as a tool for empirical study, a definition is needed to

distinguish what is to be ignored and what is to be included as a source of relevant data. Bash did not find a clear-cut, generally acknowledged definition though, either by looking for a minimum of necessary elements, or by exclusion. In vain, Bash also points out, do we look to the phenomenal world for help in arriving at conceptual clarity or definitional exactitude. Some groups included in counter culture are in no sense counter to anything at all.

Bash argues that counter culture is not an empirical concept, that it is not an observational term, but rather an interpretive construction of an observable, 'guided by some implicit and obscured pseudo-explanatory presumption' (Bash, 1972: 11). Nor is counter culture a theoretical concept as it has not been deduced logically from prior theory. To either construct new theory or to graft existing sociological theory on top of *social* (rather than sociological) concepts he considers foolish (ibid., p. 12).

> Recalling that the concept 'counterculture' is neither a theoretical nor an empirical term, but rather an interpretation of an observable, we are led to suggest that where the notion of 'counterculture' is invoked, the 'discovery' of its existential reality becomes a foregone conclusion....one analyst's 'counterculture' may be another's 'contraculture', or 'alternative life-style', or 'subculture', or 'deviant adaptation', or 'utopian community', or 'subterranean tradition', or 'adolescent rebellion/identity search', or 'social movement', or, for that matter, 'indicator of cultural change'. To venture the concept is to imply an explanatory frame which informs it, just as it is to suggest an empirical base to ground it. (Ibid., p. 27f.)

Whether or not the concept of counter culture ever *was* a suitable interpretive or a scientifically fruitful concept, I would say, it is not any longer as the phenomenon has changed into something else. As 'being counter' no longer could be regarded as a main characteristic we need a new label. Is there any? We must avoid the same mistake again, that is choosing a concept that could sound like a sociological interpretation. Roszak himself published a book in 1975 where he made a long list of the religions, therapies, wild sciences etc. flourishing in Western countries today.

> We have no word in our language to name it; we would have to concoct some impossible linguistic hybrid: 'psycho-mystico-parascientific-spiritual-therapeutic....'

Then he suggests:

> Having no better term to corral so wide and wild a range of pursuits, let us borrow an allusion from the popular mythology of the day and call the scene as a whole, with all its paths both straight and twisted, the 'Aquarian frontier', the subtle landscape and open field of contemporary spiritual adventure. (Roszak, 1976: 30)

What we need is a new label including the varieties of today; and 'Aquarian Frontier' certainly is a label but a sociological or scientific concept it is not. 'The New Age' is another term used, but both of these suggest astrological interpretations, and there are groups inside the border who reject astrology as well as they reject any other external dependence for the development of the self. Another overall term, also used by people belonging to the groups in question, is 'the Human Potential Movement'. I am not yet sure what problems this term will solve, but in my understanding this says fairly well what it is all about, at least today, and maybe ever since the sixties. The expression was coined in the growth centres which Keen in 1969 characterized as the visible outposts of what he called 'the Soft Revolution'. Whether the phenomenon can be called a revolution at all depends on whether it succeeds in establishing a new social organization. This can hardly be predicted but at least it could be regarded as a movement elaborating human potentials.

CONCLUSION AND DISCUSSION

The main conclusion to be made from this paper is that counter culture could not be studied empirically today as a distinct phenomenon. The most simple reason is that the phenomenon labelled as 'counter culture' belongs to the past, the sixties and early seventies.

The dawn and dusk of counter culture could be explained firstly by the fact that the use of this term has changed over time, secondly by internal changes in the phenomenon itself, and thirdly by some changes in the dominant society to which counter culture was contrasted.

First, the conceptual status of the term counter culture has changed. The concept of counter culture was founded when the phenomenon was recognized as one of protest, of rebellion against the technocracy. The student revolt and the experiments with different life-styles were both regarded as means of demonstrating deep dissatisfaction with all sorts of authority. A bit later the political student movement was excluded from the connotation of the concept, and emphasis in description was laid on attempts at attaining higher levels of awareness, including building alternative communes with ecological concern.

The concept of counter culture was not simply a label, however, but also implied certain optimistic expectations. By many writers the events were regarded as not only a symptom of a cultural crisis, but also as a possible solution to such a crisis. The adoption of this concept implied a hope that these counter movements would balance the technocratic development and even transform dominant society.

Second, the phenomenon originally labelled and interpreted as counter culture has changed. The main internal change observed was a decline of political actions at the university campuses; while in contrast the mystic variety, the practice of certain oriental religions and the articulation of human potentials were getting more organized and disciplined. Many previous activists or 'failed militants' shifted over to introspection, self-expression and privatism.

In retrospect one could even argue that it would have been more fruitful to keep the two varieties separate as two distinct phenomena, and perhaps not recognize the mystic as political or 'counter' at all. For instance simple anti-consumption life-style may in fact never have been a genuine act of protest or solidarity with the poor. Renunciation of mass-consumption patterns is an important technique of gaining 'expanded consciousness'. As the mystic variety survived the main orientation more clearly turned out to emphasize self-development rather than attempts at transforming society. The confusion between the two varieties may have been caused by the fact that they originally caught attention at about the same time.

Third, some changes in the dominant society to which counter culture was contrasted could be noticed. Some values and norms originally regarded as typical for counter culture were embraced by 'ordinary' people. For instance, attitudes toward work and consumption have changed.

It would be too much to conclude that these changes in attitudes were effects of counter culture alone. One could as well argue that the time was ripe to react against technocratic development and that the youth just happened to be more sensitive and had the opportunity to react first.

A final change to be mentioned is the good relations that seem to have been successively established between counter culture and mainstream society. The generally changed attitudes and the increasing demands for things like health food and courses in meditation could be seen as a support for the conjecture that the mystic and ecological variety have survived and become more organized.

These changes in counter culture and in society could be seen as the dusk of counter culture as such. What caught attention in the sixties, and was regarded as a counter culture can no longer be seen as a distinct phenomenon contradicting mainstream society. If there still is a separable phenomenon, it has developed into something else. The intentions are not mainly to create an alternative culture or transform society but simply to increase personal health by elaborating human potentials. For these reasons the concept of counter culture does not fit any longer — if it ever did.

A POSTSCRIPT

This paper was written in early 1978. Since then I have had an opportunity to study the phenomena of 'counter culture' or 'alternative life-styles', to use these imprecise labels once more, in more depth empirically in the Swedish context. As regards the spiritualist branch of this movement I think that my earlier conclusions still hold. Their counter-character is now on the whole even less pronounced than before. But the ecological branch of the movement, as represented by a number of communes and an even larger number of smaller collectivities practicing their own alternative life-style, is growing in fact, and now becoming more well-organized in their resistance to the dominant tendencies of capitalist technological and economic growth. Their beliefs not only shape their daily lives. They express their philosophy by participating in demonstrations against the use of poisonous defoliants in commercialized forestry, the development of nuclear power, the destruction of old but renewable urban living-quarters etc. The fact that the philosophy of this counter-movement is also to some extent emerging in political movements operating within established society not only in Sweden but in many other countries — *Die Grünen* in West Germany and the party of the ecologists in France are cases in point — does not gainsay the fact that those who have moved outside the mainstream of contemporary technological and economic development constitute a counter-movement. And in critical situations they are treated as such, for instance through massive police mobilization to restrain or counteract their activities.

Therefore I must amend the conclusions of my original paper on one point. Even if the concept of counter culture no longer fits reality with regard to those movements or groups who seemingly opted out from mainstream society to care for their own spiritual development, it certainly still fits the reality of the communes and collectivities on which I have been doing research in recent years. To them mainstream society is moving toward a dark and crisis-ridden future. But spontaneously counter-movements have emerged in many places at the same time which increasingly are working together to create a different future breaking the barriers of the past. Whatever you think of this movement it is certainly counter-cultural, and it is not fading away.

REFERENCES

AHRNE, G. (1976) *Den gyllene kedjan. Studier i arbete och konsumtion.* Stockholm: Prisma.

BASH, H. H. (1972) 'Toward a Sociological Theory of Counter Culture'. Paper presented at 67th annual meeting of the ASA, New Orelans.

BERGER, P. L., B. BERGER, & H. KELLNER (1973) *The Homeless Mind.* Harmondsworth: Pelican Books, 1977.

CHRISTIE, N. (1971) *Om skolan inte fanns.* Stockholm: Wahlström & Widstrand.

CURLE, A. (1972) *Mystics and Militants. A Study of Awareness Identity, and Social Action.* London: Tavistock Publications.

FLACKS, R. (1971) *Youth and Social Change.* Chicago: Markham Publishing Company.

HIMMELSTRAND, U., G. AHRNE, L. LUNDBERG, and L. LUNDBERG (1981) *Beyond Welfare Capitalism, Issues, Actors and Forces in Societal Change.* London: Heinemann.

KEEN, S. (1969) 'The "Soft" Revolution Explored', *Christian Century* 85: 1667-1669.

KORPI, W. (1972) *Varför strejkar arbetarna?* Stockholm: Tidens förlag.

MASLOW, A. H. (1970) *Motivation and Personality.* New York: Harper & Row.

MUSGROVE, F. (1974) *Ecstasy & Holiness. Counter Culture and the Open Society.* London: Methuen.

— — (1977) *Margins of the Mind.* London: Methuen.

PETTERSSON, O. (1977) *Valundersökningar. Väljarna och valet 1976.* Stockholm: Liber Förlag/Allmanna Förlaget.

REICH, C. (1970) *The Greening of America.* London: Penguin Books.

ROSZAK, T. (1968) *The Making of a Counter Culture. Reflections on the Technocratic Society & Its Youthful Opposition.* London: Faber and Faber, 1973.

III
DISCUSSION

10

SPONTANEITY VERSUS PLANNING IN SOCIAL DEVELOPMENT

Tatiana I. Zaslavskaya
Soviet Academy of Sciences

1. INTRODUCTORY NOTES

The topic of this discussion is Planning versus Spontaneity — their relationships, functions and interaction in social development. Professors Cherns and Sztompka, Dr. Akeredolu-Ale and others have put forward interesting approaches to these problems. The most important are the following four: First, changes in the role of planning and spontaneity in the historical process of human development. Second, the dependence of social aspects of planning on the concrete historical conditions under which it is implemented, above all, on class structure, on the arrangement of social forces, class and group goals. Third, problems of democracy in planning, relations between planners and those 'being planned', participation of vast masses of people in developing and implementing plans. Fourth, the relationship between centralized planning of social development, on the one hand, and personal liberty, on the other.

I am going to consider these problems from the Marxist standpoint, but first I will try to define the basic notions of the discussion, i.e. Planning and Spontaneity, since our analysis has shown that different authors understand them differently. Professor Sztompka's paper is rather interesting methodologically. It gives a deep insight into possibilities offered by different theories of social development in explaining

Planning versus Spontaneity dialectically. But his approach is philosophical and not sociological. Indeed, Sztompka understands any goal-directed intervention of a social subject into events or processes as 'planning'. Spontaneity is regarded however not as an alternative mechanism of social development but as a mere result of poor planning. Thereby the relationship between planning and spontaneity is basically reduced to that of plan feasibility and degree of implementation, thus stripping it of its social meaning.

As regards other authors, they seem to disregard planning or give it a too broad interpretation. For instance, Professor Denitch concentrates on the relationship between the spontaneous activity of masses and the organized struggle of a revolutionary party for power. He disregards the topic of 'planning'. Elizabeth Jelin does not discriminate 'planning' from current governmental policy which is, e.g. regulation of prices, employment control etc. Since these are the only elements of central planning under capitalism, her approach is understandable.

My task is to substantiate my own understanding of planning and spontaneity not because it is 'better' but in order to make easier the subsequent analysis of problems. By planning I mean institutionalized developmental goals, in working out strategies for their achievement, concentrating and allocating necessary resources among task executives as well as for the control over plan implementation. That part of development which is beyond the sphere of governmental plans I understand as spontaneous.

The activity of opposing revolutionary parties is not social *planning* though its impact on human development may be often greater than that of current governmental planning. It should be noted here the essential difference of social content in the dichotomies 'spontaneity-planning' and 'spontaneity-organization'. However, the lack of central planning in capitalist countries justifies the discussion of the latter dichotomy as well since 'organization' contains at least *elements* of planning.

2. THE CHANGING ROLE OF PLANNING AND SPONTANEITY IN THE HISTORICAL PROCESS OF HUMAN DEVELOPMENT

Professor Denitch in his paper implicitly raises a question: which is better, planning or spontaneity? But, as was correctly noted by Dr. Akeredolu-Ale, the actual interest lies rather in the analysis of their changing role in processes of human social development taking place before our eyes rather than in subjective opinions on what is 'good' and what is 'bad'.

Planning and Spontaneity can in principle be interpreted as alternative patterns of social development. The 'spontaneous' pattern is associated with automatic mechanisms. Under a certain level of productive forces — for instance in early capitalism — the action of these mechanisms provides for the economic and social advance of society. Directions and rates of this advance, however, do not depend on societal goals.

The 'planning' pattern differs from the spontaneous by conscious definition of goals, by substantiated choice of developmental strategies, concentration and optimal allocation of resources. On the strength of this, the total efficiency of planned development is higher than that of the spontaneous — at least in theory if we assume adequate plan implementation.

However, planning requires certain economic preconditions for societal development, above all, concentration of resources necessary for development in the hands of the society. For this reason, planning can become the principal developmental pattern only after the advent of socialism.

Spontaneous mechanisms of development typical of capitalist societies are adequate only up to a particular level of productive forces. Tremendous growth of production conditioned by current technological change undercuts the spontaneous mechanisms of adjustment in the sense that they cease to cope with social problems.

Under these conditions capitalist governments intensify their intervention into the economy, primarily by artificially raising spontaneously-formed market demand, as suggested by Keynes and others. But as the base of the economic system, i.e. private ownership of producer goods, is intact, the actual result of governmental planning in capitalist countries is not resolution but instead aggravation of social contradictions: inflation, unemployment, tight food situation, intensification of social differentiation and of different forms of class struggle.

Especially conspicuous become the weaknesses of spontaneous mechanisms if taken from the perspective of contemporary global problems. Over the last third of the twentieth century mankind, for the first time in its history, started an overexploitation of nature, the outcome of which will determine the whole of our future. Rapid destruction of natural environment, spread of famine, and the energy crisis make the earth's inhabitants realize that the play of spontaneous forces becomes dangerous and threatens the very existence of mankind. The necessity to plan social development on both national and planetary levels becomes increasingly clear.

Tentative steps in this direction are being made before our eyes. Large-scale cross-cultural studies aimed at finding out concrete ways for human escape from energetic, ecological and food crises are being made. Developmental alternatives of world social system are examined and compared, global models devised on which to try and test particular strategies for control over this development. Quite recently (summer 1978) an agreement has been reached in Vienna about the organization of a number of European scientific congresses on energy problems which is one concrete step to the implementation of the ideas of the Helsinki agreement.

The social and political importance of these steps is undisputed. Finding an optimal variant, however, and its practical implementation is not the same. Class, political and national contradictions and conflicts forming the picture of the contemporary world are a drag on rational and regular resolution of global problems impeding human development.

3. PLANNING TARGETS AS REFLECTION OF THE GOALS OF CLASSES, LAYERS AND GROUPS

Plans and programs of development devised by governmental bodies most often are presented by their makers as reflections of general national goals. However, in societies consisting of antagonistic classes national goals are often a mere abstraction. The real nature of governmental planning in capitalist societies was vividly shown in the papers of Professors Jomo and Jelin analyzing the experience of Malaysia and several Latin American societies. These authors very convincingly support Lenin's definition of the capitalist state as a tool of political power of the ruling classes but not by a long shot as a 'superclass national body' whose mission is to provide for social equilibrium and to satisfy the goals of all classes.

However, as is seen from these papers, the specific historical situation in particular societies conditions the class content of developmental targets. Under the pressure of a highly organized working class the bourgeois government is often forced to incorporate into common national programs some of the working people's needs. And the stronger the swing of spontaneous class struggle opposing the governmental control and planning, the more are working people's demands taken into consideration in plans and the more progressive become the plans themselves.

In connection with our concern about the class aspect of planning in a class society, I have a few words to say about Professor Cherns' recommendation to developing countries, i.e. to choose for introduction such (and solely such) technological systems which would ensure both economic efficiency of management and favourable social change, i.e. social advance. It is beyond doubt that contemporary technological systems actually possess both economic and vital social attributes so that the choice of a particular system is at the same time a choice in the technological, economic and social spheres. But the decisive role is played by the forces that underlie (and are allowed to underlie) the choice of concrete technological systems within the given mode of production. In fact such forces are objectively inherent to any economic mode: they are determined by the system of prevailing relations of production rather than by the 'good will' of planners. In particular, under capitalism, the economic interests of the bourgeoisie prevail as a rule over the goals of general national development in the solution of social problems. For this reason, the criterion of social benefit of a particular technology plays a very small part in the actual choice of developmental alternatives.

4. PLANNING OF SOCIAL PROCESSES IN SOCIALIST SOCIETIES

In socialist societies planning of social processes is a necessity since the economy is planned, and social development is closely associated with the economic sphere. Indeed, the development of a socialist economy is subordinated to social goals, and the process of combining such goals is to be planned. In order that social problems can be solved there is a need for physical and financial resources, and their source is again the economy. And, eventually, a planned socialist economy experiences a strong counter-impact of social processes which still more intensifies the need for their being planned.

Major aims of social planning in socialist societies are the growth of people's well-being, improvement of style and quality of life, reduction of social differentiation between classes and groups, further improvement of social relations, and, finally, the creation of necessary conditions for many-sided personal development offered to every citizen. All these goals are of a general nature reflecting basically general national goals. At the same time, it would be misleading to think that social classes and groups in socialist societies have no specific goals of their own. In fact the holders of such interests are classes of workers and peasants, urban and rural populations inhabitants of different regions. manual and non-manual workers, individuals with different level and source of incomes. How, then, are these heterogeneous goals balanced in plans of social development?

In a shorter time perspective such a task is not posed at all since concentration of public resources in limited crucial directions is more effective than even but slow progress in all directions simultaneously. According to this, the implementation of social targets of every five-year plan is more favourable for some groups of population and less favourable for others. For example, during the ninth five-year period (1971-1975) in the USSR, old age pensions, disablement allowances, stipends of students and wages of low paid workers in material production sphere were raised. During the tenth five-year period (1976-1980) pay of the workers in the tertiary sector of economy was raised. Apart from this, during these periods (1971-1980) living conditions of rural population were being improved at a higher rate than those of the urban.

Why does this strategy not lead to social conflicts? There are at least three reasons. First, social classes and groups forming the structure of socialist societies are not antagonistic to each other. They actively co-operate, communicate, help each other, have common social values and common interests. Second, governmental plans provide for the solution of the most imperative problems, and people quite understand it. Finally, inequality and uneven development tolerated in short-run plans are as a rule adjusted and brought to balance in a longer run.

With respect to the long run, it is extremely important to satisfy equally interests and goals of different classes and groups. And admittedly it is far from easy. Very helpful here are sociological studies permitting us to estimate accurately the degree of satisfaction of social needs among different population groups and to reveal the most urgent long-run problems of social development.

Different social processes are not planned with equal rigidity in the socialist society. Most detailed are plans of processes connected with the public economy, e.g., income level of different groups of population, production and distribution of consumer goods, the construction of housing and consumer facilities, health care, education, trade, consumer services, passenger transport etc.

Far less detailed and less rigid is planning of processes which though connected with public economy are at the same time dependent on individual behaviour too. Such are human migration, labour mobility, educational upgrading, improvement of settlement patterns etc.

Finally, there are such processes which though crucial for society do not appear as objects of directive planning due to their specific nature. Such are, for example, fertility, marriages and divorces, seasonal and daily migration, different leisure behaviours and a multitude of other individual behaviours.

Under partial and non-rigid planning of many social processes it is rather difficult to implement economic plans rigidly. Spontaneous factors occasionally may lead even to failure of plans. It is the case, for instance, when a newly constructed plant fails to recruit the required manpower.

Why, then, do we find that the area of centrally planned social processes is not expanding in socialist societies? The question rests on the connection between planning and control. The point is that particular forms of planning involve appropriate forms of control over the activity of formal organizations and individual behaviour; the forms of this control, however, are not arbitrary but set by the nature of socialist relations.

Centralized planning makes sense with regard to processes directly governed by the state. Their circle is fairly large. Socialist states have various economic, legal and administrative mechanisms enabling them to regulate the activity of plants, service establishments, business and non-business organizations, urban and regional bodies. These mechanisms are, for example, planning rates and proportions of production of different product items, regulation of wholesale and retail prices, proper distribution of scarce resources among regions and branches, establishment of incentives motivating performance and effective industrial engineering.

An important tool of state control is the development and consistent implementation of a certain policy of locating industry and social infrastructure, regulation of settlement forms, organization of education and health facilities. A special role is played by state policy in the field of research and engineering aimed at the quickest possible introduction of technological innovations.

It should be noted that all these mechanisms are more or less neutral to the degree of centralization. The latter depends on what problems are within the competence of top bodies and what are delegated to local bodies and individual organizations. Under a high degree of centralization, plants, for example, receive detailed plans of compulsory production targets for specific items from the top and are nearly altogether devoid of a chance to vary the overall structure of production. An alternative may be planning the total volume of particular groups of products in money terms, whereas the specific range of items may be decided by the plants according to demand. In this case central planning of key variables of economy would be favourably combined with 'spontaneous' efforts of local organizations to increase production efficiency.

The same applies to the distribution of plants' incomes between consumption and accumulation, to policy in technology and settlement patterns etc. Finding the proper measure for planning 'from the top' and for initiative 'from below' presents a certain difficulty on every concrete occasion and is based on trial and error methods. Either alternative has merits and demerits of its own. While central planning facilitates concentration of public resources on main targets, a lower degree of centralization would permit a fuller utilization of social resources embodied in the free creative initiative of masses.

It should be noted that free, unconstrained, spontaneous activity of masses has a great influence on the development of socialist society. This influence is twofold. On the one hand, it is not infrequent that certain non-planned and unconstrained human behaviour may be harmful for society. The examples are excessive consumption of alcohol by certain population groups, absenteeism, violation of safety rules on plants, wrong methods of child-rearing in the family, various forms of deviant behaviour.

On the other hand, many activities performed beyond the established standards and duties give additional resources for development. Thus voluntary labour inputs into private plots increase national income and improve population nutrition. Extension and other educational courses attended by workers on a part-time basis promote increase of general culture and vocational skills of manpower. This is the case when, on the initiative of some production teams, interesting socioeconomic experiments are staged which pioneer new paths of societal development, testing their pluses and minuses.

Favourable influences of an unconstrained activity of the population on the processes of social development are many times as high as negative influences. For this reason standardization and regulation of this activity should be made with great caution. In socialist societies two conceivable mechanisms for the regulation of personal behaviour are employed. The first is direct administrative-legal control prescribing certain forms of behaviour as compulsory, tolerating others as permissible and prohibiting still others as inconsistent with the societal good. This regulation of extreme forms of behaviour threatening the normal functioning of society are common to all types of society; they are not something peculiar only to socialism.

The second mechanism is indirect stimulation of desirable forms of behaviour through creating objective conditions guiding this behaviour into a certain channel. This form of control is based on the knowledge of actual behavioural patterns, on their recognition and projection. But since mass behaviour is influenced by a multitude of factors which it is impossible to anticipate, the projection may be only of a stochastic nature. By virtue of this, they cannot make a basis for directive planning of appropriate developmental variables.

Professors Cherns and Denitch are inclined, to a certain degree, to equate planning of social development with control over personal behaviour, and the spontaneity of this development with liberty. I would like to make some objections to these views. In reality the individual is or can be 'free from society' under no circumstances. The actual difference between societal political systems is in the extent of this lack of freedom and in the forms it takes. Central planning of social processes imposes limitations largely on those aspects of personal behaviour which are directly associated with work in the public economy, whereas the everyday behaviour in one's family, leisure, personal consumption are virtually outside public control.

As regards mechanisms of spontaneous development peculiar to the bourgeois society, they impose much heavier constraints on personal behaviour. It is enough to mention unemployment stripping millions of people of an opportunity not only to choose a more attractive job, but any job whatsoever. Furthermore, we have such events as mass violent exclusion of small farmers from farming, ever increasing spread of crimes in cities etc. This shows that a system of planning as such does not create or aggravate the control over individual behaviour, but only replaces some forms of this control by others, more appropriate to the nature of socialist relations.

The last point I am going to touch upon is democracy in planning. Professor Cherns has raised the question of relations between planners and those 'being planned', i.e. population groups whose living and working conditions are affected by plans. In socialist societies planners and 'the planned' are not separated by class barriers, as is sometimes the case under capitalist conditions. But though transformed, the problem still remains since the development of governmental plans of economic and social growth constitutes an autonomous field in the social division of labour. Specialists in planning may not be fully aware of concrete conditions and interests of those groups of the population for which plans are drawn up. And their values may not coincide. Illustrations can be found in plans for rural development elaborated by planners living in cities and not always accepted quite willingly by rural people.

The solution may be sought for in a possible democratization of procedures of developing and discussing the plans. This can be achieved in two ways. One way is a dialectical combination of the 'general' and the 'specific' in social planning by concurrent measures aimed at developing and improving central planning and at strengthening local social planning at enterprise and community levels. Since the beginning of the 1970s, on the initiative of the workers of a number of large Leningrad plants in the USSR, the practice of collectively making up plans of social development of production teams became common. This initiative supported at the 24th and 25th Party Congresses has acquired a mass character. At present such local plans of social development are being implemented by tens of thousands of plants, hundreds of towns and districts. Plans are being developed with the closest cooperation and participation of working people, based on thorough investigations of their opinions and needs. The other way of democratization of planning is an all-national discussion of the drafts of five-year plans of economic growth. In the course of such discussions thousands of proposals are coming from people which are carefully summarized and studied. The most valuable of them are taken into account at the stage of final elaboration of plans; other proposals are made known to departments concerned, to local bodies etc. and are implemented in their current activity.

Such are my considerations concerning the relationship of spontaneity and planning in social development which I would like to express with regard to the papers discussed. They are clearly of a general nature.

In conclusion I should note that certain mechanisms of political, economic and social regulation of the growth of a socialist society (including the regulation of personal behaviour) constitute a system, or an integral strategy, whose elements can be changed only in conjunction. This permits us to speak of alternative strategies in social development policy, differing in particular by different ratios of central planning to spontaneous activity, or, more precisely, to mass initiative. The relative efficiency of these strategies can be determined after devising appropriate long-run target programs based on scientific knowledge of the mechanisms of social growth. These programs will obviously outline different dates for the fulfilment of public goals and different costs of them, helping thus to make the final choice of the most suitable alternative of social policy.

As is seen from the above, the problems of the relationship and interaction of planning and spontaneity are equally important for different types of society, i.e. capitalist, socialist and developing. For particular social systems planning or spontaneity are developmental alternatives. In any concrete society, however, these forms of regulation are coexistent and interacting in a certain way. The increased complexity of human societies as well as global, regional and national problems faced by them, objectively lead to higher importance attached to planning. The advantages of this trend are obvious. But the main point is that in using these advantages for a distinct statement of goals and proper distribution of resources we must avoid suppressing the 'human', active, creative element in societal development, i.e. spontaneous forces within the boundaries of these plans which are necessary and useful.

11

SPONTANEITY AND PLANNING IN 'MIXED ECONOMIES' AND UNDER SELF-MANAGING LABOUR
— With an Inquiry into a Swedish Proposal on Wage-Earners Funds

Ulf Himmelstrand
University of Uppsala, Sweden

Branko Horvat, in his contribution to this volume, has argued that the spontaneity of the market and central political planning, far from being incompatible, can be combined in ways which are more beneficial for single firms, consumers and overall social welfare than when market forces or political forces operate alone or in conflict with each other. Even though Horvat mentions workers self-management, with reference to Yugoslav experiences, his contribution is primarily directed to a discussion of market and plan. Hopefully the present paper can help to elucidate how market forces are made to operate in a somewhat different manner when workers self-management replaces private capitalism on the market. The 'spontaneity' of workers self-management on the market can be shown to have a different structure and content than the 'spontaneity' of private capitalist market behaviour, and these differences in their turn affect the residual tasks taken care of by state interventions.

But before attempting to elucidate the structure and meaning of 'spontaneity' under a system of workers self-management, I will provide a background sketch of the operation of spontaneity in a typical 'mixed economy' based on private capitalism.

THE SPONTANEITY OF THE MARKET
AND STATE INTERVENTIONS

During the first post-war decades of seemingly persistent economic growth, interrupted only by 'normal' slumps and recessions, state interventions in so called 'mixed economies' could easily submit to the rules of 'market conformity' (R. Mayntz and W. Scharpf, 1975: 15f.). Their main function was to apply counter-cyclical measures, and to remove market imperfections, for instance by easing the movement of various factors of production, so that the 'spontaneity' of the market could operate in a more unrestricted fashion. Removal of 'frictions' in the labour market is an example of such state policy.

However, the 'free and spontaneous' movement of labour, as depicted by economists, in a labour market where 'frictions' have been substantially reduced through an efficient labour-market policy, can be interpreted sociologically as a combined result of pushes and pulls, of persuasions and rewards which makes the use of the term 'spontaneity' somewhat questionable.

Small enterprises, say in northern Sweden, when squeezed out of the market by more profitable competitors in the south, generate pushes on the craftsmen and workers employed by those enterprises. However, such pushes may be insufficient for moving them toward the south due to family ties, style of life and inability to recover money invested in houses subject to a sudden depreciation of value. But labour market authorities may then offer various incentives or pulls to overcome this 'friction', to make these workers uproot themselves and move as 'factors of production' to regions with more expansive and profitable industrial activities for the benefit of the overall national economy.

This is in fact what happened on a large scale in Sweden during the sixties as a result of the internationally well known Swedish labour-market policy (Martin, 1978). For economists this is an example of how market-conforming state interventions can help 'spontaneous' market forces to operate more efficiently. For sociologists and social psychologists who take account of a wider spectrum of drives and motivations than monetary incentives, the application of the notion of 'spontaneity' is at least more problematic in this context. Were not in fact the workers in northern Sweden *forced* to leave their place of domicile? Did they have a real choice in terms of a wider spectrum of motivations? Why did protests later on develop against this labour-market policy, *flyttlasspolitiken*, an untranslatable Swedish term which vividly depicts the household equipment, furniture and people loaded on a van to be moved from home to somewhere.

I am raising these questions here not as a prelude to an evaluation of the Swedish labour-market policy of 'exit', to use Albert Hirschman's (1970) fertile concept, but only to contrast a concept of spontaneity which takes only a very narrow range of economic incentives into account, and a more sociological concept of spontaneity, unexplicated as it remains, which involves much more.

Later on I will return to the implications of these various interpretations of spontaneity in the context of workers self-management. But first a few words on how the spontaneity of markets, particularly where the 'frictions' or 'imperfections' of markets are substantially removed, leads to the destruction of market forces themselves, thereby creating an increasingly deadlocked capitalism with state interventions which no longer follow the rules of market conformity. In fact this is the kind of predicament which now in Sweden (and elsewhere, for that matter) is generating demands for a new economic system involving an increasing degree of workers control over capital, and workers self-management (Himmelstrand et al., 1981: chapters 11 and 19).

First of all it is obvious that the spontaneity of the market over time brings about a concentration and centralization of capital. Marx predicted this, but this result can be derived from conventional market theory as well. When success breeds success among competing firms in an originally strictly competitive market this, over time, leads to oligopolistic, duopolistic or monopolistic structures which reduce or eliminate the competition which is supposed to be the singular and unbeatable vehicle of optimal resource allocation in a free enterprise economy.

In his book *The Visible Hand* (1977) Alfred D. Chandler Jr., an American historian, has convincingly shown that the competitive market model fits the reality of contemporary capitalism rather badly. His main thesis is that administrative coordination involving long-range plans rather than market forces determines production and distribution in big business. Chandler's study covers the development of American capitalism from its initiation in the beginning of the nineteenth century to the middle of this century. To begin with the American economy did certainly conform rather well with the image of a competitive market economy presupposed by Adam Smith and more recent economic theory. Production and distribution of commodities were handled by many small, independent economic units. Market forces determined what was produced and where production was located as well as transport and financing. The growth of big business which in itself was a result of these spontaneous market forces successively changed the picture. Planning and administrative coordination proved to be superior to the coordination attainable by market forces. Modern big business is composed of a multitude of units which theoretically could have acted quite independently; but the integration of these units within a larger unit proved to be more advantageous. By way of planning within such a larger economic unit, it is possible to attain a more stable flow of products and a better utilization of buildings, machines and labour. Costs for acquiring information about the market as well as for business transactions can be minimized. On the basis of his thorough historical studies Chandler concludes that production and distribution nowadays increasingly are determined not by market forces, as economic theory assumes, but by planning and administrative coordination. The invisible hand of market forces has been replaced by the visible hand of corporate management, if not for the whole of the American economy so at least for a most powerful section of it. J. K. Galbraith (1967 and 1974) has made the same points in his illuminating analysis of the 'technostructure' and 'the new industrial state'.

But the process of concentration and centralization of capital has developed much further in other countries than the USA. As shown by comparative studies (Bain, 1966: 48-53; Pryor, 1973), Sweden ranks the highest among advanced capitalist countries in terms of industrial concentration and centralization of capital. Pryor points out that industrial concentration seems to be inversely proportional to the size of the domestic market. In countries with a small domestic market only the largest and most concentrated industrial firms have been able to survive competition on the export market. Sweden certainly has a small domestic market, but in addition the former social democratic labour government of Sweden, supported by the Swedish trade union movement, pursued an economic policy of capitalist economic growth resulting in the industrial concentration now exhibited by Sweden, presumably not for the benefit of capitalists alone but in order to increase the size of the national income for the benefit of redistributions of income and welfare among the broad masses of the Swedish people.

But in recent years, with protracted international recessions succeeding more than two post-war decades of unprecedented economic growth, the benefits of welfare-state capitalism have been questioned. Simultaneous industrial stagnation, unemployment and inflation — so called staflation — is the most visible symptom of this capitalist predicament which, in the last instance, is the final result of the self-destructive spontaneous forces of the market, as supplemented in some cases with market-conforming state interventions. The so-called mixed-economies no longer seem workable, since the state is forced, by the development of capitalism, to disturb the basic dynamics of capitalism itself. The state now often intervenes directly in production in a manner violating the most elementary criteria of capitalist business, and also allocates increasing resources to sustaining people whom the labour-market no longer can absorb. This is done not only or even mainly for ideological reasons. Bourgeois and not only labour governments do it even though it is done with less consistency by conservative bourgeois governments. State violations of market conformity thus emanate from the contradictory development of capitalism itself. In the international debate it has often been emphasized that the sheer size of crisis-struck enterprises today makes it too costly politically and too disruptive economically to allow a free play of the classic mechanisms for advancing long term productivity — bankruptcies, unemployment, devaluation of capital etc. — and therefore the state may have to intervene to salvage 'sick companies', and to control and discipline individual capitalists as well as the working class (Wright, 1978: 177). Therefore this pattern of state intervention is a latent force even in countries which have not pursued this approach to the same extent as Sweden.

However, state medication of 'sick' capitalist enterprises may have effects as serious as the original illness of capitalism itself. Does this mean that we are now approaching the final crisis and demise of capitalism — or as Marx wrote: 'The knell of capitalist private property sounds.'?

Two Marxist social scientists, Sam Bowles and Herbert Gintis (1979: 17) have sarcastically remarked that Marxists have 'successfully predicted nine out of the last three final collapses of the capitalist order.' But capitalism has survived. Contemporary capitalism can survive due to state interventions and other arrangements, however contradictory, which both assure survival and contain collective uprisings. The crucial point of societal transformation in mature capitalism therefore is not a dramatic collapse of the system, but the trivial fact that mature capitalism is performing badly, and that the relative strength of the labour movement and its allies within the framework of political democracy at least in some countries could make it possible to articulate the demands for a better economic system. We stand at a crossroad, and the issue is not to wait for any spontaneous break-down of capitalism, but to be aware of the crossroad itself, and to make a political choice of the right way in order to reduce and eliminate the contradictions of capitalism. But if the transition to a new system is not entirely spontaneous then a plan for such a transition is needed, a plan which does not look at plan and spontaneity as incompatible principles in societal transformation and reproduction. Of course the challenge to formulate such a plan of transition is too great to be dealt with comprehensively in this context. But the end-result of such a transition can still be discussed in broad theoretical terms.

SPONTANEITY AND PLANNING
IN WORKERS SELF-MANAGEMENT

Assume that the fault of capitalism lies not mainly in its reliance on market mechanisms — at least not as far as commodity markets are concerned. Assume that the main fault lies with the type of spontaneity involved, that is with the *actors* responding to market forces. Modern capitalism operates with a number of different actors: capital owners and speculators, managers responsible to capital owners, workers in direct production, consumers (working or not), and the state responding both to the conflicts among these actors and to the needs of capitalist system-maintenance. Among these actors there is an asymmetry of power in the capitalist system. Capitalists are most powerful — not because they 'command' or are most 'influential' but because the system is theirs. They have the systemic power (Himmelstrand et al., 1981: chapter 16).

Ideally the actor we are looking for must be directly and locally involved in production, must depend directly on success and innovation in production at his place of work. At the same time our actor must be personally concerned with employment, with prices of consumer goods, with the quality of working life, and with the environmental effects hurting common people, families and children. In short the main actor must be able to integrate into one multidimensional judgement the requirements of capital accumulation and investment, the requirements of the commodity market, the effects of productivity and wage levels on employment and on commodity prices, and the requirements of quality of life both at work and in leisure. Finally he must know that no deliberate sacrifice of satisfactions on any of these dimensions will be unduly exploited by other actors, because otherwise he could not properly balance the various interests involved in his multidimensional judgement. In fact, if he is exploited he may not at all be interested in taking responsibility for such a multidimensional judgement but may instead decide to wage a struggle against the exploiter.

Does such an actor really exist? Not if an optimal multidimensional judgement is required. As Herbert Simon (1968: xxv and chapter 5) has pointed out most actors in the real world can only 'satisfice', not optimize. Our next task therefore is to rank the actors mentioned above in terms of their capacity for multidimensional satisficing in the context of the enterprise. This capacity will be evaluated primarily on the basis of rather conventional structural criteria, that is in terms of the pattern of incentives which operate on actors with different positions in the given mode of production.

The main incentives of capital-owners and speculators are profit, or perhaps stability and predictability of profit. When profitability declines capital owners and speculators are therefore likely to spontaneously move their capital into more profitable production elsewhere, or into unproductive speculation in diamonds, art etc. in the case of a more general decline of profitability. This is done without concern for the destruction of productive capital, and the unemployment which may ensue.

To managers who are responsible to capital-owners, profit is also a main incentive, but they are likely to be somewhat more concerned with capital investments which in the short run may somewhat detract from profits. Managers may also have a marginal concern for maintaining smooth relations with workers in direct production in order to sustain productivity and the predictability of production. But when profitability shows a tendencial decline, managerial incentives for investments also tend to decline.

To workers in direct production *profitability* is also an important incentive since a profitable company is more likely to pay reasonable wages. But if increasing profits are siphoned off to shareholders rather than to *wages* and *investments* for improvements of production at a given plant, workers are less likely to look at profits as an incentive. Unlike shareholders who can easily move their money to other companies or to improductive speculation, workers can view profit as an incentive only if most of it remains in the company for the benefit of further investments and wages. Workers have no incentives allowing the *movement of capital abroad*, to Swiss bank accounts or fictitious customers in Lichtenstein. In addition continued and stable *employment* is a main concern of workers in production. Therefore if workers are assured that the wage restraint ensures employment and productivity, and is not exploited by 'profiteers', we may even find incentives for *wage restraint* among workers, when that is required. But if wage restraint is seen as conducive only to the 'excess profits' of shareholders, then obviously incentives for wage restraint will be less pronounced. In his capacity as consumer the worker is more concerned with *consumer prices and living costs* than other actors. Basic living costs account for a larger proportion of the expenses of workers. And furthermore workers to a much less extent than capital-owners and even managers can convert part of their costs into tax deductibles. Workers are also more exposed to environmental hazards and dangers in and outside of their work, and therefore would have more of an incentive to reduce such *environmental effects.*

From this it is obvious that workers, particularly in a system of workers self-management, are subject to a much wider spectrum of productive and social incentives than the traditional owners and managers of capital. The present system of capitalism (1) divides different incentives between actors who hold contradictory positions in the system, (2) gives most systemic power to the actor(s) with the most limited repertory of incentives and, as a result, (3) requires costly state interventions to rectify the imbalances and negative externalities ensuing from the operation of these limited incentives in their competition with considerations of social welfare.

Workers self-management operating within competitive commodity markets implies a shift of power in the production for such markets. *Most systemic power is given to the category or class of actors which exhibit the least limited spectrum of productive and social incentives, that is to workers.* Within this relatively wide spectrum of incentives, many incentives remain contradictory, but here these various incentives are instantaneously integrated in the multidimensional satisficing process of a *single* collective actor. In contrast to this we have the non-integrated separate processes of satisficing, with *different* actors responding to different and partly contradictory incentives, which characterizes the present system of private enterprise and which calls for constant and costly corrections when more or less irreversible damage has already been done as a result of non-integrated satisficing processes dominated by the actors least capable of multidimensional satisficing.

Our conclusions about structurally determined differentials in multidimensional satisficing capability among actors, could also be formulated in more political terms. In view of the wider spectrum of incentives operating on workers, relevant as these inventives are both to productivity, to human fulfilment and social dignity, any plan for the transformation of a deadlocked 'welfare capitalism' should allocate most power over the economy to workers. The idealistic slogan 'power to the people' has here been replaced by the analytic formula 'power to those most capable of multidimensional satisficing'. It may sound less appealing in contexts of political rhetoric, but in a scientific analysis of options available to move beyond 'welfare capitalism' it is more informative.

I will not here discuss whether a system of workers self-management (and among workers I include white collar employees, of course) deserves the label 'democratic socialism'. There are socialists who refuse to consider workers self-management within a commodity market economy as an instance of genuine socialism, and instead characterize such a system as a refinement of capitalism only, or as 'capitalism without private capitalists'. I have discussed these matters in another context (Himmelstrand et al., 1981: chapter 21). Here our intention has been only to intellectually explore whether the efficiency of a decentralized market economy could be salvaged in a manner which integrates social and human considerations not by bureaucratic state interventions but through a redistribution of power among the actors within the capitalist system according to the principle of maximum multidimensional satisficing capability. A Swedish economic historian, Bo Gustafsson (1978: 12) has indicated that the system thus emerging may be most adequately characterized as 'democratic collectivist capitalism' rather than socialism — but he also suggested that such a system might be a crucial step toward a democratic form of socialism. After all Karl Marx himself did assume that a refinement of capitalism is a precondition for a socialist transformation of society: 'No social order ever disappears before all the productive forces for which there is room in it have been developed; and new higher relations of production never appear before the material conditions of their existence have matured in the womb of the old society.'

But even though a system of workers self-management may eliminate some of the contradictions of present-day capitalism — particularly with reference to the whole pattern of capital accumulation, investment rates, job motivation, wages, prices, employment, content of production, and negative externalities — thus relieving the state of many of the tasks which it today must undertake, some problems will remain which require state coordination and intervention. In an increasingly complex economy there is always a need for coordination, corrective redistributions and some degree of overall planning; and the state could partly meet such needs by setting the parameters of economic activities rather than by detailed regulation (Brus, 1972: 132ff), and rely on regulation only in specific cases.

Various ways of combining workers self-management and state planning have also been discussed in Branko Horvat's contribution to this volume. In particular he emphasizes the concept of 'participatory planning' where workers participate in the formulation of the plan as well as in its implementation. But these ideas are not simply idealizations of a Yugoslav system of workers self-management or only the visions of some free-floating architects of an utopian future. The system of *wage-earners capital funds* (Meidner, 1978), and *social development funds* recently proposed by LO, the Swedish Federation of Trade Unions, and by the Swedish Social Democratic Party, does not go quite as far as suggested in this paper, but could quite possibly provide a starting point for a movement in that direction. This proposal is presently being investigated together with other related proposals by a Swedish government commission. Depending on the outcome of future political elections, a system with at least some of the general characteristics indicated above may be introduced over the next ten or fifteen years in Sweden — but not without struggles. We will then have another empirical case, in addition to Yugoslavia, which could be analyzed to throw more light on the relationships between spontaneity and planning in a certain type of market socialism.

WAGE-EARNERS FUNDS AND 'ECONOMIC DEMOCRACY'

A crucial factor determining the future outcome of the political struggle for or against wage-earners funds in Sweden is of course the strength of resistance to be expected from bourgeois parties, and leaders of the business community. Since I have discussed this factor elsewhere (Himmelstrand et al., 1981: part III), I will here only indicate that this resistance is far from monolithic. Prompted by the proposal for wage-earners funds from the Swedish labour movement, and by the increasing intensity of the conflict between labour and capital in the present period of recurrent and protracted slumps and recessions, some progressive or at least pragmatic business leaders, with the help of a professor of financial law, have made an alternative proposal supposed to go a long way to accommodate the demands of labour (L. Lidén and G. Lindencrona et al., 1979). Since their proposal is of some theoretical interest, I will quote a crucial passage from their book (my translation from Swedish):

> If you wish to reduce the power of present owners there are two possibilities. You can retain the present legal linkage between ownership and power, but transfer the rights of ownership to somebody else. The best known example of this method in Sweden is Meidner's proposal of wage-earners funds.
>
> Another method is to dissolve the linkage between ownership and power. As far as the big companies are concerned this implies that you transfer the administrative and management rights of owners to some other group without therefore depriving the owners of their shares, and the economic rights associated with these shares. (Lidén, Lindencrona et al., 1979: 24)

What these authors seem to have in mind is a tripartite division of power in company boards, with representatives of shareholders, labour and community or societal interests sharing the seats on the board. However, the proposal for wage-earners funds is more radical in the long run, and comes closer to the principle of maximum multidimensional satisficing capability of *one* dominant collective actor, namely labour, espoused in this paper. It is not enough to cut the legal link between ownership and economic power through new legislation, and replace it with some kind of tripartite power structure, as suggested by Lidén and Lindencrona. Rather the power over use of capital must be successively transferred to collective labour, by making labour the decisive owner of capital, according to the proponents of wage-earners funds.

At the 1971 Congress of LO, the Swedish Federation of Trade Unions, Dr. Rudolf Meidner, a senior economist employed by LO, was invited to head a working-party to study the problems of wage-earners funds in depth. When Meidner and his collaborators submitted the first version of their report in August 1975, suggesting a legislated transfer of a certain percentage of yearly company profits to wage-earners funds, it became obvious that Meidner's proposal addressed itself not only to the lofty ideals of equality and economic democracy, but also to the concrete realities of capital concentration and centralization, and to the inability of the capitalist system to ensure stable investment and employment rates.

In the ensuing debate the emphasis was shifted to the problems of power over decisions on investment and employment. In the words of the programme of the Swedish Social Democratic Party: 'Decisions affecting the development of the entire country and the living-conditions of individual citizens are still the prerogative of a limited number of persons guided by considerations of capitalist profit.' And furthermore:

> Decisions concerning the orientation of production are coming to have more and more far-reaching and wide-ranging effects. Consequently the need for democratic control of the economy is being thrown into progressively sharper relief. Both national economic planning and local initiatives are needed. One of the central tasks of social democracy must be to reconcile planning for society as a whole with local and individual aspirations.

These extracts from the programme of the Swedish Social Democratic Party were quoted in the opening paragraph of a revised proposal for wage-earners funds submitted jointly by LO and the Social Democratic Party in February 1978. This revised proposal contained not only Meidner's original proposal of collective profit-sharing by successively transferring a certain portion of yearly company profits to wage-earners funds, but also a proposal for the creation of a system of national and regional development funds based not on company profits, but on fees based on incomes from wages and salaries. The aim was to increase collective savings for the benefit of industrial investments, particularly in the export-oriented industry. Henceforth we will call this joint proposal of LO and the Swedish Social Democratic Party (SAP) the LO-SAP Report of 1978.

The proposal for national and regional development funds was added to the original profit-sharing scheme in order to cope with the trend toward decreasing rates of public savings after 1972. During the sixties and early seventies the General Pension Fund, created by the social democratic government in 1960, contributed significantly to the expansion of the investments in Swedish industry. After 1972 this role of the General Pension Fund became less significant as the paying of pensions became more extensive.

Incentives for *private* savings, and an increasing solidity of *private* industrial firms through increasing profits, as a means to satisfy the needs for industrial investments, could not be accepted unconditionally by LO and SAP. In view of their wish to decrease distributive inequality, and to influence investment allocations, only collective savings under joint labour and public control were acceptable. The Meidner scheme of profit-sharing alone would not be sufficient to increase savings, however, and therefore the scheme of national and regional development funds based on fees from income was added.

Even though the profit-sharing component of the LO-SAP Report was tabled at the 1978 SAP Congress, the congress accepted the main idea, but did not find the 1978 version sufficient as a basis for political decisions. The congress decided to continue to study the profit-sharing scheme in preparation for a decision at the next party congress in 1981. However, since the general outline of Meidner's profit-sharing scheme is of considerable interest from the point of view of this paper, I will now give a more detailed account of some of its details.

The figure on page 212 summarizes the 1978 version of Meidner's profit-sharing scheme. Business firms with more than 500 employees — all in all about 200 concerns in the whole country — would be required by law to issue shares every year amounting to 20 percent of their profits to wage-earners funds. In Meidner's original proposal firms with more than 50 or perhaps 100 employees were included. To prevent 'business egoism' tied to each firm, the increasing number of labour seats at shareholders meetings to which labour would be entitled by virtue of their increasing ownership of shares, would be allocated equally between representatives of the local union and a provincial labour-representative body, until the representation of labour attains 40 percent of the seats at the shareholders meeting. From that point on all additional seats would be allocated to representatives from the provincial body of labour representatives, according to the LO-SAP Report.

The shares are kept by a Distributive Board which also is responsible for keeping track of the size of labour representation on shareholders meetings, and for allocating seats between local and provincial bodies.

Shares in wage-earners funds cannot normally be sold on the stock market. They are the collective ownership of labour, and therefore no individual dividends will be paid to workers. A main objective of wage-earners funds is to increase and consolidate the collective control of labour over their firms through representation on shareholders meetings, and in the appointment of company boards. However, it has been suggested that yields from wage-earners funds, once they have become large enough, could be paid to workers for specific purposes.

Today it is usually sufficient to own about 10-15 percent of the shares in a Swedish company to have a decisive influence over the deliberations of shareholders meetings, and the appointment of company boards. If wage-earners funds are introduced in the future, it is quite possible, however, that this limit may be displaced upward. Larger shareholders may try even harder than today to obtain the right to vote by proxy for smaller shareholders who usually do not attend

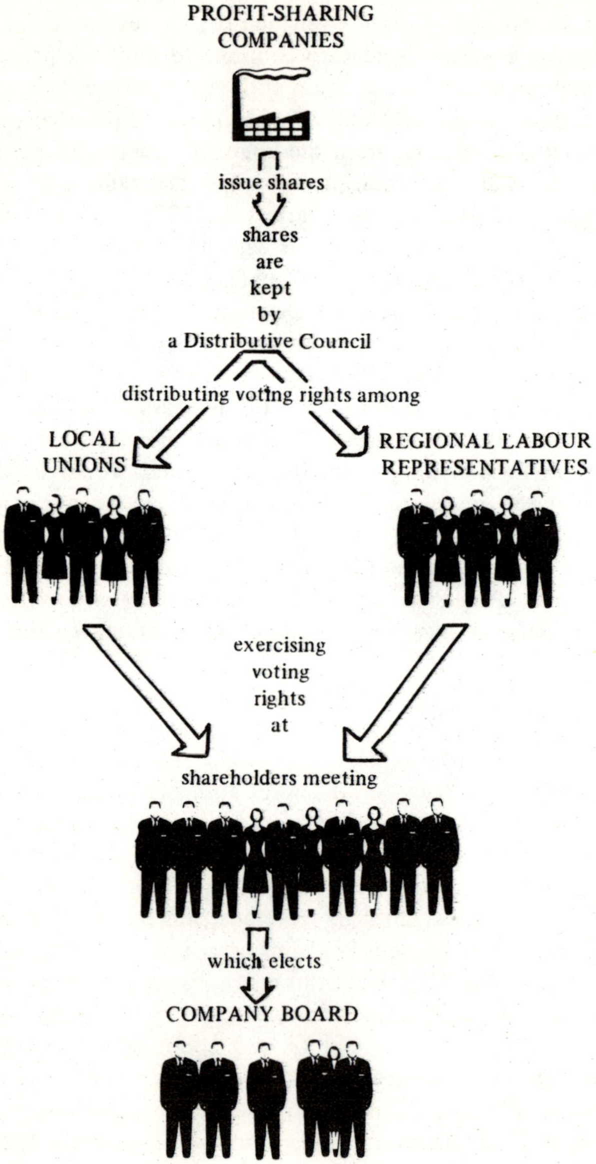

PROFIT-SHARING
COMPANIES
issue shares
shares
are
kept
by
a Distributive Council
distributing voting rights among
LOCAL
UNIONS
REGIONAL LABOUR
REPRESENTATIVES
exercising
voting
rights
at
shareholders meeting
which elects
COMPANY BOARD

shareholders meetings. In any case it will take quite some time before labour attains a crucial vote at shareholders meetings, with the profit-sharing scheme outlined in the LO-SAP Report. With 20 percent of the profit issued as wage-earners shares as suggested, it will take ten years before labour attains 17 percent of the vote, if the profit is 10 percent. If the profit is 15 percent about 24 percent of the vote will be attained by labour in these ten years. In order to attain 50 percent of the vote it will take 25 years in companies with an average profit of 15 percent, and as much as 29 years in companies with an average profit of 10 percent (LO-SAP 1978: 37 f.).

It is anticipated that the arrangements outlined above will be reviewed by Parliament every five years to oversee the functioning of the system, and to improve it if necessary, and perhaps extend it to companies with less than 500 employees.

Obviously this profit-sharing proposal will meet resistance from private shareholders who quite possibly may consider the issuing of shares from 20 percent of yearly company profits to wage-earners funds as a confiscation of part of their 'property'. In order to placate private shareholders, and also to stimulate their continued interest in buying and holding shares during a long transitional period, the LO-SAP Report suggests a number of measures which will not be discussed in detail here. For instance the LO-SAP Report supports Meidner's original suggestions that companies should be allowed to deduct the shares issued to wage-earners funds from taxable profit. This would largely neutralize the effects of the issuing of wage-earners shares, from the point of view of private shareholders.

The fact that companies with wage-earners funds, for the foreseeable future, also would need privately-owned capital is probably as important as these legal measures and guarantees. It would thus be counter-productive for labour representatives, even where they have a decisive vote at shareholders meetings and in company boards, to tamper with dividends to private shareholders who contribute risk-assuming capital to the company. Wage-earners funds are not designed to deprive present shareholders of their current assets, but only to distribute future increases in wealth and profits so as to make it possible for labour eventually to take decisive control over the use of capital.

The LO-SAP Report suggests that such a change in the distribution of power over capital in fact may turn out to be quite beneficial to smaller shareholders in the long run. Increasing solidity combined with greater equity and labour control — a combination which is impossible within the present capitalist system — and the wider range of economic and social incentives of labour as compared to private capital, could be more conducive to a stabilization of investment rates, to a diminishing flow of capital abroad, to wage restraints when such are needed to combat inflation, to a greater tolerance of increasing profits, since part of the profit then would go to labour, and to a greater involvement in work and productivity generally. The LO-SAP Report seems so convinced of these long-term benefits of wage-earners funds even for minority private shareholders interest, that it seriously considers the possibility that business firms with less than 500 employees (who will not automatically become part of the system) *spontaneously* join the system to reach these benefits — including the tax deductions derived from the issuing of wage-earners shares.

Some space should also be devoted to the new national and regional development funds proposed to supplement the Meidner scheme in the LO-SAP Report. As we have mentioned earlier these development funds will be based not on a profit-sharing scheme but on incremental fees to be paid yearly by every company on the basis of a certain percentage of wages, salaries and other income deriving from each company. In return LO has accepted the idea of wage restraints roughly corresponding to these fees in collective bargaining. These fees will be so constructed that the development funds would attain a level of savings amounting to about 40 percent of gross investments in the manufacturing industry within four or five years.

The LO-SAP Report emphasizes that in the short-run it would be justified to give labour a significant influence over the management of development funds in view of the fact that these funds require some wage restraint on the part of labour corresponding to the fees paid. At least two competing *national* development funds would be set up, one with an earmarked labour majority, and one with a majority for representatives of public interests, to be appointed by government. These representatives will of course include representatives of labour parties in some proportion to their strength in Parliament. The governing bodies of *regional* development funds would be appointed by regional political bodies. In the long-run when the influence of labour over the economy may have increased considerably as a result of the increasing number of labour representatives on shareholders meetings and in company boards, the earmarked majority representation of labour in one of the national development funds, could be reduced in favour of members appointed by government, to represent broader societal interests. It is of some interest in this context to take account of some critical voices on Meidner's profit-sharing schemes heard even within the Social Democratic Party itself. Some social democratic intellectuals have maintained that the type of wage-earners funds proposed by LO-SAP would violate the following passage in the Social Democratic program: 'the Social Democratic Party wishes to transform society in such a way that the right of determination over production and its distribution is placed in the hands of the entire nation....' Keeping this objective of Swedish social democracy in mind, it would seem illogical to allow the employees of Volvo, for instance, to make their own decisions on investments and production within a system of wage-earners funds, since such decisions may have consequences for the economy of the nation as a whole. Some social democratic proponents of this critical view have suggested the building of 'citizens funds' as an alternative to wage-earners funds. The boards of such 'citizens funds' would be elected on a separate ticket in connection with elections to Parliament (Korpi, 1978: 333).

This approach places citizens' rights in opposition to the rights accruing to man by virtue of his work. This latter right has been derived by some proponents of wage-earners funds from Marx's labour theory of value (Abrahamsson and Broström, 1980), by others from the simple fact that most people spend most of their time awake at work. In my view neither line of argument seems particularly relevant to the problem at hand, quite regardless whether you otherwise accept the usefulness of the concepts of citizens' or workers' rights.

Proponents of wage-earners funds, and of the kind of workers self-management which can be envisaged in the future as a result of this reform, rarely claim that decision making in firms controlled by local or even regional labour is sufficient to meet the needs of 'the entire nation'. Such a claim could be based only on a strange combination of syndicalism and classical Manchester liberalism. The LO-SAP proposal for wage-earners funds quite explicitly rejects the 'egoism of the firm' by requiring not only local but also a more broad-based representation at shareholders meetings, and by suggesting a parliamentary representation in the boards of regional development funds and in at least one of the national development funds. Furthermore, even where local and regional labour control predominates, the economic activities of any firm take place not only within the constraints of the commodity market (which assures the interests of consumers if the market is sufficiently competitive), but also within the parameters of economic activity determined by a democratically elected government supposed to cater for the needs of the nation as a whole.

However, since labour has a broader spectrum of interests and incentives than has private capital, as we have suggested above, state interventions into a system where there are considerable elements of workers control will, firstly, have a much more limited task to perform than in contradictory capitalism. Secondly, where such state interventions are necessary anyhow, they will meet with less resistance and more understanding where labour is in control both in single firms and in Parliament and government. It is only the operation of this multi-level system of decentralized labour control, competitive commodity markets and the determination of significant economic parameters by the democratic state which can assure that production is determined in a way which reasonably satisfies broad national interests rather than only the interest of private capital accumulation, the interests of local or national unions, or the interests of a new class of state bureaucrats. Locating the control only on the national level of parliamentary decision making under the slogan of 'citizens' rights' would imply a system of bureaucratic planning and regulation which most probably would hamper the dynamics of the economy, to the disadvantage of 'the entire nation', including the working class.

What we have outlined above is in essence the multi-level structure and logic of the new 'economic democracy' which the Swedish labour movement now suggests as a replacement of the contradictory system constituted by a crisis-ridden capitalist order which combines broad-ranging societal consequences with a narrow focus of decision making in the interest of private capital accumulation only, and which requires constant and costly state interventions, and an intensified and also very costly class struggle, in order to safeguard the interests of the majority of people. If properly implemented such a structure of economic democracy could combine spontaneity and planning in a new and less contradictory way than before.

In January 1981 when Reagan in the US joined Barre of France and Thatcher of England to form the now fashionable 'Milton Friedman Minstrels', the Swedish labour movement, with majority support in public opinion polls, submitted a third and probably final proposal for wage-earners funds, with a less complicated design but based on the same principles mentioned here — a challenge to the myths of neo-liberalism and the realities of centralized capitalist planning.

REFERENCES

ABRAHAMSSON, B. and A. BROSTRÖM (1980) *The Rights of Labour*. Beverly Hills Ca: Sage Publications.

BAIN, J. S. (1966) *International Differences in Industrial Structure. Eight Nations in the 1950s*. New Haven/London: Yale University Press.

BOWLES, S. and H. GINTIS (1979) 'The Crisis of Capital and the Crisis of Liberal Democracy: The Case of the United States'. Paper presented to the Round Table on The Subjective Forces of Socialism, Cavtat, Yugoslavia (September).

BRUS, W. (1972) *The Market in a Socialist Economy*. London: Routledge & Kegan Paul.

CHANDLER, A. D. (1977) *The Visible Hand*. Cambridge, Mass.: The Belknap Press of Harvard University Press.

GALBRAITH, J. K. (1967) *The New Industrial State*. London: Hamish Hamilton.

– – (1974) *Economics and the Public Purpose*. London: André Deutsch.

GUSTAFSSON, B. (1978) 'Kapitalismens kris – och vägen framåt', *Socionomen*, no. 17.

HIMMELSTRAND, U., G. AHRNE, L. LUNDBERG and L. LUNDBERG (1981) *Beyond Welfare Capitalism. Issues, Actors and Forces in Societal Change*. London: Heinemann.

HIRSCHMAN, A. (1970) *Exit, Voice and Loyalty*. Cambridge, Mass.: Harvard University Press.

KORPI, W. (1978) *The Working-Class in Welfare Capitalism*. London: Routledge & Kegan Paul.

LIDÉN L., G. LINDENCRONA et al. (1979) *Ägarmakt på avskrivning?* Stockholm: SNS.

LO-SAP (1978) *Löngagarfonder och Kapitalbildning – förslag från LO-SAPs arbetsgrupp*. Stockholm: LO-SAP.

MARTIN, A. (1978) 'The Dynamics of Change in a Keynesian Political Economy: The Swedish Case and its Implications', *British Political Yearbook* 4.

MAYNTZ, R. and F. W. SCHARPF (1975) *Policy-making in the German Federal Bureaucracy*. Amsterdam: Elsevier.

MEIDNER, R. (1978) *Employee Investment Funds, An Approach to Collective Capital Formation*. London: Allen & Unwin.

PRYOR, F. (1973) *Property and Industrial Organization in Non-Communist Nations*. Bloomington, Indiana: Indiana University Press.

SIMON, H. (1968) *Administrative Behavior*, 2nd ed. New York: Macmillan/ The Free Press.

WRIGHT, E. O. (1978) *Class, Crisis and State*. London: New Left Books.

NOTES ON CONTRIBUTORS

E. O. Akeredolu-Ale is Research Professor in Social Development at the Nigerian Institute of Social and Economic Research. He is the author of *The Underdevelopment of Indigenous Entrepreneurship in Nigeria*, 1975, and the editor of *Social Development in Nigeria*, 1980.

Albert Cherns is Head of Department and Professor of Social Sciences at Loughborough University, UK.

Bogdan Denitch is Professor of Sociology and Executive Officer, PhD Program in Sociology at the Graduate School of City University of New York. He is primarily interested in working class parties of Western Europe and developments in Eastern Europe. He is co-editor of *The Opinion-Making Elites in Yugoslavia*, 1973, editor of *Legitimation of Regimes: International Frameworks for Analysis*, 1979, and author of *The Legitimation of a Revolution: The Yugoslav Case*, 1975, and *Society and Social Change in Eastern Europe*, 1978.

Ulf Himmelstrand is Professor of Sociology, University of Uppsala, Sweden, and President of the International Sociological Association (1978–82). He is former Professor of Sociology at the University of Ibadan, Nigeria and has published various works in the fields of political sociology, mass communication and development studies. He is the principal author of *Beyond Welfare Capitalism. Issues, Actors and Forces in Societal Change* (1981).

Branko Horvat is Professor of Economics at the University of Zagreb and President of the International Association for the Economics of Self-Management.

Elizabeth Jelin is Director of the Center for the Study of the State and Society, Buenos Aires, Argentina.

K. S. Jomo is a lecturer in the Faculty of Economics, National University of Malaysia, and director of the independent Institute for Social Analysis (INSAN) in Malaysia. Oxford University Press will soon publish his book, tentatively entitled *Class Formation in Malaysia: Capital, the State and Uneven Development.*

Britta Jonsson is a doctoral student in the Department of Sociology at the University of Uppsala, Sweden.

Piotr Sztompka is Professor and Director of the Institute of Sociology at Jagiellonian University, Krakow, Poland. He is author of *System and Function: Toward a Theory of Society*, 1974, and *Sociological Dilemmas: Towards a Dialectic Paradigm*, 1979.

Lars Udéhn is Researcher in the Institute of Sociology at the University of Uppsala, Sweden. Currently he is working on a dissertation for the doctor's degree called *Individuals or Society? – A Critical Appraisal of Methodological Individualism.*

Tatiana I. Zaslavskaya is Professor at the Institute of Economics and Industrial Engineering, Novosibirsk, USSR.